by Rich & Sue Freeman

Published in the United States of America by Footprint Press, Inc.

Footprint Press, Inc., 303 Pine Glen Court, FL 34223
www.footprintpress.com or info@footprintpress.com

Cover Design by Lynch Graphics and Design (www.bookcoverdesign.com)
Maps by Rich Freeman
Pictures by Rich & Sue Freeman
Author photo by Andrew Olenick (www.fotowerks.com)
ISBN: 1-930480-19-9 (13 digit ISBN 9781930480193)
Manufactured in the United States of America
Library of Congress Control Number: 2005924920

Every effort has been made to provide accurate histories and up-to-date road and building descriptions in this book; however, historical records often offer conflicting information. Most of the properties listed here are private property. Please stay only on the public roads unless the public is expressly invited to visit, such as at a museum. Please drive or bicycle with care, following all traffic regulations.

Follow these routes at your own risk. Void where prohibited, taxed, or otherwise regulated. Contents may settle during shipping. Use only as directed. Discontinue use if a rash develops.

The authors, publishers, and distributors of this book assume no responsibility for any injury, misadventure, fines, arrests or loss occurring from use of the information contained herein.

Large front cover photo: 30 Lyons Road, Macedon (not on a tour)
Small cover photos, left to right:

- Railroad Pumphouse, Fishers, Tour 9
- Lima District #6 Schoolhouse, 6679 Jenks Road, Lima, Tour 7
- Mendon Academy, 16 Mendon-Ionia Road, Mendon, Tour 9
- Cobblestone Barn, 513 Route 238, Attica, Tour 6

Large back cover photo: Cobblestone Barn, 513 Route 238, Attica, Tour 6
Small cover photos, left to right:

- Clark Smokehouse, 2029 Kendall Road, Kendall, Tour 3
- 8524 Ridge Road, Alton, Tour 12
- Webster Baptist Church, 59 South Avenue, Webster, Tour 10
- 751 Crowley Road, Farmington, Tour 9

Cobblestone *Quest*

Footprint Press publishes a variety of outdoor recreation guidebooks. See a complete list and order form at the back of this book.

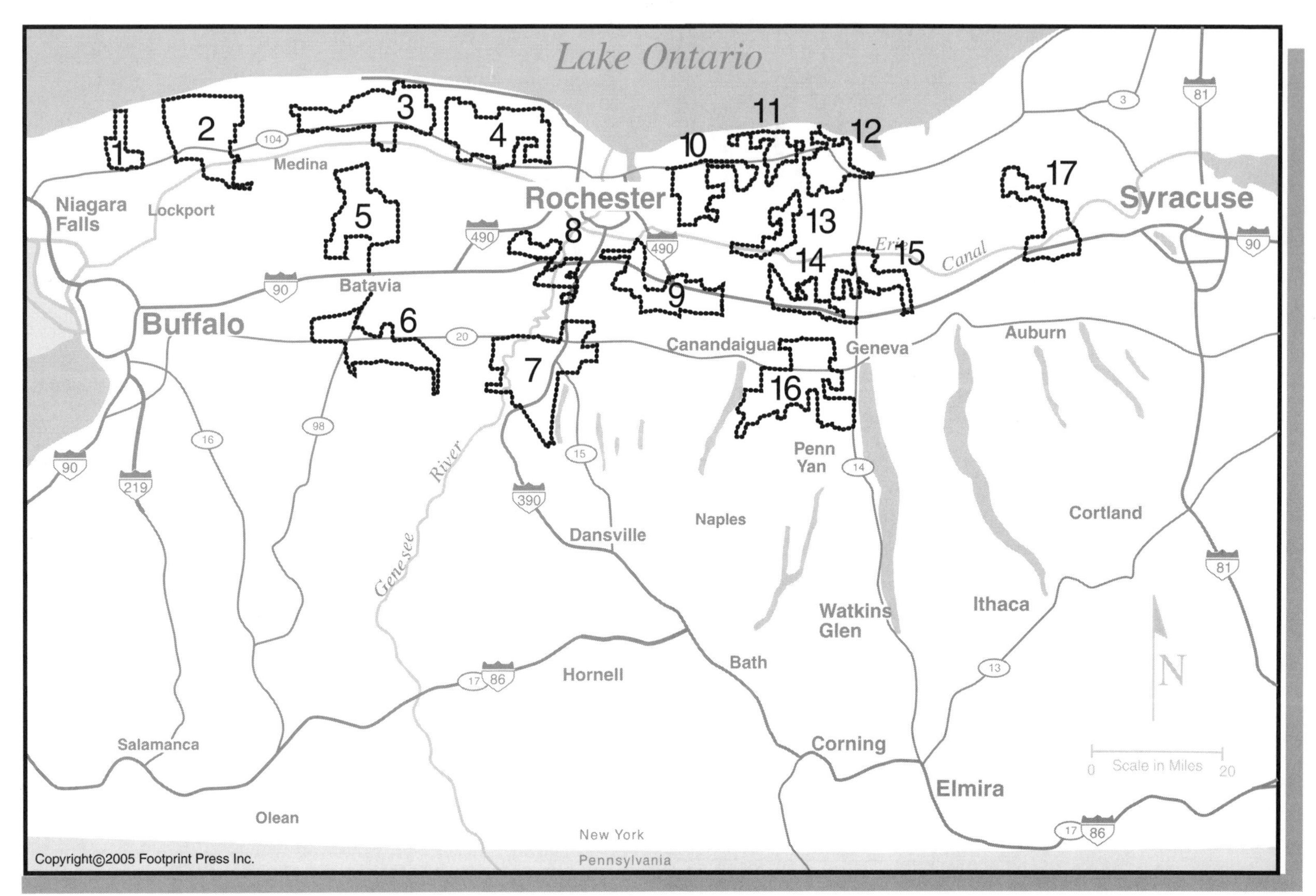

Overall Tour Locations

Contents

Acknowledgements

We were blessed with the assistance of so many people during our search for historical information on the cobblestone buildings and extend our thanks to each and every one of them. Cobblestone homeowners openly shared their love of their cobblestone homes, the histories of the homes, and even invited us inside. Cynthia Howk of The Landmark Society of Western NY and Delia Robinson of The Cobblestone Society helped us with library research. Cynthia Howk and C. W. Lattin of The Cobblestone Society reviewed our cobblestone background information and assisted us with architectural terms. Many others graciously reviewed our draft manuscript for errors and supplied additional historical information. They include:

Carolyn Adriaansen, Town of Marion Historian
Liz Albright, Town of Ontario Historian
Jeanne Baker, Brutus Weedsport Historian
Lynn Barton, Town of Webster Historian
Lorraine Beane, Town of Greece Historian
Gale Conn-Wright, Town of Batavia Historian
Chris Davis, Newark-Arcadia Historical Society
Fran Dumas, Yates County Historian
Florence A. Field, Town of Wheatland Historian
Douglas Fisher of the Victor Historical Society
Kathleen Goodman, Town of Alexander Historian
Doris Greco, Village of Lyons Historian
Diane Ham, Town of Mendon Historian
Margaret Hartsough, Town of Farmington Historian
Beth Hoad, Town of Palmyra Historian
John G. Horner, Town of Elbridge Historian
Charles F. Horton, Town of Wilson Historian
Babette Huber, Victor Town Historian
Leigh Jones, Town of Hopewell Historian
Jean Keplinger, Town of Perinton Historian
Joette Knapp, Town of Kendall Historian
Kathy Knauer, Town of Penfield Historian
Norman LaJoie, Town of Hartland Historian
Barbara Lamb, Town of Geneva Historian
C. W. Lattin, Orleans County Historian
Anne Leach, Town of Chili Historian
Mary Melious, Town of Gorham Historian
Richard Nellist, Town of Ridgeway Historian
David Oliver, Town of Rush Historian
David W. Parish, Town/Village of Geneseo Historian
Richard Ransley, Town of Sodus Historian
Mary E. Smith, Town of Hamlin Historian
Margaret Sweetman, Village of Cato Historian
Don Tiffany, Town of Phelps Historian
Mary Townsend, Village of Hilton Historian
Larry Turner, Town of Groveland Historian
Lorraine Wayner, Town of Somerset Historian

We also extend our thanks to Bonnie Hayes from Historic Palmyra for supplying us with a copy of *Palmyra - A Bicentennial Celebration*, and to D. Brooks McKinney from the Department of Geoscience at Hobart & William Smith College in Geneva for giving a lecture on the history of cobblestone building. Finally, we are indebted to Susan Domina for her proof-reading expertise. This book was improved by her attention to detail.

Introduction

Residents of upstate New York drive by cobblestone houses as a routine and don't give them much thought. We barely recognize that our home turf was the pre-Civil War birthplace of a new form of construction. And, that it's a method that remains peculiar to our region with over 90% of cobblestone buildings in the U.S. residing within a 65-mile radius of Rochester, New York.

The cobblestone craft that developed around Rochester flourished, spread, and died out all within less than half a century. But it left its stamp permanently on the region. And it holds its place in history as the last generation of completely hand-built houses.

Estimates vary, but approximately 700 to 1,200 cobblestone buildings were built in the United States. 600 to 900 of them are in New York State, spread over 25 counties, spanning from the Hudson River to Niagara Falls. The southernmost cobblestone building in New York State is on Hill Street in Hornell. It is an Italianate style residence, built for the local newspaper publisher.

Some (~70 known) cobblestone buildings are in Wisconsin, Ohio, Illinois, Vermont, Colorado, Michigan, and Ontario, Canada. The masons probably migrated west in the 1840s and 1850s and carried their craft with them.

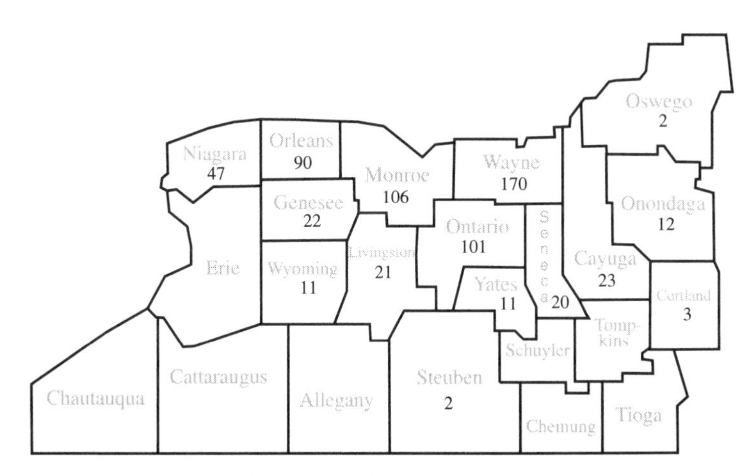

Approximate number of cobblestone buildings per county.

What is a Cobblestone?

The simplest definition of a cobblestone defines it by size. It's a stone that can be held in one hand. In contrast, a pebble can be held between 2 fingers and a boulder takes 2 hands to hold. Geologists define cobblestones by measurements: 64 to 256 mm or 2.5 to 10.1 inches.

The word comes from Middle English. A *cob* is a rounded lump. A *ston* is a small rock. Together they create *cobelstons* or rounded stones used for paving roads.

Geologically, New York cobblestones are a variety of rock types; often sandstone, limestone, quartzite, gneiss, and igneous and metamorphic rocks.

Cobblestones are often differentiated as either fieldstones (field cobbles) or water-rounded stones. Fieldstones are angular stones gathered from glacial till and outwash deposits. Water-rounded (or lake-washed) stones are also glacially derived but have been wave rounded either along the Lake Ontario shore, or long ago by a glacial lake and left in an outwash deposit.

From Where Did the Cobbles Come?

All cobblestones are the result of water action — either ground by the ice of glaciers, rounded by the torrents of water as glaciers melted, or rounded by the wave action of streams and lakes.

Millions of years ago, upstate New York was covered by a succession of at least 17 glaciers, some almost a mile thick. The action of the ice created rough and sometimes squarish cobbles in a variety of sizes, shapes and colors. These were the first to be used; collected as the land was cleared. The last of the glaciers to recede left ancient Lake Iroquois, which eventually receded to the shore of today's Lake Ontario, leaving cobbles rounded by wave action. The receding waters also deposited a ridge of cobbles, many of them red sandstone, along what is Ridge Road (Route 104) today. Lake Iroquois was 150 to 250 feet deeper than Lake Ontario is now.

Water-rounded stones were also gathered from creekbeds and from beaches along Lake Ontario and the Finger Lakes.

Cobblestone Building Periods

The cobblestone building era is divided into 3 periods that serve as convenient groupings, not absolute timelines.

Early Period: 1825-1835

In early period cobblestone buildings, the cobbles vary in color, size, and shape. Masons predominately used glacial field cobbles and built with crude, irregular designs. Most mortar joints were flat and unembellished. Some had V shaped mortar joints formed by the mason holding the trowel at an angle and striking the joint. The horizontal V made the line between the cobbles appear straighter and made the stones appear to project beyond the wall surface, which highlighted the stones in sunlight. Some of the houses using early period construction were built as late as 1846.

Middle Period: 1835-1845

Cobblestone buildings from the middle period used smaller (1.5 to 2.5 inches high, 2 to 4 inches long), rounded or oval water-washed stones in addition to and sometimes mixed in with glacial fieldstones. The masons competed for design originality such as setting oval stones horizontally, vertically, or diagonally. And, they began setting vertical V joints. In the early 1840s someone made a metal form to create a bead or half circle about 1 inch wide to form a rounded joint between the courses.

Late Period: 1845-1860 (the Civil War)

Late period cobblestone buildings were built with very uniform, small (1 to 1.5 inches high), single color stones, especially on the front. The cobbles became a veneer against a structural rubble stone wall. Construction from this period is often criticized for taking on a monotonous, machine-made appearance. Some say craftsmanship gave way to skill. The masons developed intricate patterns such as the introduction of herringbone and striped patterns. The mortar joints were narrow Vs or beaded joints.

Demise of Cobblestone Construction

The demise of cobblestone construction coincided with the outbreak of the Civil War, which caused inflation, so masonry labor became expensive. The supply of small stones became more difficult to come by and costs rose, as they had to be sourced from farther away. Cobblestone construction was replaced by more efficient technologies such as wooden balloon frame construction, fast-drying Portland cement, and mass-produced bricks.

Did Cobblestone Construction Originate in New York?

As far back as the 3rd century, the Romans built massive walls as part of their coastal fortifications, using water-worn flint cobbles that were abundant in the English countryside. They perfected natural lime mortars but didn't lay the stones in defined courses. The Saxons and Normans built walls using flint cobbles (called flint-heads) in rough courses in the 11th century.

Beaded horizontal mortar joints between courses of lake-washed cobblestones. (956 Kent Road, Kent)

Then, in the Middle Ages, cobblestone streets, houses (called flints) and outbuildings were constructed all over Europe and England, particularly in Southeast England and Normandy (northwest France), still using flint. In the 14th century masons knapped (or split) the cobbles and used limestone mortar in a flush treatment. This differed from the mortar Vs and pyramids commonly found on U.S. cobblestone buildings. Flint cobbles can be found laid in coursed, uncoursed, rough coursed, dual coursed and herringbone patterns. No effort was made to select stones of a common size or shape.

Cobblestone construction, based on a European precedent, was adapted and refined by American craftsmen to become a uniquely American form of building construction.

Settlers in the U.S. used fieldstones gathered from the fields to build fences and foundations with flush faces. Sometime between 1825 and 1830 an unknown mason built a house using smaller stones in horizontal courses. This design idea spread rapidly.

U.S. History of Cobblestone Building

After the American Revolution, settlers pushed west into central and western New York. They cleared land for farming and built log or hand-hewn frame cabins from materials on hand. Streams were dammed to power mills to process more lumber.

Lumber mills, brickyards and limekilns sprang up as the first industries. By 1820 brickyards, stone quarries, limekilns and glass factories were prevalent. They provided a choice of building materials (wood, brick, stone).

The location and mason of the first cobblestone building remains a mystery. By charting the dates of construction, it appears the epicenter of cobblestone building was south of Lake Ontario with the earliest buildings in the towns on this map:

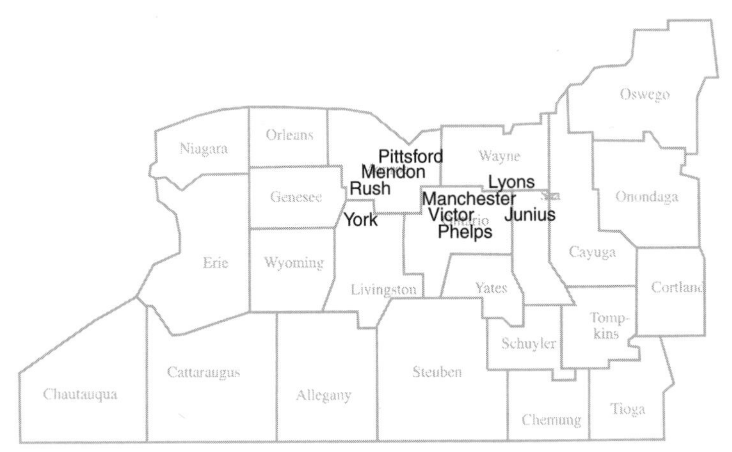

Towns with evidence of
very early cobblestone construction.

What is known, is that cobblestone buildings began on farms and later migrated to the villages. It remained a predominately rural construction method, with only a small number being built in villages.

Why Build Cobblestone Buildings?

Settlers came to the wild frontier and built their log cabin homes. As they prospered with the boom from the Erie Canal and increasing family sizes, they looked to build bigger, more prestigious homes. Lumber was hard work to procure and was needed for fences, barns, animal shelters, carriage sheds, wood sheds, granaries, etc. Also, according to an account in *Pioneer History of Orleans County* by Arad Thomas, "the lumber of the country found a ready market and floated away on the Erie Canal." Bricks were expensive, but stones could be gathered for free. In fact, they needed to be cleared from fields to allow plowing.

The Erie Canal created an economic boom. Wheat prices jumped so farmers cleared more land and prospered. Rochester became known as the "flour city" with a proliferation of mills to grind the wheat from the famous Genesee Country.

Cobblestone homes offered several benefits. They were fireproof and were built with an air of permanence. Paint was expensive so cobblestone homes were easier and less expensive to maintain. Best of all, the building material was free. It could be gathered from plowed fields or brought home in oxcarts after delivering wheat to Sodus for shipment on Lake Ontario.

Gathering & Sorting Stones

Gathering stones was the responsibility of the future homeowner, not the mason. For field cobble houses, boys were often paid $0.10 a day to walk beside a *stoneboat* or sled pulled by oxen or other draft animals, to collect stones turned up by plowing.

Lake-washed cobblestones line the Lake Ontario shoreline.

For lake-washed cobbles, wheat was often taken to Sodus in oxcarts and cobblestones gathered from the lakeshore were brought back in the returning cart.

The stone gathering process could take several years. Once gathered, the stones had to be sorted by size and sometimes color. This was a job for children and women using beetle rings or a sorting board. Neighborhood "bees" were sometimes held to gather and sort stones, followed by a big supper, music and dancing.

Most tools used in cobblestone construction were ordinary ones found on farms, such as mason's trowels, straight edges, calking irons, and hammers. Three specialized tools were developed for cobblestone masonry:

Beetle Rings: A beetle is a heavy wooden mallet used to force stones into sand. The head is often bound with 2 iron rings (or beetle rings) to prevent splitting. These rings were readapted to sorting stones by size.

Sorting Board: A board or plank with various sized holes cut into it. This tool was designed to sort stones by size.

Bead Form: A metal form used to create a 1-inch-wide bead or half circle on a mortar joint. This first showed up in the middle period of cobblestone construction.

Mortar Magic

Soft lime mortar is the glue that holds the cobbles together. In its most basic form, mortar is made of lime, sand and water. But, each mason's mortar recipe was unique and guarded closely as a trade secret. Wide variations occurred in the proportions of ingredients, the quality of ingredients, the method of obtaining and mixing the ingredients, and even in storage methods. Experimentation was encouraged.

The magic of soft lime mortar was that it cured slowly and let stones settle and bear weight. Soft lime mortar took up to 35 years to fully harden, which gave the building time to settle without cracking. These were pre-Portland cement days. Cobblestone buildings can't be repaired with modern mortar (Portland cement) because it dries too hard, too fast, and pushes the cobbles out.

To make soft lime mortar, local limestone (calcium carbonate) or local dolomite (magnesium carbonate) was broken into pieces, and burned within heaps of logs (early primitive method) or in a limekiln. Limekilns were built 20-feet high, sometimes into the side of a hill, so it was easy for a cartload of limestone to be loaded in the top at road level. A fire was built in the bottom. Flame passed up through the stone and out the top. Burning took 2 to 3 days to create quicklime. When water was added to quicklime it created heat and produced a hydrated lime sludge. This process was called slaking.

Masons needed coarse, pure sand to mix with hydrated lime sludge to create a strong cement (5 to 9 bushels of sand to 1 bushel of lime). Some darker mortars may have had local earth mixed in. Some masons aged the mortar in a ground pit covered by sand or cow manure for up to a year.

Limekiln operators sold quicklime by the bushel. It was used as fertilizer, for tanning, as a whitewash, for plaster, and in making mortar. Limekilns were common in this region throughout the 19th century. In 1860, Orleans County had 15 limekilns.

Who Were the Masons?

That's a very good question. To this day, most of the cobblestone masons remain anonymous. Records from only a few masons survived — none from early buildings. It is unlikely that masons brought the skills from Europe. Early cobblestone construction lagged the skill shown in England by 50 years.

Because of the number of houses built over a short period, there must have been many masons. Evidence we have shows that only a few masons built more than 3 or 4 homes. Many houses were built by their owners who learned construction techniques by word of mouth, from periodicals, or from work on the Erie Canal. The evolution of buildings shows increasing skill & sophistication in masonry.

Building Techniques

A good mason could lay 4 courses, or about 18 to 24 inches of wall per day. Generally, only 1 mason worked on a house at a time, so work would progress slowly and allow the mortar to begin to set. Some were built in a season, but it could take 2 to 3 years to build a house. A mason might work on 2 or 3 buildings concurrently per season. Each mason had his own style of selecting and assembling the cobblestones so it's possible to look at houses and find others (often nearby) that resemble each other and were built by the same mason. In 1850 a mason's pay was $1.00 to $1.50 per day plus board, for working 10 to 12-hour days.

Construction methods as well as building materials advanced with each of the three periods.

Early period cobblestone buildings were constructed with an 18 to 20-inch thick, solid coursed rubble wall with 3 rows of field cobbles tied together with elongated or triangular shaped stones. The inner 2/3rds of the wall used large stones. There was complete integration of the cobblestone surface with the interior wall — the whole wall was laid up as one. To finish the inside, horsehair plaster was applied to the stone.

Middle period cobblestone buildings were constructed with a rubble core. A facing of cobblestones was laid on front of the core, which included longer cobbles extending into the core for bonding. Again, the entire wall was laid up as one.

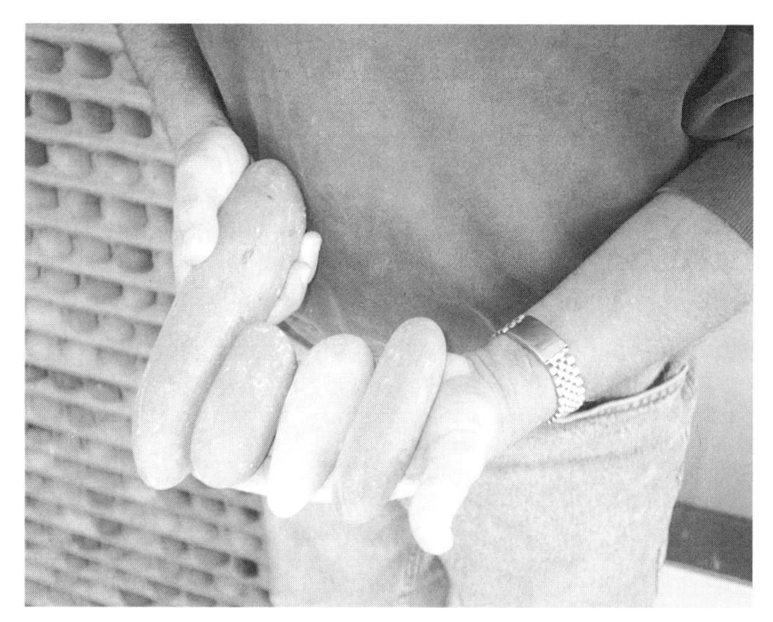

Elongated cobbles were sometimes set with only their ends showing. The long parts served to tie the wall together. (956 Kent Road, Kent)

Some late period cobblestone buildings were constructed with a rubble wall laid first, with a mortar and small stone veneer laid separately. There was no bonding between the two. This was the least permanent design. Wall thickness varied, with one mason using 20-inch cellar and first floor walls and 18-inch second floor walls. Another mason used 16-inch walls throughout. Firing strips were applied to the interior walls to provide an air space (sometimes 2 to 3 inches thick) between the stone and interior wall. The interior wall was then finished with lath and plaster.

Myth Buster

Commonly believed folklore states that canal masons, particularly Irish or Scottish masons, left unemployed by the completion of the original Erie Canal in 1825, turned to cobblestone masonry. But, the original Erie Canal was an immediate economic success and enhancements to widen and deepen it began in 1832 and continued through 1862, offering plenty of work for canal masons throughout all three cobblestone building periods. Almost half of the cobblestone buildings were built between 1836 and 1846 when canal masons would have been employed.

The demand for masons on the canal was primarily for building locks and aqueducts. Over 65% of these structures were east of Syracuse on the original Erie Canal but only 4% of cobblestone buildings are found there.

Masonry for locks and aqueducts on the canal consisted of working with large blocks of stone, not with small cobbles. In Lockport where canal masons built a series of 5 locks to climb the Niagara Escarpment, they built their homes of cut stone blocks, not of cobblestones.

It certainly wasn't Irish canal masons who built the cobblestone houses, as mythology states. Only 3 Irish workers were documented to have worked on the original Erie Canal. The wave of Irish immigration did not begin until the late 1830s. There was not even a large Irish labor force available for the first enlargement of the canal in 1836.

Although the exact date of the earliest cobblestone building isn't known, there is evidence that some were built before 1825 and possibly as early as 1810, predating the canal.

Some canal masons may well have built cobblestone houses. But, more commonly, it was probably local masons or even local farmers themselves who learned the skills and built their own and their relatives' homes. A periodical called the *Genesee Farmer* published a series of inquiries and responses from farmers asking about the process of cobblestone building. The responses say nothing about needing specialized masonry skills or about locating a skilled mason.

You Are There

Step back in time and listen to the account of building a cobblestone house from the perspective of a man who, as a child, helped his family build their home in Arcadia, Wayne County:

> *"Father had accumulated a large quantity of stone and lumber including one very large whitewood tree, about four feet in diameter, and thousands of feet of basswood and hemlock and had carefully piled it up with sticks between each board and built a shed over it that it might be thoroughly seasoned. On the last sleighing that spring there was a 'bee' and a large pile of sand was taken from back of the woods where Mr. Farnsworth's farm now stands, it being the first ever taken from there. It kept one or two men shoveling snow on the bare spots by thawing so fast. We got two or three loads of cobblestones from the lake for the facing of the wall. The 'cut stones' (caps and sills) came from Phelps (then Vienna)."*
>
> *"The job was let to a Mr. Skinner, not including the inside work, have forgotten the price, but I think it was less than $200. They came and laid the cellar wall; then went away and did other jobs to let this harden; then returned and laid the first story; then went away again for several weeks and so on until it was finished. Meanwhile, the carpenters prepared the window and door frames, the sleepers and joists. As the walls were ready for them they did the plaining (sic) and matching the flooring (every board in the house being plained by hand) and nearly all but the floors were sandpapered."*
>
> *"While they were absent father would have to draw more stones from Phelps besides doing a little farming and all the other work and business accompanying such building. He also went with two teams to Italy Hollow, south of Geneva, and got about 2,000 feet of pine lumber for about $10 per thousand, being about all of the pine used in the house."*
>
> *"The first stone he drew from the lake, he took a man with the team and went to the bar off the bluff across the bay on ice. I went with him and we reached home about one o'clock in the morning. Father went about 20 times but sometimes being rainy he got only part of a load and often reached home 10 or 12 o'clock at night. Parkings the carpenter only did the work until it was enclosed, which was late in the fall. One of my jobs was to flatten the nailheads as there were no finishing nails then; also had to putty the nailheads after being driven."*
>
> *"In laying the walls after getting out of reach from the ground there were poles set about 6 or 8 feet from the wall and about as high as the walls were to be, then long poles were lashed to them with hickory witches an inch or an inch and a quarter in diameter and six to eight inches long and then scantling laid across them to the wall and planks laid on them making a scaffolding all around the house. Then a crane and tackles and rope were*

fastened to the northeast post (it being larger than the rest). Buckets a little larger than a molasses cask cut in two would be filled with either mortar or stones and hoisted up, using a horse, to the scaffold and their contents distributed with a wheelbarrow. When they were above reach from a scaffold the staging would be raised again. The inside work was done by Ruel Taylor and his men. They did their work evenings and were here all winter."

"The doors were made by hand. Father went out southwest of Newark and bought a butternut tree for stair railings and all connected with them — the house was not ready for occupancy until May the next year. The frame part was not moved until fall, the crane and tackles were used in digging the well in the fall, which was in 1845."

from *Cobblestone Structures of Wayne County*
by Verlyn Edward Klahn, 1955

Types of Structures Built

Cobblestone construction was used to build many homes. But that's not all. This technique was also used in building churches, schools, mills, barns, stores, shops, factories, carriage houses, garden houses, gate and toll houses, smokehouses, pumphouses, hophouses, privies, stables, turniphouses, piggeries, decorative walls along roadways, and even cemetery markers and cemetery receiving vaults. Examples of many of these structures still exist and can be seen on the tours that follow.

Architectural Style

Cobblestone is a construction method, not an architectural style. In terms of architectural style, most cobblestone buildings are Greek Revival. Some are Federal, Gothic Revival, Italianate, Post Colonial, and Victorian styles.

Each cobblestone building is handcrafted and unique. The doors on a house were often not interchangeable — each built specific to an opening. Carpenters used hand tools and their own creativity to create moldings, fireplace mantles and doors.

Components of a Cobblestone Building

(See definitions on page 179.)

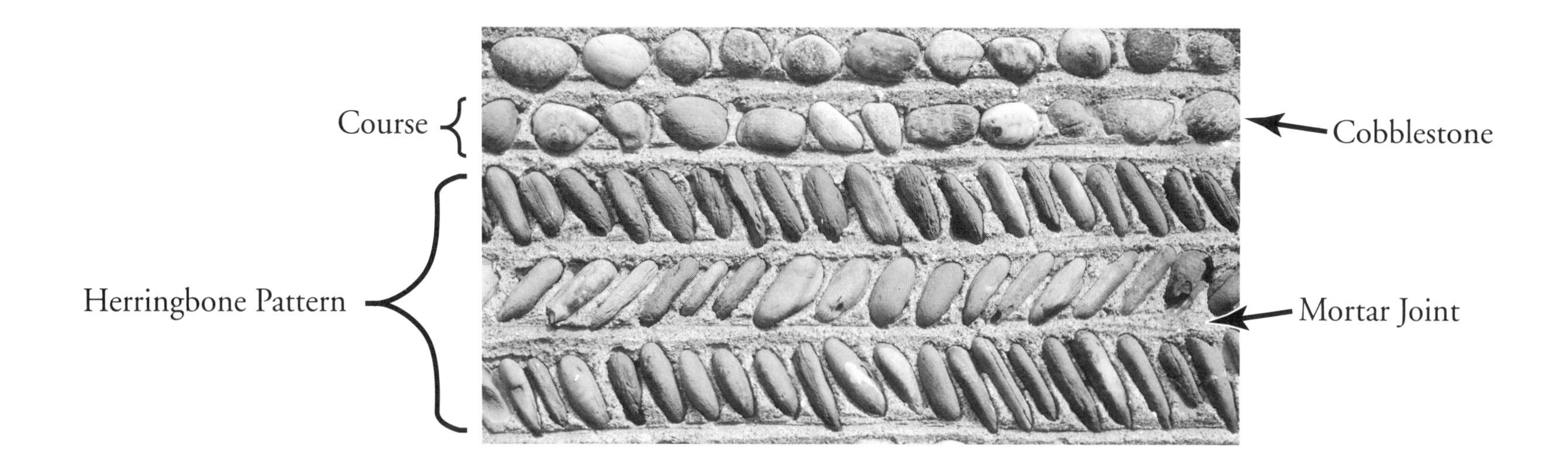
Course
Cobblestone
Herringbone Pattern
Mortar Joint

Cornice
Frieze
Frieze Window
(colloquially called
a Belly Window)
or Decorative Grill
Foundation

What Are The Tours?

The cobblestone tours in this guidebook are not an accounting or an updating of the historical record of all the cobblestone buildings in the area. We selected buildings that can be seen from the road, ones that offer a particularly good example of cobblestone construction, or offer unique features. And, they are in a cluster with others that make a reasonable driving route. On the maps you'll see little gray house shapes that denote other cobblestone buildings within the area covered by the map but not specified on the tour. Cobblestone buildings specified on the tour are noted on the maps with a circled number.

House names used are generally the name of the original owner, where known. Often in historical records, houses are named according to the owner at the time of the research, but this can be very confusing.

How to Spot a Cobblestone Building

The instructions for each tour give directions, landmarks and distances for locating the cobblestone buildings. A general clue is to look for big, old trees. The trees were planted in the 1800s when the houses were built and have grown to stately sizes. You may also spot a haggard-looking owner. We're just joking, of course, but cobblestone buildings do consume significant time and money for maintenance. But, we believe you'll agree with us that cobblestone buildings are well worth the effort. Have fun on the tours and enjoy the diversity and uniqueness of the cobblestone buildings. Then, do whatever you can to help preserve them for future generations to enjoy.

Map Legend

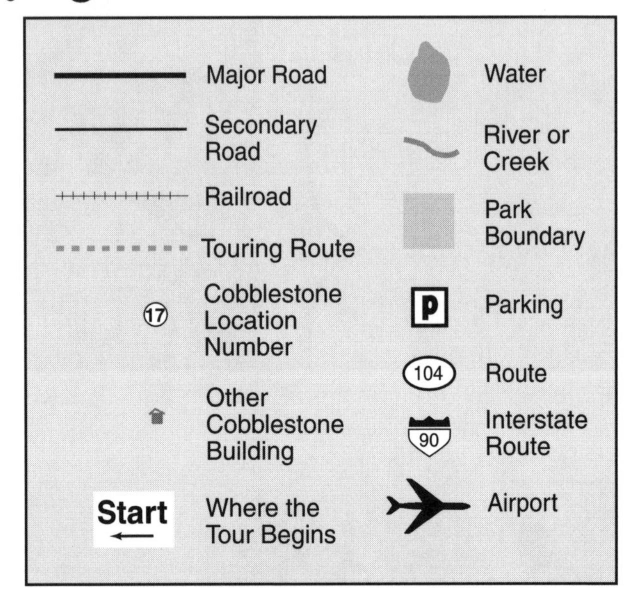

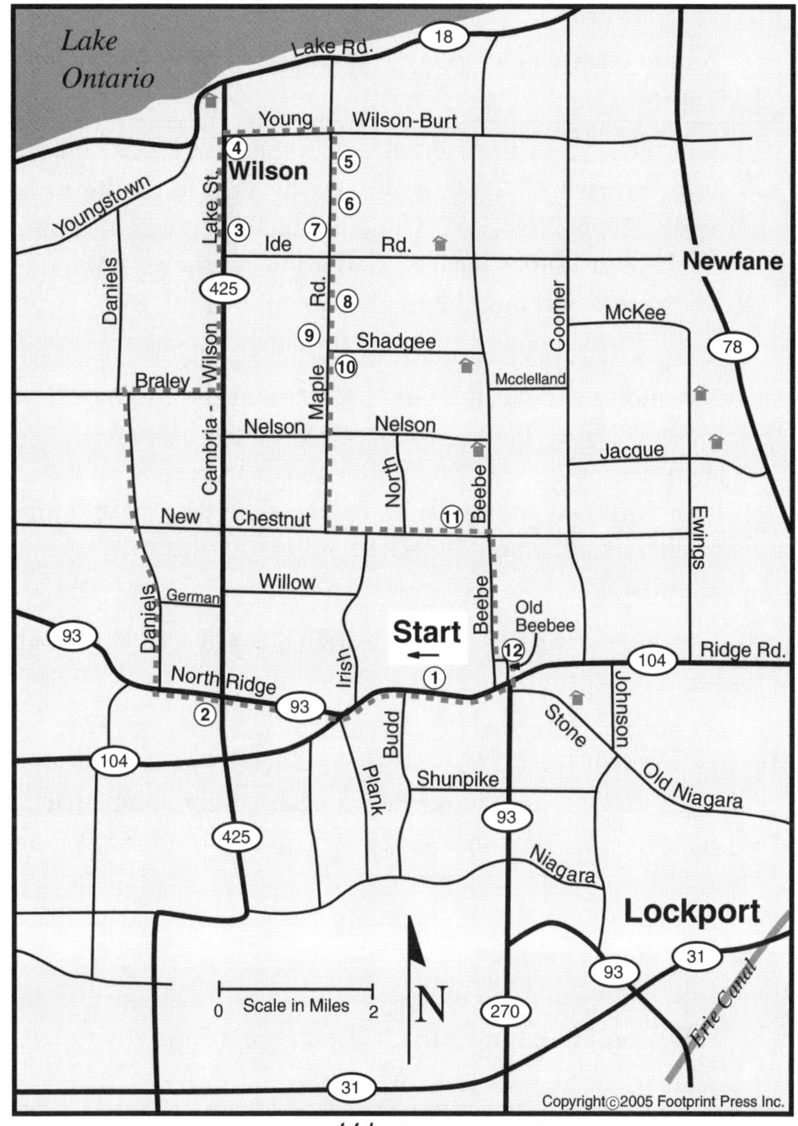

Cobblestone Tour 1

Cobblestone Tour 1

Northwest of Lockport in Niagara County
Total Distance: 22 miles
Approximate Time: 1 hour

On this tour you'll find several examples of cobblestone houses in the Greek Revival style, with belly windows, and an unusual lintel design called the "Holland hat" effect.

Begin the tour northwest of Lockport, heading west on Route 104. 0.8 mile west of the Route 93/270 junction, watch right.

1.
Address: 4975 Ridge Road (Route 104), Lockport

This 2-story, L-shaped home was built with small, lake-washed cobbles on the front and sides, and cut limestone lintels, quoins, sills and water table. Belly windows can be seen in the wide frieze on the sides. The front door is surrounded by sidelights with a unique round-pattern glass. A porch covers the front of the wing and there's a fan in the front gable end.

Continue west on Route 104, then turn right onto Route 93 west (North Ridge Road). After the traffic light at

Cambria-Wilson Road (Route 425) pull into the parking lot of the church on the left.

2. North Ridge United Methodist Church
Address: 3930 North Ridge Road (Route 93), Lockport, Town of Cambria
Year Built: 1847-1848
Style: Greek Revival

This gorgeous church with stained glass windows and a white steeple was built for the Methodist Society. It has small, rounded cobbles on the front and large field cobbles on the sides. This building was added to the National Register of Historic Places in 2002.

Continue west on Route 93, then turn right (north) onto Daniels Road. At the end, turn right onto Braley, then left onto Route 425 (Cambria-Wilson Road, which will turn into Lake Street). After passing Ide Road, watch right.

3. Johnson House
Address: 2533 Cambria-Wilson Road (Route 425), Wilson
Original Owner: Morgan Johnson
Year Built: 1844-1845
Period: Middle
Style: Greek Revival

Morgan Johnson was a ship captain when he built this home in 1844. His ship, the "Milly Cook" caught fire and sank in Wilson Harbor. The spot is still known today as Milly Cook Cove.

An anchor from the schooner Franklin Pierce, rests on the lawn, northwest of the house, giving this house the nickname "Anchor House." The Franklin Pierce was anchored off shore in 1840 when a sudden storm cut the anchor loose. The anchor was found near the Wilson pier in 1897.

Note the especially fine workmanship on the ornate lintels and quoins and cut limestone columns at the entrance. The recessed center is unusual, along with the limestone steps and stone railings. The house sports wide Greek Revival cornices with cast iron grills in a wide frieze that mask a full-height second floor. Especially unique is the herringbone foundation.

The one-story wing out back originally was a service wing. Inside, the home has a circular staircase.

Continue north on Route 425 (Lake Street) into Wilson and turn right onto Young Street at the traffic light. Immediately turn right into the parking lot. It's the parking lot of the Wilson House Inn restaurant. It's best to walk around this building to view it. This is an operating restaurant, so you may want to plan a visit for lunch or dinner.

4. Wilson House (now the Wilson House Inn)
Address: 300 Lake Street, Wilson
Original Owner: Luther Wilson

Year Built: 1844
Period: Middle

This building was built as a home for Luther Wilson, the son of Reuben Wilson, who founded the Town of Wilson. In 1890 the double funeral of Captain Luther Wilson (age 92) and his son Reuben F. Wilson (age 68) was held in this house. Next the house became a club house, called the "Wilsonian Club" when a group of businessmen purchased the house. They built bowling alleys in the basement and held dances in the large room on the second floor. It first became a restaurant in 1947, and remains so today.

Notice the small, mixed color, water-rounded cobblestones (6 courses per quoin on front and 5 courses per quoin on the side). On the front you can see how the building has shifted and settled. Below the water table the foundation has been updated with cement blocks.

Continue east on Young Street, passing a traffic light, then turn right onto Maple Road and watch left in a grove of large trees. Three houses on this road were all built around the same time period, but each has a distinctively different look.

5. The Whitlock House
Address: 2449 Maple Road, Wilson
Original Owner: Nehemiah Whitlock
Year Built: ~1835
Period: Middle

Style: Greek Revival

Two Doric columns adorn the porch at the front door, which is framed by sidelights and a transom. Four wooden grills are set in the wide frieze. Notice that both the front and sides sport tiny water-rounded cobbles (5 courses per quoin) and the lintels and quoins are precisely cut. Square fieldstone was used as the foundation below the water table and as a wall in the front yard.

A grill in a wide frieze, above courses of field cobbles.
(Exley House, 2546 Maple Road, Wilson)

Continue south on Maple Road and look at the next house on the left.

6. Pettit House
Address: 2471 Maple Road, Wilson
Original Owner: Clinton Pettit
Year Built: ~1835
Period: Middle
Style: Greek Revival

This is a farmhouse with markedly different craftsmanship. It's a 1.5-story field cobble building with a 1-story wing, and a wide frieze containing 2 belly windows.

This house was the boyhood home of Ira S. Pettit, born in 1841, as noted by the historical marker in front. Ira died at age 23 as a Union soldier in Andersonville prison during the Civil War. His story is the subject of a novel by Jean P. Ray, *Diary of a Deadman.*

Continue south on Maple Road and look at the next house on the right.

7. Exley House
Address: 2546 Maple Road, Wilson
Original Owner: Thomas Exley
Year Built: ~1835
Period: Middle
Style: Greek Revival

This is a 2-story fieldstone building (3 courses per quoin) with a single story wing on the left. It has a colonial blue

Exley House, 2546 Maple Road, Wilson

front door and white painted lintels and quoins. Note the grills in the frieze.

This house looked significantly different in the late 1800s. The Exleys added many rooms onto the house. Reportedly there was no door on a north wing. The residents, Mrs. Exley's sister, Mrs. Harness and her daughter, are said to have gone in and out via a window by means of a small ladder. Mr. & Mrs. Arthur Gifford (who cared for the Exleys) lived in a wing off the back of the house, that was built three steps lower than the main house.

Ten rooms had been removed before Mr. Goodman bought the house in 1921, then he removed three more in 1922. Mr. Goodman reported some visitors from Canada told him there were 2 loose boards under a bedroom where the Exleys used to hide cans of money. The Exleys were wealthy. They gave substantial money to the Exley Methodist-Episcopal Church in Wilson and willed their 2 farms to the church upon their deaths.

Continue south on Maple Road. Cross Ide Road and watch left.

8. Morse House
Address: 2773 Maple Road, Wilson
Original Owner: James Morse
Year Built: ~1845
Period: Middle
Style: Greek Revival with English Gothic window caps

Somewhat hard to see behind trees, this farmhouse was built with tiny water-washed cobbles, five courses per quoin. It's a 2-story house with a wing on the left. Belly windows are found in the frieze on the wing and a porch spans its front. The stone lintels have the 'Holland hat' effect that is English Gothic. They were made in Lockport and hauled here for $10 each. A stone barn still stands, north of the house.

Continue south on Maple Road to the second house on the right.

9. Wilson House
Address: 2804 Maple Road, Wilson
Original Owner: William Wilson
Year Built: 1861

Don't be fooled! This is not an official cobblestone building but is being pointed out for comparison. The square stones and square quoins were created by the mason splitting field-stones to replicate the English cut stone methodology. Two families originally occupied this house, totalling 13 people.

Continue south on Maple Road. Pass Shadgee Road and watch left.

10. Smith House
Address: 2995 Maple Road, Wilson
Original Owner: Jesse Smith
Year Built: 1833 or 1840
Style: Greek Revival

Did you learn the difference? Just like house #9 on this tour, this home isn't an official cobblestone either. The square stone on front is cut brown ledge rock (fieldstone), approximately 4 inches high per course. Otherwise, it shows all the characteristics of a cobblestone building. There is recent mudding on the sides. It has belly windows in the frieze.

Continue south on Maple Road to the end. Turn left onto Chestnut Street. Pass North Road then watch left.

11. Woodcock House

Address: 4831 Chestnut Road, Wilson
Original Owner: William Woodcock Sr.
Year Built: ~1836-1840
Period: Middle
Style: Greek Revival

William and Fanny Woodcock came from England and settled on the Old Niagara Road. In 1835 they and their 3 children moved to East Wilson and built a log cabin on a 100-acre plot of land on Marsh Settlement Road (as Chestnut Road was then called). This was a wilderness with swamps in the surrounding areas. Bears and wolves roamed about freely.

The Woodcocks hauled stones by wagon from Lake Ontario over trails cut through the woods and began construction of their 2-story cobblestone house in 1836. Four years later the home was complete and the Woodcock clan lived here for over 100 years.

Look carefully at this unique structure. From the ground up you'll find fieldstone on the main house, but small, water-washed cobbles set on edge between the quoins. The quoins, lintels and water table are painted white. Unfortunately segments of the cobblestones have been mudded over. As usual there are larger stones on the sides.

At the next intersection turn right (south) onto Beebe Road. 1.4 miles from the corner, turn left onto Old Beebe Road and look left at the bend.

12. Four Towns Cobblestone

Address: 3999 Old Beebe Road, Wilson
Original Owner: F. Capen
Year Built: ~1835
Period: Middle

The house and outbuilding, now a garage, are both cobblestone. It's unique to have a cobblestone garage. Unfortunately, it has seen better days. Four town boundaries intersect here and many refer to this building as the "Four Towns Cobblestone."

Continue south on Old Beebe Road. The next intersection is the junction of Routes 104 and 93.

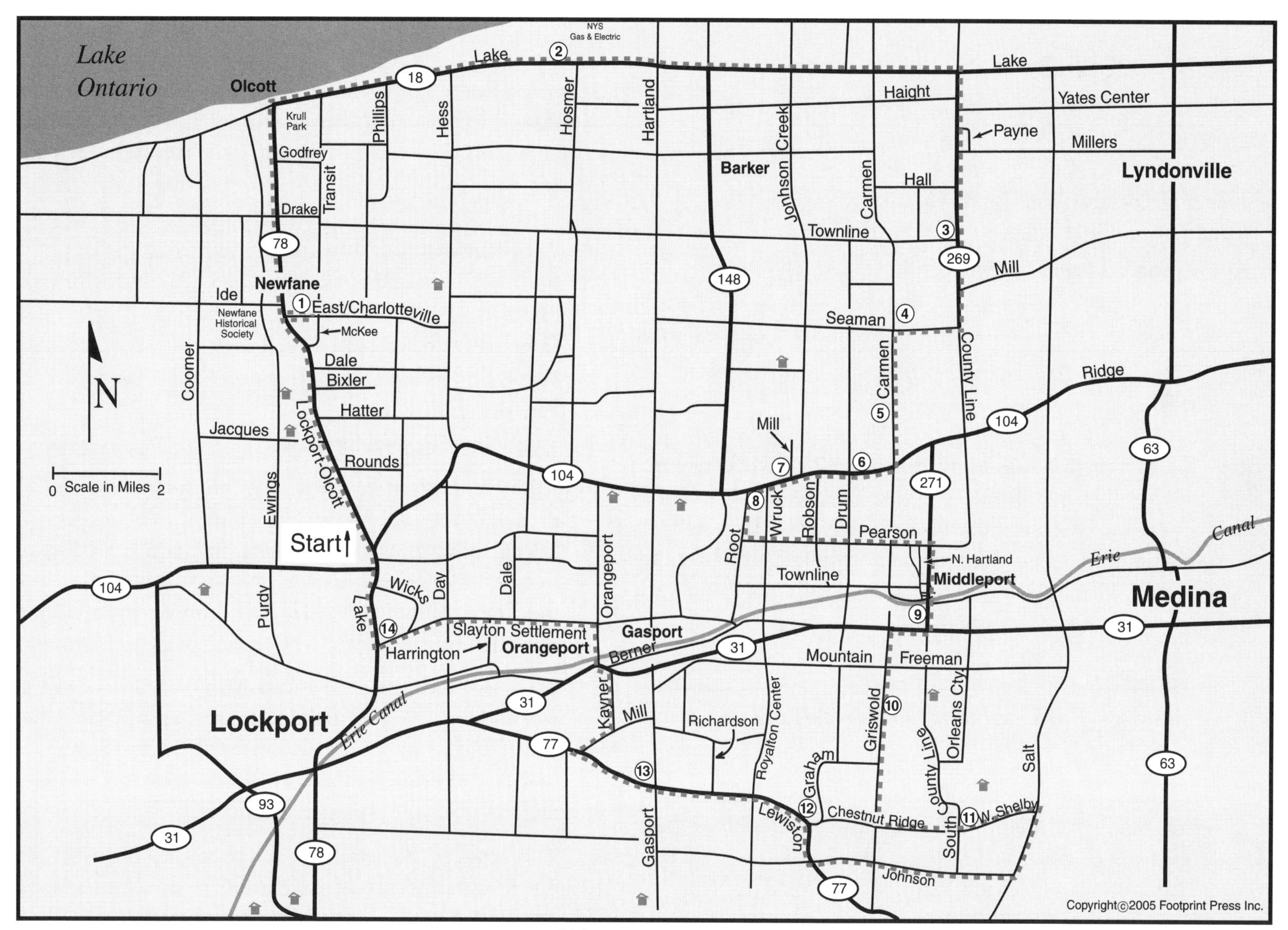

Cobblestone Tour 2

Cobblestone Tour 2

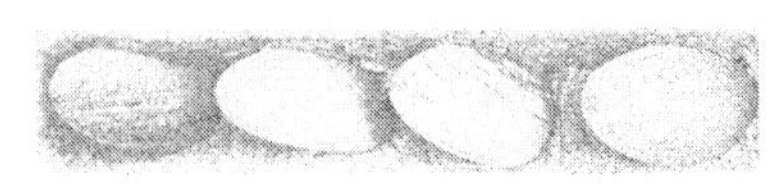

North of Lockport in Niagara County
Total Distance: 63 miles
Approximate Time: 1.5 hour

On this tour, you'll be able to get out of your vehicle and get a close-up look at churches, a house that's now a museum, and a schoolhouse.

Begin the tour by heading north on Route 78 from Lockport. Continue north past Route 104. Route 78 becomes Lockport-Olcott Road and leads into the village of Newfane. Turn right at the traffic light onto East Avenue/Charlotteville Road. Take the first left onto Maple Avenue. Look at the church on your left. Park in the church parking lot.

1. First Baptist Church
Address: 6047 East Avenue (Charlotteville Road), Newfane
Year Built: 1843

The oldest church in Newfane was built with field cobbles set 3 courses per quoin. The front tower with stained glass windows was added in 1907. An addition on the right was added at the end of World War I.

Go back out Maple Avenue. Turn right onto East Avenue, then right onto Route 78 north. At the traffic light, turn right (east) onto Route 18. 5.1 miles from the turn, (after Hess Road) watch left for a "Babcock House Museum" sign. Turn into the parking lot here.

2. Babcock House Museum
Address: 7449 Lake Road (Route 18), Appleton, Town of Somerset
Original Owner: Jeptha W. Babcock
Year Built: ~ 1848 (some references say 1840)
Period: Middle-late
Style: Greek Revival farmhouse

Jeptha and Mary Babcock were prominent citizens when they built their farmhouse. In addition to being one of the largest wheat growers of the area, Jeptha was the first postmaster in the western section of Somerset and Supervisor to the Town of Somerset. He went on to be a NY State Assemblyman. The Babcocks raised 4 children in this house.

Outside notice the wide friezes with 5 crème colored grills that light the second floor bedrooms and Doric columns and sidelights that frame the front door. It was built with multi-colored lake cobbles laid horizontally that vary in size, ranging from 4 to 6 courses per quoin.

The Town of Somerset Historical Society (716-795-9948) operates this gorgeous old farmhouse as a museum. It is open on Saturday and Sunday 1 - 4 PM from the last

Saturday in June through the second Sunday of October. Major restoration work was completed on this home in 1983. Inside you can see a bread oven, wrought iron fixtures that are handcrafted replicas of authentic 19th century pieces, light fixtures that resemble candles, as well as the deep windows and doors that are standard on cobblestone buildings. The Somerset Old Fashion Farm Festival is held here the Sunday of Memorial Day weekend and a Victorian Christmas is held the second Sunday of December.

Continue east on Route 18 for 7.0 miles, then turn right (south) on Route 269. Pass Haight Road and Hall Road on the right, then look right just before the corner of Townline Road for a cobblestone building.

3. Fisher House
Address: 2134 County Line Road, Town of Somerset
Original Owner: Joseph and Mary Fisher
Mason: Fred Shy (The same mason who built the First Universalist Church, #9 on this tour.)
Year Built: 1850-1852

This 1.5-story building has wings on the right and back. Notice the frieze on the side with belly windows and below it a coffin door, now painted white, facing Townline Road. This building has red sandstone quoins and lintels. The small, water-rounded cobbles on the front are set on edge, 5 courses per quoin. Larger field cobbles were used on the sides.

Joseph and Mary Yoeman Fisher married in England in 1826 and set sail for America the next day, on a 6-week journey. They originally purchased 10 acres of land and added to it over time. The Fishers and their 10 children moved into their cobblestone house the day before Christmas, 1852. It was heated by a wood stove, lit with oil lamps and had a pump in the kitchen for water.

This house remained in the Fisher family until 2001 when it was purchased by John and Alma Miller, an Amish family from Ohio.

Continue south on Route 269, then take the next right onto Seaman Road. Watch to the right as you approach Carmen Road, and pull into the driveway of the Hartland Historical Society District 10 Schoolhouse, before the stop sign.

4. Hartland Historical Society District 10 Schoolhouse
Address: 9713 Seaman Road, Hartland
Year Built: 1845
Style: Schoolhouse

This building, dubbed the "little gray schoolhouse" is a simple, single story structure build of field cobbles and limestone quoins, lintels and sills. You can park and walk around the building and peer inside to see it still set up as a schoolhouse.

Turn left (south) onto Carmen Road at the stop sign, and watch to the right.

5. Bixby House
Address: 2888 Carmen Road, Hartland
Original Owner: Riley W. Bixby
Year Built: ~1850-1852

Notice the very small, water-washed cobbles on edge on the front of this building and larger field cobbles on the sides. The wide frieze has 3 belly windows and the lintels, quoins and trim are painted white.

This house is on the State and National Register of Historic Places.

Continue south on Carmen Road. At the next junction, turn right onto Route 104, and watch to the right.

6.
Address: 9491 Ridge Road (Route 104), Hartland
Year Built: ~1836

This 2-story house that sits near the road has squarish, rough field cobbles and rough Medina sandstone quoins and lintels. Notice the rows are not perfectly straight.

Continue west on Route 104, passing Drum, Robson and Johnson Creek Roads. Then watch right after Mill Street.

7. Harrington House
Address: 8993 Ridge Road (Route 104), Town of Hartland
Original Owner: Harrington family
Year Built: ~1845
Period: Early

This plain, early period home was built with field cobbles laid 3 courses per quoin.

The wing and portico were additions. This house is a candidate for the State and National Register of Historic Places (application pending).

Continue west on Route 104. Pass Wruck Road and watch left.

8. Quaker Meeting House
Address: 8856 Ridge Road (Route 104), Town of Hartland
Year Built: 1836
Period: Early

This plain, early period building was built as a Quaker meeting house. Today it's a private residence called "Cobblehurst." Feel free to explore the Quaker cemetery next door.

Take the next left onto Root Road. Take the next left onto Pearson Road. Pass 4 crossroads, then pass Chase and N. Hartland Streets to the right, then turn right onto Route 271 (Stone Road which will become Main Street). Cross over the Erie

Canal and watch to the right for a church in the village of Middleport.

9. First Universalist Church
Address: 48 South Main Street, Middleport, Town of Royalton
Mason: Fred Shy (The same mason who built Fisher House, #3 on this tour.)
Year Built: 1841
Period: Late
Style: Greek Revival topped with a hexagonal cupola

Congregational picnickers from the Universalist Society collected stone for this church from the shores of Lake Ontario and transported them by ox cart. Notice the tiny lake-washed cobbles set vertically. The mason followed a design from Asher Benjamin's *The Builders' Guide,* first published in 1839. An unusual feature is that the quoins are all equal size and form a pilaster effect at the corners of the building. Two large, white Doric columns at the front, frame inset doors. The sides have a wide frieze. 5 stained glass windows can be found on the north side.

Continue south on Route 271, then turn right (west) on Route 31 at the flashing light. Take the first left onto Griswold Street. Pass Freeman/Mountain Road, then watch to the left.

Decorative Italianate scrolling on the eves of Boudreau House, 4585 Griswold Street, Royalton.

10. Boudreau House
Address: 4585 Griswold Street, Royalton
Year Built: ~1848-1850
Style: Italianate Ornate

This is a 2-story building with an inset porch between the sections. The eves have decorative Italianate Ornate scrolling. Look closely at the lintels. They're angled at the top, and cobbles were selected that are progressively smaller toward the point so the rows remain straight. The front has small cobbles set on edge and fine cut limestone quoins. Two unequal sized gables can be found on each side.

Continue south on Griswold Street, then take the first left onto Chestnut Ridge Road. Cross South County Line Road and look left immediately after the intersection.

11. Schulps (or Shelp) House
Address: 10181 West Shelby Road, Middleport
Original Owner: John and Mary Schulps (or Shelp)
Mason: Oliver Cohen
Year Built: 1836
Period: Middle
Style: Colonial Revival

Revolutionary War soldier Oliver Cohen (or Cone) purchased this land for his daughter Mary who married John Schulps. Cohen was a minuteman from Connecticut. The large fieldstones and lake stones in neat rows suggest a middle period building. The 12-inch lintels are cut gray limestone. A fan shaped window at each gable end lets light into the attic. The wooden addition was built in the early 1900s, and the rounded porch in front was added later. Note the three stories in the back. Inside there's a dirt floor basement that contains a beehive fireplace with a large crane used for baking.

Schulps House, 10181 West Shelby Road, Middleport

Continue east on West Shelby Road, and take the first right onto Salt Road. Take the next right onto Johnson Road. Pass South County Line Road then Griswold Street. Turn right onto

Lewiston Road (Route 77). Watch right after Route 77 turns left at the stop sign.

12. Guernsey House
Address: 9065 Chestnut Ridge Road (Route 77), Royalton
Year Built: ~1832
Style: Colonial

Sitting at Gilbert's Corners, this house sports large field cobbles and white shutters. Limestone blocks set at an angle with a keystone are used in place of lintels. Quoins are rough blocks. Note the interesting fan-shaped vents on side eves.

Continue west on Route 77. Pass Royalton Center Road and Richardson Road, then watch right at the corner of Gasport Road, just after the signal light.

13. Stagecoach Tavern
Address: 7971 Chestnut Ridge Road (Route 77), Royalton
Year Built: ~1830

This small 1-story home has large field cobbles and a large, 2.5-story brick addition. It was once the historically famous stagecoach tavern at McNalls Corners. It sat along an Indian trail that became Lewiston Trail or Road, and is known today as Route 77. Note the large lintels with a chiseled surface and the two large carriage openings. The lower level one has been replaced with a window. The upper one still serves as a doorway.

Continue west on Route 77, then take the first right onto Mill Road. Take the first left onto Kayner Road (unlabeled). Turn left onto Rochester Road (Route 31). Shortly, take the first right onto Orangeport Road, and cross over the Erie Canal. Take the first left onto Slayton Settlement Road. Pass 2 cut-stone houses on the right, then Dale Road, Harrington Road, Day Road and Wicks Road. Watch right.

14. Goodrich House
Address: 6567 Slayton Settlement Road, Lockport
Original Owner: James Goodrich
Year Built: ~1830-1835
Style: Greek Revival

This 2.5-story house with a 1.5-story wing on the left is easy to see. The cobblestones are 4 courses per quoin on the front. Notice the unusual door over the front door, white painted limestone lintels, quoins and water table, and a medium size frieze. Look behind the house to see a fieldstone smokehouse.

Continue west on Slayton Settlement Road. and you'll run into Route 78 (Lake Avenue.) north of Lockport, your starting point.

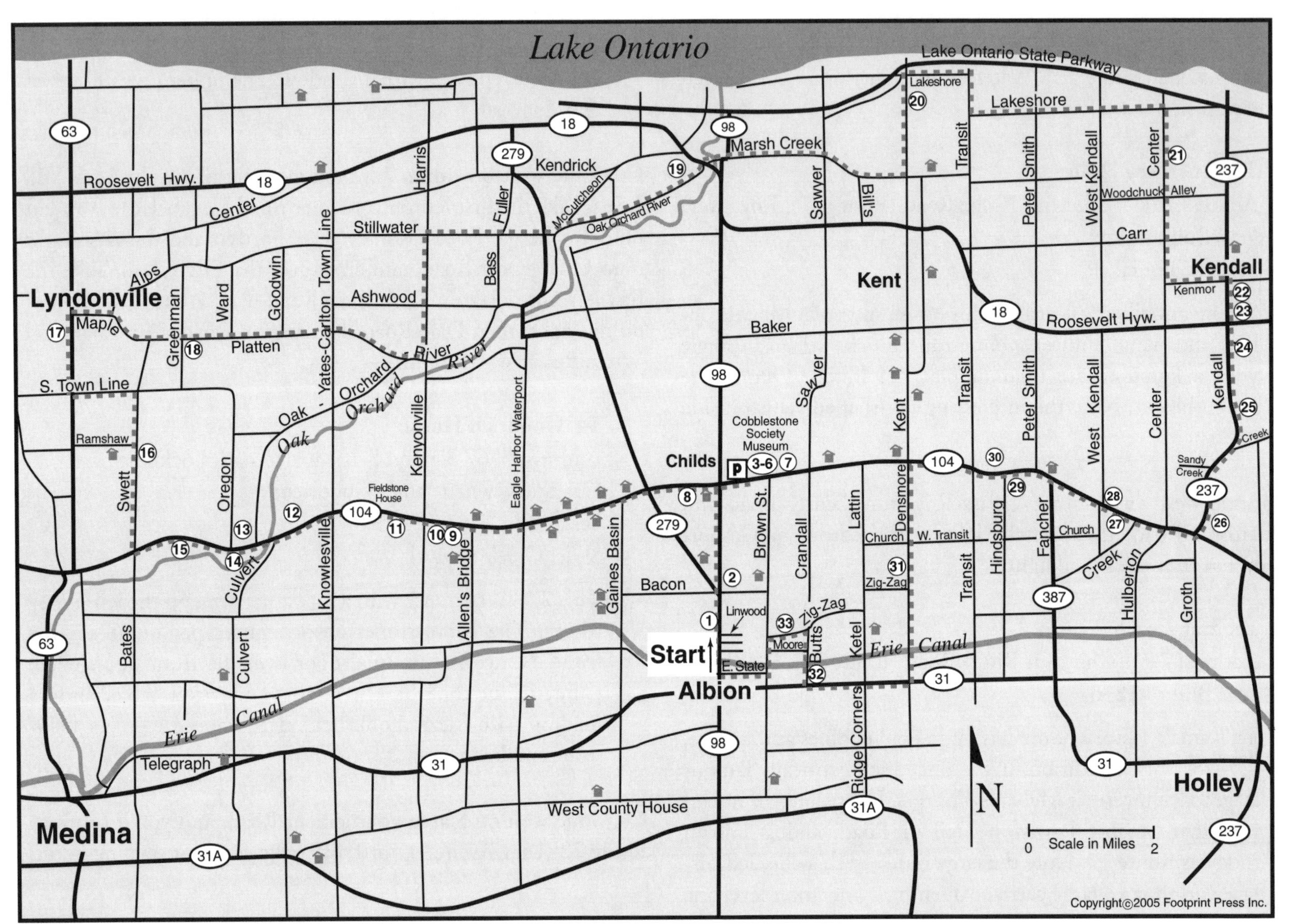

Cobblestone Tour 3

Cobblestone Tour 3

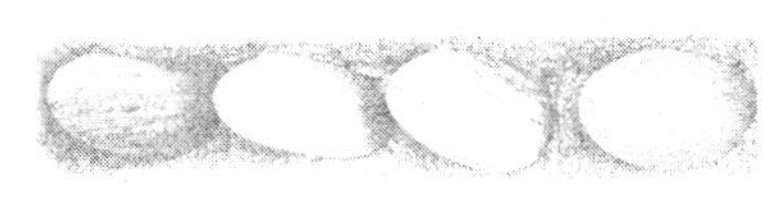

North of Albion in Orleans County
Total Distance: 64 miles
Approximate Time: 3 hours

Ridge Road (Route 104), originally an Indian trail, became a principle east-west route following the ridge created by the shoreline of a prehistoric lake, called Lake Iroquois. Houses along Ridge Road were built between 1825 and 1860, spanning the range of early, middle and late cobblestone construction.

On this tour, watch for the creativity of a local mason who did not like to emphasize the horizontal mortar joints. Instead he placed cobbles in horizontal rows but formed a concave depression around each stone to make it project. This effect was to emphasize highlights of light and shadow on each stone. This has been called the Gaines pattern or depressed hexagonal pattern and is believed to have originated here.

Begin by heading north out of Albion on Route 98. Outside the village limits, after North Street, watch for the first cobblestone building on the left.

1. Hill House
Address: 3278 Oak Orchard Road (Route 98), Albion, Town of Gaines
Original Owner: Samuel Hill
Year Built: late 1830s

Samuel Hill married Olive Knight in 1815 and moved to a log cabin in Gaines in the spring of 1823. In the late 1830s they had their 2-story cobblestone house built using field cobbles. Look for the herringbone pattern high on the front and side walls, between the tops of the second floor windows. The Gaines pattern (depressed hexagonal) was used on the side walls.

Continue north on Route 98. Past the junction of Route 279, watch right.

2.
Address: 3077 Oak Orchard Road (Route 98), Albion, Town of Gaines

This 2-story home was built with small, lake-washed cobbles on the front and sides. Look closely. They're a mix of round stones and oblong stones set vertically within each row to maintain a common row height. The lintels, quoins, sills and water table are finely cut sandstone. The building has a wide frieze and sidelights and transom that surround the front door. There's a cut stone addition on the back.

Continue north on Route 98 to the intersection of Route 104 and The Cobblestone Society Museum complex in Childs. At the intersection turn right onto Route 104. Turn left to park in the museum parking area. The museum complex is open for touring from June 23rd through Labor Day, 11 AM - 5 PM Tuesday - Saturday, 1 PM - 5 PM Sunday, closed Mondays. You can visit the outside of the buildings anytime. (www.cobblestonesocietymuseum.org)

Three of the cobblestone buildings have been designated National Historic Landmarks by the National Park Service. There are also four additional frame construction buildings to tour: a circa 1921 blacksmith shop, a circa 1875 print and harness shop, and an exhibit hall of farm tools built in 1855.

3. The First Universalist Church
Address: 14393 Route 104, Childs, Town of Gaines
Original Landowner: John Proctor
Year Built: 1834
Period: Early
Style: Federal

The First Universalist Church is the oldest cobblestone church in North America. This building has changed little over the years. It was built with cobbles of various sizes and shapes, gathered from area fields. The quoins are rough-cut limestone. The sills are wood planks. The lintels are brick. The stone and brick terrace and front steps were added in the 20th century. The original tower was removed in 1919 when it required repairs. The present tower, built to look like the original, was a gift of John D. Brush in 1965. Threatened sale of the church in 1960 led to the formation of The Cobblestone Society.

The date stone reads "Erected by the First Universalist Society A.D. 1834, GOD IS LOVE." The founding fathers of the church included Joseph Billings, John Hutchinson, Chauncey Woodworth and John Proctor, three of whom had cobblestone homes. In 1877 this meeting house was named "The Church of the Good Shepherd."

4. Ward House (located to the right (east) as you face the church)
Address: 14393 Route 104, Childs, Town of Gaines
Original Landowner: John Proctor
(owned this land 1811-1861)
Year Built: 1836
Period: Middle
Style: Federal

John Proctor was influential in building the church next door. He pushed for development of his town "Fair Haven," which is now called Childs. It's reasonable to assume that John Proctor offered his land for this parsonage. In 1861 Mr. Proctor sold the land to Benjamin and Mary Ann Dwinnell of New Hampshire, the aunt and uncle of Horace Greeley. Mr. Greeley, newspaper editor of the NY Tribune

Cobbles set in a Gaines or depressed hexagonal pattern.

and one-time presidential candidate, held the mortgage on this cobblestone parsonage for his relatives, until 1863. Mrs. Inez Ward was the owner in 1975 and sold it to The Cobblestone Society.

The parsonage was built with lake-washed cobblestones and a Medina sandstone quoins. The Gaines pattern can be seen below the first floor and on the sides. The hip roof, built over a single floor house on a high basement, is rare for western New York. The wooden wing was added in the 1930s. This 1.5-story cottage originally had the kitchen and two rooms partially below ground level. The parlor and two bedrooms were on the floor above.

5. Simmons House
Address: 14403 Route 104, Childs, Town of Gaines
Mason and Original Owner: John Simmons
Year Built: 1842
Period: Early

In the early 1840s, John Simmons purchased a ¼ acre lot from John Proctor and built his small house in 1842. Mr. Simmons was listed in the census as a farmer, but he was also an accomplished mason. He built his cobblestone house, the brick blacksmith shop in Gaines, and the Baldwin's Corners District #6 cobblestone school in the town of Carlton. For his house, Mr. Simmons used large lake-washed cobbles of varied sizes and colors, set in the Gaines pattern. The house has sandstone quoins and brick lintels.

6.

Address: 14407 Ridge Road (Route 104), Childs, Town of Gaines
Original Owner: unclear
Year Built: 1840s
Period: Early
Style: Greek Revival

The original ¼-acre plot on which this house sits, was sold to George Smith by John Proctor in 1844 for $60. Six years later, Smith sold it to William B. Cook for $700. Somewhere within that span, the cobblestone house was built. William Cook was the Universalist minister who lived here rather than in the parsonage because of his large family: 12 people, including one servant. By 1860 John Proctor was once again the landowner. He sold it to his daughter and son-in-law, Clarissa and Josiah Proctor.

The 2-story house with a 1-story wing, was built with lake-washed cobbles in front and large field cobbles on sides, set in the Gaines pattern. The quoins are sandstone, lintels are brick, and sills are wood. This home has been considerably changed by alterations and additions. The 2nd story windows have original wood plank sills and wood beamed lintels. Those on the 1st story were replaced with painted concrete.

Continue east, still on the north side of Ridge Road.

7. District 5 Schoolhouse

Address: 14447 Ridge Road (Route 104), Childs, Town of Gaines
Year Built: 1849
Period: Late
Style: Greek Revival

There were approximately 50 cobblestone schoolhouses constructed in New York. Most were one-room and many have been converted into cozy homes. This schoolhouse was in use for 103 years, until 1952. John Proctor sold this land to the school district in 1847. It was across the street from a smaller schoolhouse which was built in 1817.

This cobblestone building has unusual construction. The walls are only 10-inch thick. Over a wooden frame covered with vertical planks, sits a 6-inch veneer of lake-washed cobbles. The only other cobblestone building constructed like this is #11 on this tour (12818 Ridge Road). The water table, quoins, lintels and sills are red Medina sandstone.

Notice also that the building has a boys and girls entrance and that the floor is sloped allowing those students in back a better view of the teacher and blackboard. Finally, the marble tablet inscribed "School District No. 5 — Town of Gaines A.D. 1849. Wm. J. Babbitt, Esq. Gratuitously superintended the erection of this building and made the district a present of this bell." The bell resides in the domed cupola.

The Cobblestone Society acquired this building in 1961, and it now serves as a museum of 19th century education.

Elongated cobbles set in a herringbone pattern surround this window with a limestone lintel and sill. (2499 Swett Road, Lyndonville, house #16 on Tour #3)

Return to your car, and head west on Route 104. The third house past the corner of Route 98 (Oak Orchard Road) was part of John Proctor's land holdings. Today it looks like a brick house. The cobblestone lower level is obscured by bushes. In 1825 John Proctor sold this lot to Jeptha Wood. By the mid-1800s it was again owned by Proctor and was listed as tenant property. John Proctor was probably the one who had the cobblestone house built (14308 Ridge Road). Cyrus Witheral (or Witherel) was the mason. In the 1930s Ferrin and Beatrice Fraser were the owners. Ferrin Fraser wrote scripts for radio series including *Lights Out*, *Terror*, *Nick Carter*, and *Little Orphan Annie*. He also wrote books with Frank Buck and wrote over 500 articles for popular magazines. His wife Beatrice played organ for the Eastman Theater in Rochester.

Continue west on Route 104 to the 5th house from the corner, on the left.

8.

Address: 14268 Ridge Road (Route 104), Childs, Town of Gaines

This 2-story house with a 1-story wing on the side, has a wide frieze and cut limestone lintels, quoins and water table. Notice the fan in the gable end.

Continue heading west on Route 104 and pass 7 additional cobblestone houses. Because there are so many fine examples of cobblestone buildings along Route 104, we won't pause to detail each one.

Watch left, after passing Allen's Bridge Road.

9. Saunders House
Address: 13194 Ridge Road, Town of Gaines
Original Owner: Isaac V. and Roxanna Saunders
Mason: Cyrus Witheral (or Witherel) (One of the masons, who probably did the herringbone in the center section, was paid $75 for his work on this house.)
Year Built: 1840
Style: The entrance is Greek Revival, but the fan-shaped ornamental in the gable is Federal Style. There's a mix of Greek Revival and Federal moldings.

This home was built for Isaac V. Saunders and his wife Roxanna in 1844 and was owned by Miss Florence Harmer in 1961. It's a rare 3-part home consisting of a central 2 ½-story with 1 ½-story wings. There's a heavy wood cornice and cut limestone lintels and quoins. On the front and side above the porches the mason used long, thin oval cobblestones in a herringbone pattern. All the horizontal joints are Vs. Only some of the vertical joints are beaded, others are plain. The quoins, lintels and sills are sandstone.

Proceed west, still looking left.

10. Whipple House
Address: 13076 Ridge Road, Town of Gaines
Original Owners: Samuel and Mary Jane Whipple
Mason: Cyrus Witheral (or Witherel)
Year Built: ~1844
Period: Late

Samuel, the original owner of this cobblestone home, died in 1851 and, as was the custom of the time, an inventory of his possessions was done. Property set aside for Mary Jane and his children included 1 cow, 10 sheep, 2 hogs, 1 spinning wheel, 2 stoves, cooking utensils, 1 bible, family pictures, the family library, 3 bedsteads, 4 beds, bedding, clothing of the family and widow, 1 table, 6 chairs, 6 knives, forks, spoons, plates, tea cups and saucers, 1 sugar dish, 1 milk pot, and 1 tea pot.

This 2-story house was built with long, thin water-rounded stones set in a herringbone pattern, cut stone lintels, and 12-inch high sandstone quoins. The horizontal joints are wavy Vs and the vertical joints are plain.

Continue heading west on Route 104, past Kenyonville Road and watch left.

11. Lyman House
Address: 12818 Ridge Road, Town of Gaines
Original Owner: William and Betsy Lyman
Year Built: 1849
Period: Late
Style: Greek Revival, cottage-style house

William and Betsy Lyman came from Vermont to settle in Gaines in 1826. They purchased this land in 1842 and built the cobblestone cottage for their 7 children.

The exterior walls of this home are only 6-inches thick. First a plank frame was erected. Then a layer of cobblestone veneer was laid on the exterior, resting on a 3 1/4 -inch thick wood plate at grade. The same unusual construction method was used to build the District 5 Schoolhouse (#7 on this tour). Oval cobblestones and some fieldstones were used for the veneer. The horizontal joints and some of the vertical joints are Vs. Notice there are no quoins. Wood pilasters form the corners. The lintels and sills are also wood.

Continue west 1.4 miles, passing Knowlesville/Town Line Road, then watch right to view a cobblestone house on the north side of the road.

12. Steward House
Address: 12387 Ridge Road, Town of Ridgeway
Original Owners: Witter (Wilbur) and Betsey Steward
Year Built: Late 1830s
Period: Late
Style: Greek Revival cottage-style house originally, now with Italianate exterior woodwork

Witter (Wilbur) and Betsey Steward moved here from Connecticut in 1831. In 1864 John Amos purchased this property. His descendants lived here for at least 100 years.

The house was built with rounded fieldstones of varied sizes and colors, showing fine craftsmanship. The horizontal joints are Vs and vertical joints are pyramidal shaped. The wing to the west is faced with smaller, water-rounded cobbles. The wing has an inset porch with square columns. The Italianate style exterior woodwork was a later addition. The quoins and lintels are sandstone. The sills are wood. Notice the four hitching posts and the carriage step in the front yard.

Continue west to the corner of Oak Orchard River Road, still watching right.

13. Spencer House
Address: 12225 Ridge Road, Town of Ridgeway
Year Built: 1840s
Period: Late
Style: Greek Revival

Before the opening of the Erie Canal, Oak Orchard on the Ridge, as this area was known, was a thriving business center.

It had a tannery, a distillery, a gristmill, a sawmill, an ashery, 3 taverns, 3 stores, and 3 inns.

In its original form, this big, L-shaped, 2-story building had 22 rooms and steep gables. As was typical of cobblestone buildings, it had finer workmanship on front and was rough on the back. It was built with fieldstones, V mortar joints, and red sandstone quoins, lintels and sills. A long porch was added to the side at one point. The main cornice was characteristic of Greek Revival era of the Victorian period.

This building has been the Cobblestone Inn (bar) and Speedy's Hotel. It is currently undergoing renovations under new ownership.

Continue west and watch left.

14. Howell House
Address: 12184 Ridge Road, Town of Ridgeway
Original Owner: Gilbert Howell
Year Built: 1845

Gilbert Howell was one of the first settlers at Oak Orchard. Evidence of a more recent owner, "W. Mesler" is carved in a stone sign in the front yard.

This 1.5-story building has a 1-story wing with an addition over it, and Greek columns on the porch. It was built with a combination of lake-washed and field cobbles with V mortar joints. The quoins, lintels, and sills are gray and reddish-brown sandstone.

Continue west on Route 104, watching left for a white farmhouse and a barn that is ½ cobblestone.

15. Cobblestone Barn
Address: 12054 Ridge Road, Town of Ridgeway

This fieldstone barn has a major wooden addition. Notice the cut stone arch over the carriage door.

Continue west, then turn right (N) onto Swett Road. In 1.3 miles, watch right.

16. Tolford House
Address: 2499 Swett Road, Lyndonville, Town of Ridgeway
Original Owner: Charles Tolford
Year Built: 1845

Charles Tolford bought 432 acres of land from his father in 1842 and built his house, with a herringbone pattern on the front and in the gable ends of the side walls. Notice the arch over the opening in the gable end on the sides, surrounded by herringbone. The house was built with unusually large sandstone quoins, measuring 18 inches high by 22 inches long. Most quoins are 12 inches high by 18 inches long. The horizontal mortar joints are Vs and the vertical joints are plain. The quoins, lintels and sills are sandstone. The stained

Tolford House, 2499 Swett Road, Lyndonville

glass in the front door is recent. The wooden wing in the rear has a cobblestone foundation.

Proceed north and take the second left onto South Town Line Road. Take the next right onto Route 63 (Lyndonville Road) to the village of Lyndonville. The next house will be on your left within the village.

17. Blood House
Address: 142 S. Main Street, Lyndonville, Town of Yates
Original Owner: Jackson and Mary Blood
Year Built: 1847
Period: Late
Style: End of Greek Revival era

Jackson and Mary Blood traveled for 27 days from New Hampshire to Batavia in 1817 by canvas covered wagon, pulled by oxen. Mary rode in a chair suspended as a swing from the top bow of the wagon. After 2 months, they moved to Yates. A relative, Seldon Blood, told of hearing about going to Lake Ontario and spending a whole day gathering 3 bushels of stone the right size and shape for this cobblestone home.

This 2.5-story home has a massive Greek Revival cornice. The front and sides have a very small, carefully sized, lake-washed cobblestone veneer, whereas the rear wall used field-stone of various sizes, laid in the Gaines pattern. The dark solid stones are local red sandstone. The speckled or mottled cobbles are hard Canadian metamorphic rocks. The mortar joints are beaded. The cut stone arch that connects the second floor windows is unique.

Continue into the village and turn right onto Maple Avenue. Bear right as Maple passes Alps Road and turns into Platten Road. Pass Swett Road and look right at the corner of Greenman Road.

18. District 14 Schoolhouse
Address: 1870 Platten Road, Yates, Town of Yates
Year Built: 1846

On November 28, 1846 William Greenman sold this parcel of land for $400 to the trustees of School District 14. The community used lake-washed and rounded fieldstones laid horizontally, vertically, and diagonally with V mortar joints. The quoins are pink sandstone. This school closed in 1938 when the district centralized to Lyndonville. It is now a private residence.

Continue east on Platten Road as it merges with Oak Orchard River Road. Turn left onto Kenyonville Road at the stop sign. Turn right onto Stillwater. Cross Route 279 and continue straight on Oak Orchard River Road. Watch left down a bit.

19. Shipman House
Address: 1402 Oak Orchard River Road, Town of Carlton
Original Owner: Israel Shipman

John Shipman of Connecticut came to the frontier with Elijah Brown and his family in 1804, via a sailboat on Lake Ontario from Sodus. John married Ann Tomblin, and they had a son named Israel. John died in 1833 and deeded this land to Israel. Israel and his mom lived here until the land was deeded to George Curry.

The cobblestone house was built using red and gray, long, thin water-rounded cobbles set in a herringbone pattern. Mortar joints are Vs, the quoins are sandstone and the sills are wood. The mansard roof on the wing was added around 1880.

Continue east on Oak Orchard River Road. You'll pass the Brown farm (1285 Oak Orchard River Road). To the right, but hidden from view, is a cobblestone farm outbuilding that was built in the 1830s. It has no mortar embellishment. Its unusual cellar was used as a root cellar. The Brown family used the outbuilding as a cooperage to make apple barrels.

The Brown family has a long history in this area. Elijah and Bathshua Brown sailed to Carlton from Sodus, via Lake Ontario in 1804. Before arriving in Carlton, Elijah (age 57) died. Bathshua buried him on their new property, the first burial in Orleans County. Bathshua and her large family lived in the frontier wilderness until her death in 1826.

At the end of Oak Orchard River Road, turn right onto Oak Orchard Road (Route 18) and immediately bear left onto Marsh Creek Road toward the "Village Inn" sign. Cross Oak Orchard River on a one lane bridge. Go straight on Route 98, but continue straight onto Marsh Creek Road when Route 98 turns left. Pass Sawyer Road, pass Bill's Road, and turn left (N) onto Kent Road. In 1.1 miles, watch right.

Warren House, 956 Kent Road, Kent

20. Warren House
Address: 956 Kent Road, Kent
Mason: Silas and Lucinda Warren
Year Built: ~1840
Period: Late

It took 3 years to build this 2-story house with a 1-story wing. Oblong cobbles were laid so just the ends show. Larger stones were used on the sides of the house (5 courses per quoin), and very rough rectangular stones were used on back of house. The mortar joints are beaded. Cut Medina sandstone for the lintels, quoins and sills came from the Huberton quarry. The full basement, once housed a cistern to collect rainwater. The 18-inch-thick walls are actually 2 walls with an air space between them. The step block and hitching posts in front lawn are all original.

In 1838 Silas and Lucinda Warren bought 234 acres of land. Silas was a justice of the peace and a Baptist church deacon, known locally as "Deacon Warren." This house was originally built for two families. Deacon Warren, who lived on the north side (died in 1914 and is buried in Mt. Albion Cemetery) kept 25 cows and was known for making cheese and butter. The eldest son, Reuben, lived on the south side. Reuben stayed; the other sons dispersed. Rueben married Eunice Joy in 1846, and they had 3 daughters.

The current owner, Pete Consler repointed many of the cobbles, keeping the original look. The west wall gets the worst of the acid rain and incurs the most damage. Pete's dad added the sandstone and cobble front steps. Porch columns were boxed in at some point. Pete didn't realize it until he went to resurface the porch floor. Pete had his name carved into the step stone. He believes the rounded bump-out on the side was once a side entrance. The bumpout had glass block when his parents bought it. His parents only used this as a summer cottage. At one time it had coal heat. Pete's dad added the fireplace.

Pete stripped 100 years of old paint off the living room walls and repainted it in 3 shades of peach/orange to match the original colors. The insides of the windows are boxed in with fancy trimmed wood.

Continue north on Kent Road, then turn right onto Lakeshore Road. At the end, take a right onto Transit Road, then take the first left back onto Lakeshore Road. Take the third right onto Center Road and watch left.

21. Barber House

Address: 1351 Center Road, Kendall, Town of Kendall
Original Owner: Ryan and Roxanna Barber
Style: Greek Revival farmhouse

Ryan and Roxanna Barber purchased this lot in 1844 and built this 2-story farmhouse with a 2-story wing. They used water-rounded, oval cobbles, beaded mortar joints, wide friezes, a herringbone pattern under the water table, and red sandstone quoins and lintels. There's a date stone in the front gable and major additions on the back.

Continue south on Center Road passing Woodchuck Alley and Carr Road. Turn left onto Kenmor Road. Take the next right onto Kendall Road (Route 237) and watch left. You can pull into the Fireman's meeting hall to get an up-close look.

22. Temperance Lodge

Address: 1879 Kendall Road, Kendall, Town of Kendall

In 1848 the Sons of Temperance Lodge organized in Kendall with 12 members. In 1850 Captain John Hall donated a ¼-acre lot for the building of this cobblestone meeting house. The Lodge disbanded after 8 years and the land and hall reverted to the Alanson Whitney estate. In 1852 Whitney sold it to J. C. Johnson and C. H. Barnum with the agreement that it was only to be used as a Temperance Lodge. In 1853, a second temperance organization — Good Templars Lodge — organized. It lasted 4 years and referred to its meeting lodge as the "stone jug." In 1847 the building was deeded to the Masons for the Masonic Social Lodge and was used as such until 1904. Independent Order of Odd Fellows used the meeting hall until 1911, then it served as temporary classrooms, and for meetings of the Red Cross and Home Bureau. In 1947 it became an annex and meeting hall for the fire department, as it remains today.

This building is an example of lake cobbles on the front with horizontal beaded mortar joints and vertical V joints, and rough fieldstone on the sides with no mortar embellishments. It provides a good contrast with the next house.

Continue straight (S), still watching left.

23. Spicer House
Address: 1889 Kendall Road, Kendall, Town of Kendall
Original Owner: Ezra and Mary Spicer

Orman, Numon, Darius, and Ezra Spicer and their families moved here from Washington County, NY. Ezra and Mary Spicer purchased this land from the State of Connecticut in 1836. The Spicers were part of 50 settlers who formed the Methodist Episcopal class of 1831, part of an Episcopal religious revival movement. In Kendall, this revival was known as the "big barn revival" because meetings were held in Ezra Spicer's big barn.

This small one-story home with an addition out back, was built with small field cobbles that vary in size and color. The mortar joints are unembellished. Irregular quoins are of mixed stone. Sandstone lintels are set on edge. The original floor plan had the kitchen in the basement and a parlor and bedrooms on the 1st floor.

Continue straight (S) on Route 237. Pass Roosevelt Highway (Route 18) at the flashing light, and look left between the first white house and its red barn and garages.

24. Clark Smokehouse
Address: 2029 Kendall Road, Kendall, Town of Kendall
Original Owner: Robert and Anna Clark
Year Built: early 1820s

Clark Smokehouse at 2029 Kendall Road, Kendall

This smokehouse was built by farmers Robert and Anna Clark. Robert's dad, William, came from Connecticut in 1823 along with Caleb and James and their families. They settled Clark's Settlement between Kendall and Hamlin.

Small elongated cobbles on front and left side (the sides facing the house) are set horizontal. The right and back sides used large, rough stones. The smokehouse has sandstone quoins.

Continue straight (S) for another 1.2 miles, and watch left.

Stevens House, 2443 Kendall Road, Kendall

This home was built on a sandstone block foundation with a rough sandstone water table. Above that are tiny, uniform size lake-washed cobbles. The horizontal mortar joints are beaded; vertical mortar joints are Vs. Notice that this house doesn't have visible stone quoins. Instead, it's constructed using 13-inch-wide wooden pilasters. The house has wide friezes with frieze windows and herringbone pattern over the lintels.

Continue straight (S) on Kendall Road (Route 237) passing Creek Road and Sandy Creek Road. Shortly before the flashing light at Route 104, watch left.

25. Stevens House

Address: 2443 Kendall Road, Kendall, Town of Kendall
Original Owner: Samuel and Caroline Stevens

The Stevens brothers, Samuel, Hiram and William, settled this area. Samuel married Caroline and built this cobblestone home in the mid-1840s. At least one of the Stevens brothers was a mason by trade. A Stevens daughter remembers carrying mortar to the masons. She said stones were gathered from Lake Ontario and sand came from a site on the Ridge.

District #2 Schoolhouse, 2889 Kendall Road, Murray

26. District #2 Schoolhouse
Address: 2889 Kendall Road, Murray, Town of Murray

This former schoolhouse is now a private residence. It was built with water-rounded fieldstones of various sizes, colors and shapes. The quoins, lintels and sills are red sandstone.

Turn right onto Ridge Road (Route 104). Pass Hulberton/ Center Roads and Creek Road, then watch left.

27. Colt House
Address: 16184 Ridge Road, Murray, Town of Murray
Original Owner: Lyman Colt
Year Built: ~1840

This land was first purchased from the State of Connecticut by Lyman Colt in 1840. By the 1860s it was owned by William Smith who farmed 20 acres of fruit trees and other produce.

The 2-story house was built with fieldstones and water-washed cobbles of varied size, shape and color. Three bands of elongated stones were laid in a herringbone pattern between the windows on the first and second floors. The quoins and lintels are red sandstone. The lintels are oblong cobbles set on edge.

Continue west on Ridge Road and watch right before West Kendall Road.

28. Spaulding House
Address: 16131 Ridge Road, Town of Murray
Original Owner: Oliver Spaulding
Year Built: 1844
Style: Greek Revival

The datestone on the front says “1844 O. Spaulding.” This was once a fancy home as evidenced by the herringbone stripes and horizontal stripes mixed in small cobble rows on the front. In the gable peak, each row of stones is shaped a little differently. The sides have large, rough cobbles and flat mortar. The quoins, lintels and sills are red sandstone. Extensive wooden additions were added in the 20th century. Hitching posts remain in the front yard.

Continue west on Ridge Road, passing a cobblestone house (16035 Ridge Road) on the right, whose front is hidden by a cream-colored addition. Pass Route 387, then Peter Smith Road, then watch left just before Hindsburg Road. This house is mostly obscured by additions.

29. Hinds House
Address: 15698 Ridge Road, Albion
Original Owner: Joel and Darius Hinds
Year Built: ~ Late 1830s

In 1830 Joel Hinds began a settlement by building a produce warehouse. Two years later his warehouse was a thriving marketplace on the Erie Canal. Settlers voted to name the community Hindsburg in honor of Joel and his brother Jacob. In 1835 Joel built a 2-story wooden frame tavern and built the first store. Joel and his brother Darius Hinds co-purchased this property in 1846. In 1853 Joel bought full ownership from Darius' estate. This house was built with field cobbles.

Continue west on Ridge Road. Pass Hindsburg Road, then watch right.

30.

Address: 15545 Ridge Road, Gaines
Mason: Alfred Rugar (He built cobblestone buildings, per oral tradition.)
Year Built: 1851(may be earlier)

This property was purchased in 1835 by Oliver VanKirk. It's not known if he built the cobblestone house.

Built with large, rough fieldstones, this house has mortar without joint embellishments, brick lintels, small quoins and a brick arch over the door. The quoins are large fieldstones. The cellar floor is made of handmade brick. Other floors in the house are pegged chestnut.

Continue west on Ridge Road. Pass Transit Road, and turn left onto Densmore/Kent Road, and head south. Pass West Transit/Church Road, then watch right.

31. Beebe House

Address: 3118 Densmore Road, Albion, Town of Gaines
Original Owner: Aaron and Lovinia Beebe
Mason: May have been James Grear who built several cobblestone houses north of this one.
Year Built: Mid to late 1830s
Period: Early
Style: Federal center entrance house. Victorian exterior woodwork was added later.

Aaron and Lovinia Beebe purchased this land in 1834 and raised 10 children.

This cobblestone house is in good shape and is easy to see from the road. It's a 2-story, with Victorian wood scrolls under the eves and on the porch over front door. The fact that the stones are not in defined rows, the mortar is flush even on front, and 3 courses of cobbles were used per quoin, are all indications of early period construction. The quoins are cut gray sandstone. A 1920s addition on the left used large stones in a modern cobblestone adaptation

Continue south on Densmore Road. Pass Zig-Zag Road, cross over the Erie Canal, and turn right (west) onto Route 31. Pass Ketel/Ridges Corners Road, then turn right (north) onto Butts Road. Watch right just before the green canal bridge.

32. Lake Manse
Address: 3505 Butts Road, Albion

This gorgeous home has some unique properties. Notice the herringbone pattern in the cobbles below the water table. The 2-story home was built with small lake-washed, round and oval cobbles. The mortar joints are beaded. The side friezes sport metal grills. Near the road, look for the sandstone pillars with metal rings — old hitching posts. The Medina sandstone trim most likely came from quarries near the property. A sandstone-colored wash was painted over the exterior cobblestone work which is now very hard to detect.

Continue north on Butts Road and cross the Erie Canal. Pass Moore Street. Turn left onto Zig-Zag Road and watch right.

33. Brown House
Address: 14615 Zig-Zag Road, Albion, Town of Gaines
Original Owner: Daniel and Mary Brown
Period: Early

Daniel and Mary Brown moved to Gaines in 1816 from Canada where Daniel was acquitted on charges of treason for refusing to bear arms against his native U.S. when the War of 1812 began.

Water-rounded cobbles are not in defined rows, but look closely at the front to see mortar set around each stone in the Gaines pattern on this beautiful home. The sides sport flush field cobbles. The quoins are limestone. A hitching post can be found in the front. A porch wraps around the front and right sides. A modern addition is on the back.

Continue west on Zig-Zag Road to the end. Turn left onto Brown Street. Cross the Erie Canal. Turn right onto East State Street and follow it to Route 98 at the traffic light. You are now in the Historic Court House District where there are 34 buildings, including the Orleans County Courthouse and seven historic churches, on the National Register of Historic Places.

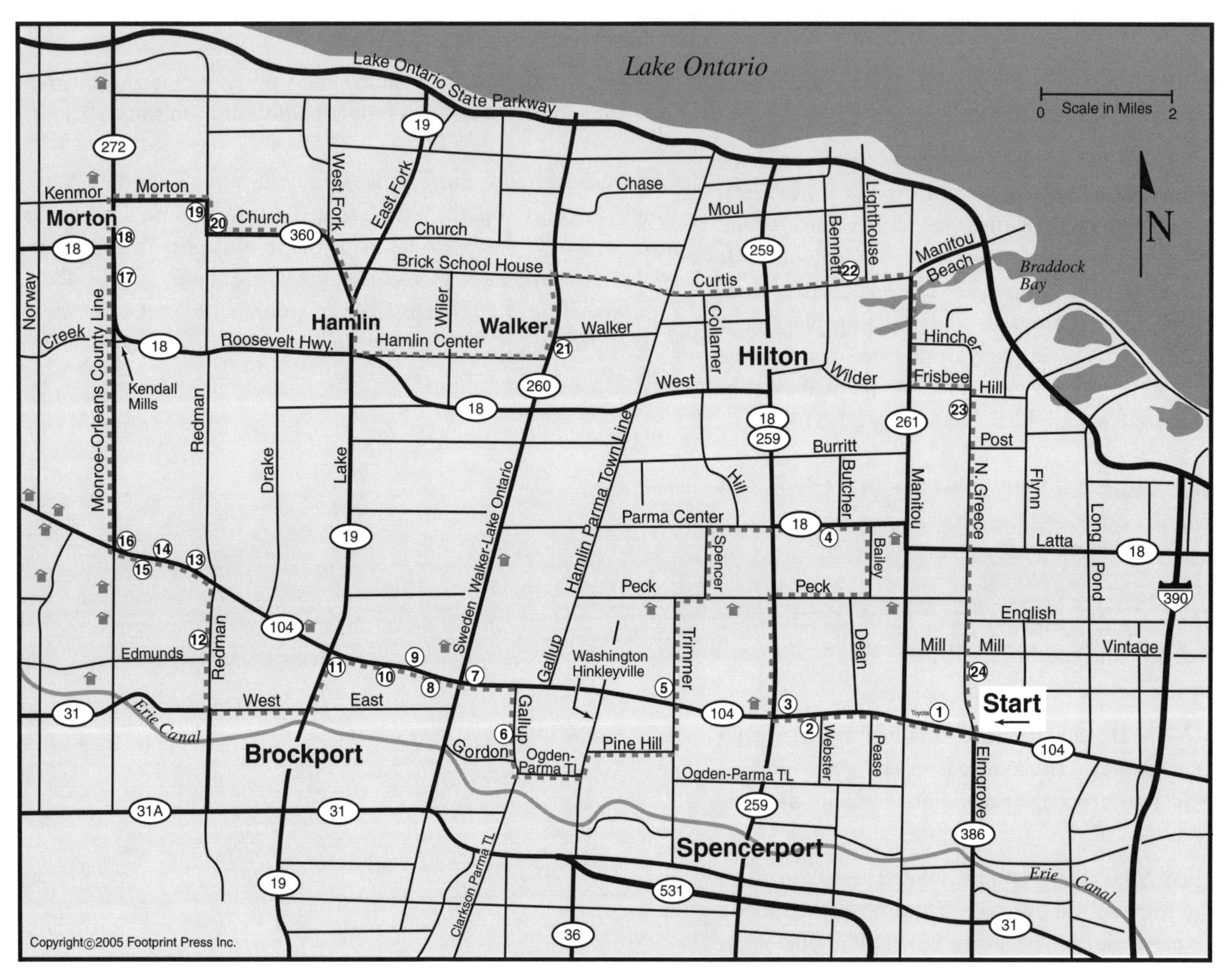

Cobblestone Tour 4

Cobblestone Tour 4

Greece, Hilton, Hamlin, Clarkson and Parma in Monroe County
Total Miles: 55 miles
Approximate Time: 2.5 hours

Ridge Road (Route 104) opened in 1809 and became a principle east-west stagecoach route following the ridge created by the shoreline of a prehistoric lake, called Lake Iroquois. Houses along Ridge Road were built between 1825 and 1860, spanning the range of early, middle and late cobblestone construction. It will be difficult to stop on this busy road.

Begin the tour heading west on Route 104, from Greece. Pass North Greece Road/Elmgrove Road, then in 0.8 mile watch right (just east of the Toyota dealership).

1.
Address: 4350 Ridge Road (Route 104), Greece

Will this house survive? It is surrounded by retail development and currently sits vacant with its future questionable. The small, rough fieldstone 1-story house with white trim is set back from the road. It has a sandstone block foundation and limestone lintels and quoins.

Ray Mercier, a long-time owner of this property ran a cat boarding business here and called this house "The Cat Nap."

Continue west on Route 104, passing Route 261, Pease, Dean and Webster Roads, then watch left.

Thrall House, 4929 W. Ridge Road, Spencerport

2. Thrall House
Address: 4929 Ridge Road West, Spencerport
Year Built: 1845
Period: Late

The smokehouse at 4929 West Ridge Road, Spencerport

Style: Greek Revival version of a 5-bay, center-entrance house of Georgian-Federal period

Here's a pretty 2-story house with a white porch at the front door supported by square pillars. The porch was restored around 1950. The wooden panels below the first floor windows are unusual. The house sports a cut stone foundation, multi-colored, water-rounded cobblestones and a water table. Wide friezes hold rectangular belly windows that open into the attic. Behind the house is a cobblestone smokehouse. The back on the house and smokehouse are both made of cut sandstone blocks. The back part of the house, which forms an L, was most likely the carriage house.

Continue east Route 104 and watch right just before the corner of Route 259. After viewing the house, you will be turning right onto Route 259.

3.
Address: 4968 Ridge Road (Route 104), Spencerport
Year Built: Late 1840s

This 2-story building has small cobbles on the front under a full-width porch. Notice the herringbone pattern on part of the front and the wide frieze over the porch. The thin oval stones in the herringbone pattern are sandstone.

Turn right to head north on Route 259, then take the first right onto Peck Road at the blinking light. Take the first left onto

Bailey Road and left again onto Parma Center Road (Route 18). Pass Butcher Road and watch left.

4. Cobblestone Barn
Address: 293 Parma Center Road, Parma

A cobblestone barn — unusual among cobblestone buildings — sits at the end of the driveway to a white farmhouse. The front has cobbles, although somewhat hard to see. Notice the large, rough fieldstones (Medina sandstone and boulders) used on the side. The quoins have been painted.

Continue west on Parma Center Road, passing a flashing light, as Routes 18 and 259 head north. Take the next left onto Spencer Road. At the end, turn right onto Peck Road, then the next left onto Trimmer Road. Watch to the right at the corner of Route 104.

5. Parma District #8 Schoolhouse
Address: 5346 Ridge Road (Route 104), Parma
Year Built: 1847
Style: Greek Revival

This small building has small, multi-colored cobblestones on the front and cut limestone lintels and quoins. This is a good place to view the variation in cobble sizes, with small stones on the front and large stones on the back. The foundation in the back, below the cut sandstone water table, is fieldstone of various sizes and shapes.

Continue south on Trimmer Road, crossing Route 104. Take the next right onto Pine Hill Road. Pass a large quarry — a good source of glacial cobblestones from the Ridge? At the end, turn left onto Hinckleyville Road, then take the first right onto Ogden-Parma Town Line Road. At the end turn right onto Gallup Road. Pass Gordon Road at the stop sign, and watch left.

Gallup House, 357 Gallup Road, Spencerport

6. Gallup House

Address: 357 Gallup Road, Spencerport
Original Owner: Eli Gallup
Year Built: Mid-1830s

Here's a gorgeous treat for your eyes. This 2-story home has green shutters, a porch on the left side of the front and an inset door flanked with sidelights and dual pillars. The limestone lintels and quoins are chiseled. It has a water table and a wide frieze. The cobblestones, which were gathered from the surrounding farmland, are multi-colored, but uniform in size. The wing on the left contains a mixture of cobblestones and cut sandstone, which is unusual.

The Gallup family owned this house and farm until 1940, when they sold it to Mr. and Mrs. Cornelius J. Van Neil.

Continue north on Gallup Road to Route 104, and turn left. Watch to the right just before Route 260.

7.

Address: 7528 Ridge Road W., Clarkson

This cobblestone building now functions as a garage. It was built with field cobbles of varied colors and sizes on the front and larger fieldstones set in flush mortar on the sides. The quoins are rough-cut and vary in size. It sits on a sandstone foundation.

Continue west on Route 104, past Route 260 and watch left in a grove of large trees, just past an old cemetery.

8.

Address: 7785 Ridge Road W., Clarkson
Year Built: ~1835
Style: Federal

This home is harder to see, blocked by bushes. It has sandstone quoins and lintels and small eves. The cobblestones become smaller as the courses proceed to the peak.

In 1910 Charles Coller bought this house and the surrounding orchards from Harry Wilson. The large wooden wing was added in 1919. The property remained in the Coller family as the Coller Fruit Farm, at least through 1975.

Continue west on Route 104, to the next house on the right.

9. Jones House and Carriage House

Address: 7816 Ridge Road, Clarkson
Original Owner: David Jones
Year Built: Late 1830s for the cobblestone cottage and carriage house; the north cobblestone wing was attached in the early 1840s

The house began as a small, 1-story cottage, but it has been engulfed by modern additions. The multi-colored field cobblestones on the cottage get progressively smaller toward the top. Look closely at the left corner of the cottage. There are

7816 Ridge Road, Clarkson

no quoins. Instead you'll find a rounded cobblestone corner. Also unusual, the windows don't have lintels and the door has a single row of bricks for its lintel. The sills are wood. The back wing with its wide frieze, was added at the turn of the 20th century.

Inch forward along Route 104 to see a large cobblestone carriage house in the side yard, set back a bit from the house. The carriage house has large but uniform cobblestones. It also has the unique rounded cobblestone corners. Originally barns stood west of the carriage house.

This home has had many owners, most of whom had daughters, so it didn't get passed down through the generations like many other cobblestone homes did. Also, the land was poor for farming. In the 1900s this property was owned by the Coller family. The cobblestone cottage was used to raise chicks and the frame house was rented out. In 1962 Kermit Mercer bought the property from Art Coller. Inside the floors had caved in, so the whole interior had to be gutted and renovated.

Continue west on Route 104, watching left for a 2-story brick house. The cobblestone portion is a wing on the back.

10.

Address: 8107 Ridge Road, Clarkson

The 1.5-story cobblestone building now serves as a wing off a large 2-story brick building with an ornate white porch spanning the corner. Again, notice the lack of quoins, a sign that this home and the home at #7816 Ridge Road (#9 on this tour) were built by the same builder, around the same time. This house has cut limestone lintels.

Continue west on Route 104, and turn left onto Route 19 at the traffic light. Near this corner, pull into the post office parking lot on the left.

11.

Address: 3726 Lake Road (Route 19), Brockport

You can walk or drive around this building. Built as a commercial building with rough cobblestones, it now houses

Deats Woodworking Shop. The building is in poor shape with parts mudded over and a cinder block section added to raise the roof. From the post office parking lot you can see the front façade. The quoins are sandstone.

Continue south on Route 19, and take the first right onto West Avenue. At the traffic light, turn right onto Redman Road. Pass Edmunds Road and watch left.

12.
Address: 3797 Redman Road, Brockport

This is a 2-story main building with a 1-story wing. A white porch spans the front of the wing. It has small cobblestones on the front and sides, cut limestone quoins and white painted lintels. Notice the sandstone foundation and a wide frieze on the sides.

In the 1902 atlas this house was listed as being owned by Chauncey Allen. Chauncey was the son of Isaac Allen, an early Clarkson-on-the-Ridge settler, who built cobblestone house # 15 (9787 Ridge Road) on this tour.

Continue north on Redman Road. Turn left onto Route 104 and watch right.

13. Schoolhouse
Address: 9410 Ridge Road (Route 104), Brockport
Year Built: 1830s
Period: Early

This simple, 1-story former schoolhouse was built with a mixture of large field and water-rounded cobbles with an air space between the walls. The mortar joints are plain. It has cut sandstone lintels and quoins. A poor repair has been made to the bottom right section of the front. This school closed in 1927 when the Brockport school system centralized.

Continue west on Route 104, watching right.

14. Crowell House
Address: 9626 Ridge Road (Route 104), Clarkson
Year Built: Early 1830s

Crowell was a doctor who had his office in the left wing. This building is similar in construction to the previous one. Its field cobbles get smaller as they go up from the ground to the roof. The window and door lintels are 4 rows of brick, and the quoins are rough, irregular red sandstone. From the side you can see a sandstone block foundation and a segment where the cobbles are flush in the mortar, progressing to protruding cobbles. It has plain mortar joints.

The wing is fieldstone, not cobbles and may predate the main house. The small openings in the gable end on the right, below the second floor windows (2 inches high by 12 inches long) were reportedly for the beehives kept in the attic.

Continue west on Route 104, watching left.

15. Allen House
Address: 9787 Ridge Road (Route 104), Clarkson
Original Owner: Isaac Allen
Year Built: 1825
Period: Early

This simple house was built with rough field cobbles and irregular sandstone quoins. Its lintels are formed by 4 rows of brick, similar to house #14 (9626 Ridge Road) on this tour, suggesting a common mason. The addition on back was built in the 1870s.

Isaac Allen, an early Clarkson-on-the-Ridge settler, was born in Connecticut in 1794 and apprenticed as a hatter at a young age. He emigrated west in stages, finally buying land in Clarkson Corners in 1816. He returned to Connecticut, found a woman to marry and brought her back to Clarkson Corners in 1817. Isaac Allen bought and sold land several times in the area before building his cobblestone home here, in 1825. The Allens raised 10 children in this house. In addition to making hats, Mr. Allen farmed the land with melons being his specialty.

Continue west on Route 104, and watch right at the next junction (Monroe-Orleans County Line Road/Route 272). After viewing this home, you'll be turning right onto Route 272.

16.
Address: 9996 Ridge Road (Route 104), Clarkson

This plain, 2-story building has large, rough cobbles. The front has cut sandstone lintels and quoins. Irregular sandstone quoins were used on the back.

Head north on Monroe-Orleans County Line Road (Route 272). Watch right after it merges with Route 18. You're now in Morton, a pioneer settlement originally called Clark's Settlement. It was established by seven families between 1811 and 1816, including the families of three Clark brothers: Caleb, James and William.

17. Clark House
Address: 1560 Monroe-Orleans County Line Road, Hamlin
Original Owner: Orrin Clark
Year Built: ~1841

This simple, 1.5-story farmhouse is quite different from the previous one. It has larger cobbles and irregular sandstone quoins and lintels made from a single row of brick. Like the previous ones, the front and sides use the same size cobbles. Belly windows can be seen in the frieze across the front. The foundation is made of sandstone blocks.

Orrin Clark lived in a log cabin on his 75-acre plot of land for over 10 years before finishing payment and receiving the deed to the land. Shortly after receiving the deed in 1841 he commissioned the construction of a cobblestone addition to his log cabin, then lived here another 10 years.

According to Mrs. Raymond Seaman, a 20th century owner, it's evident that the cobblestone portion was an addition to a log cabin because in the dining room of the frame portion "one log is boxed in."

Continue north on Route 272, watching right.

An early period, field stone wall with rough limestone quoins. Notice the crack that has developed in the wall. (513 Route 238, Attica, #6 on Tour 6)

18. Johnson House

Address: 1350 Monroe-Orleans County Line Road, Hamlin
Original Owners: Samuel and Polly Johnson
Year Built: ~1838-1842
Style: Greek Revival

Here's a gorgeous 2-story home with horizontal mortar joints that protrude half an inch. The tiny, water-rounded cobbles are 5 courses per quoin on the front. Notice that they're set with long sides horizontal. What's unusual is that the small water-rounded cobbles are used on the south side as well as the front. Slightly larger cobblestones were used on the north wall, and the rear is a flush rubble wall. The lintels and 10-inch high quoins are red sandstone, and there's a cut sandstone foundation below the water table. A wide frieze graces the front.

Samuel W. Johnson, a tailor, and his wife Polly moved to Clark's Settlement in 1824. Polly was the daughter of Col. Caleb Clark, one of Clark's Settlement's founding pioneers. The Johnsons completed payments on their land in 1838 and built their cobblestone house, utilizing their log home as a rear wing containing the dining room, kitchen, pantry, store room and 2 bedrooms. The Johnsons needed the 8 large cobblestone house rooms to house their family of 11 children.

In addition to raising children, Samuel Johnson became a successful farmer, owning over 1,000 acres of land and raising fruits, grains, livestock, and less commonly, tobacco and hops.

Continue north on Route 272, then take the next right onto Morton Road (Route 360). Watch to the right, just before the flashing light where Route 360 turns.

19. Williams House
Address: 25 Morton Road, Hamlin
Original Owner: William Williams
Year Built: ~1838

This L-shaped, 2-story building with a 1-story wing, sports very small oblong cobbles. It has a wide frieze and cut limestone quoins and lintels. The inset front door has sidelights.

William Williams settled in Clarkson Corners around 1804 and worked as the community blacksmith. He served in the War of 1812 where he volunteered to carry away the dead after the city of Lewiston burned. In 1838 Williams completed his payments ($500) on his 60-acre plot of land and began building a cobblestone house to replace his log cabin. He lived in this house until his death in 1850, at which time the cobblestone house, a frame house and the land were sold to his sons John and Thomas R. Williams for $1,612.

At the end of Morton Road, turn right onto Redman Road at the flashing light, then left onto Church Road (still on Route 360). The next cobblestone building is at this corner.

20. Hamlin School District #12 Schoolhouse
Address: 3108 Church Road (Route 360), Hamlin
Year Built: 1836-1837

Built as a one-room schoolhouse, this small, simple 1-story structure has rough, irregular quoins. Lake-washed cobblestones were gathered by district taxpayers and students. The side of the building (toward Church Road) has oblong cobbles set on their sides.

The school's 19th century furnishings consisted of a stove, a top-opening desk for the teacher, a single blackboard made of ordinary wood painted black, and long benches with board backs for the students.

The Hamlin school system centralized with Kendall before 1957 and this has been a private residence since that time. Notice the repair work that has been done.

Continue east on Church Road (Route 360) and follow Route 360 to its end. Follow the road as it bears right (south) onto Route 19. Turn left onto Route 18 at the traffic light, but continue straight (onto Hamlin Center Road) when Route 18 bends to the right. At the end, turn left onto Sweden Walker - Lake Ontario Road and watch right.

21. Blossom House and Cobbler Shop
Address: 1486 Sweden Walker - Lake Ontario Road (Route 260), Hilton

This building has wide friezes on the front with rectangular frieze windows and a full-length front porch. Notice the small cobbles near the side peaks. This home was unusual in that it had 3 front doors.

It was built in the heart of the business district of East Hamlin, near a store, blacksmith and carriage shop, and an inn. Originally built as a double house and cobbler shop, it housed Allen Douglas Blossom, his wife Elizabeth Smith Blossom and the families of 4 of their 13 children at various times. All the men were shoemakers, including son Warren, daughter Caroline, who married her first cousin Peter Blossom, daughter Julia, who married her first cousin James Blossom, and daughter Lois, who married John Goodrich. In an 1855 census, the building was valued at $1,500.

Continue north on Sweden Walker - Lake Ontario Road, past Walker Road, and take the next right onto Brick School House Road. Continue east as Brick School House Road becomes Curtis Road. Pass Route 259 (North Avenue) and Bennett Road, then watch left.

22. Curtis House
Address: 204 Curtis Road, Parma
Original Owner: Philander Curtis
Year Built: 1848

This house is comprised of 3 stages. The first stage is a 2-story building with wide friezes and belly windows. Next comes a 1-story, then the final 1-story building, which has large cobbles at the base. On the far right wing, the cobbles get smaller as the structure goes up and then are large again toward the top. Look for the cut sandstone foundation.

Continue east to the end of Curtis Road, and turn right (south) onto Route 261 (Manitou Road). Take a left onto Frisbee Hill Road at the flashing light. At the end, turn right onto North Greece Road and watch right.

23. Davis House
Address: 149 North Greece Road, Greece
Original Owner: Edwin Davis
Year Built: 1845
Style: Greek Revival

This 2-story farmhouse, built in 1845 for the Davis family, serves today as a home and doctor's office. During its early years, teachers at the Frisbee Hill School often boarded at this house. In 1856 it was purchased by Lucius Bagley and remained in his family until 1942. The Bagleys pastured 8 cows and grew beans, corn, wheat and hay on their 100-acre farm. Henry Joel Bagley, son of Lucius, worked the farm until his death in 1942 at age 90. He often recounted the tale of a Civil War veteran named John Stothard who paid frequent visits to this house. Mr. Stothard claimed he had gathered cobblestones for the Davis family as a small boy.

Lucius Bagley's great grandson, also called Lucius Bagley was a custodian at the Greece Town Hall for many years and was one of the first volunteers in the U.S. to enlist during World War I. He served on the Navy battleship U.S.S. Iowa.

In the 1970s the Hazon's (owners at the time) hired Carl Schmidt, renowned cobblestone expert, to assist with renovations, to assure retention of the original cobblestone character.

This home was built with water-rounded cobblestones. The lintels and quoins are red sandstone, and the foundation is sandstone block. The building has wide friezes. The porch has square wooden columns that support a wood cornice in Greek Revival style. Look closely to the right of the driveway, near the house to see a cobblestone smokehouse with rough cobbles and sandstone quoins. It's one of only a few surviving cobblestone smokehouses in Monroe County.

Continue south on North Greece Road. Cross Route 18, and watch left after passing Mill Road.

24. Covert House
Address: 978 North Greece Road, Greece
Original Owner: William Covert
Year Built: 1832-1835
Style: Greek Revival

After the Covert family built their home, it passed through a succession of owners. Then in 1914 it was purchased by Walter Brodie. After his death, his daughter Helen Brodie-Pollok dedicated her life to the restoration and care of this home. Due to her efforts, this home became the first and to this date, only landmark in Greece, listed in the Federal, State and Local Register of Historic Homes.

The 1.5-story house has a center entrance flanked by sidelights, under a porch with Doric columns. It has a wide cornice and frieze with iron grills. Multi-colored, water-rounded cobbles were used. The wing in the back was the original carriage house. The fireplace inside was not original to the home. It was saved from a house being demolished during the construction of I-390 and rebuilt here. The original house was heated with potbelly stoves. Behind the house is a cobblestone well.

Continuing south on North Greece Road will take you back to Route 104.

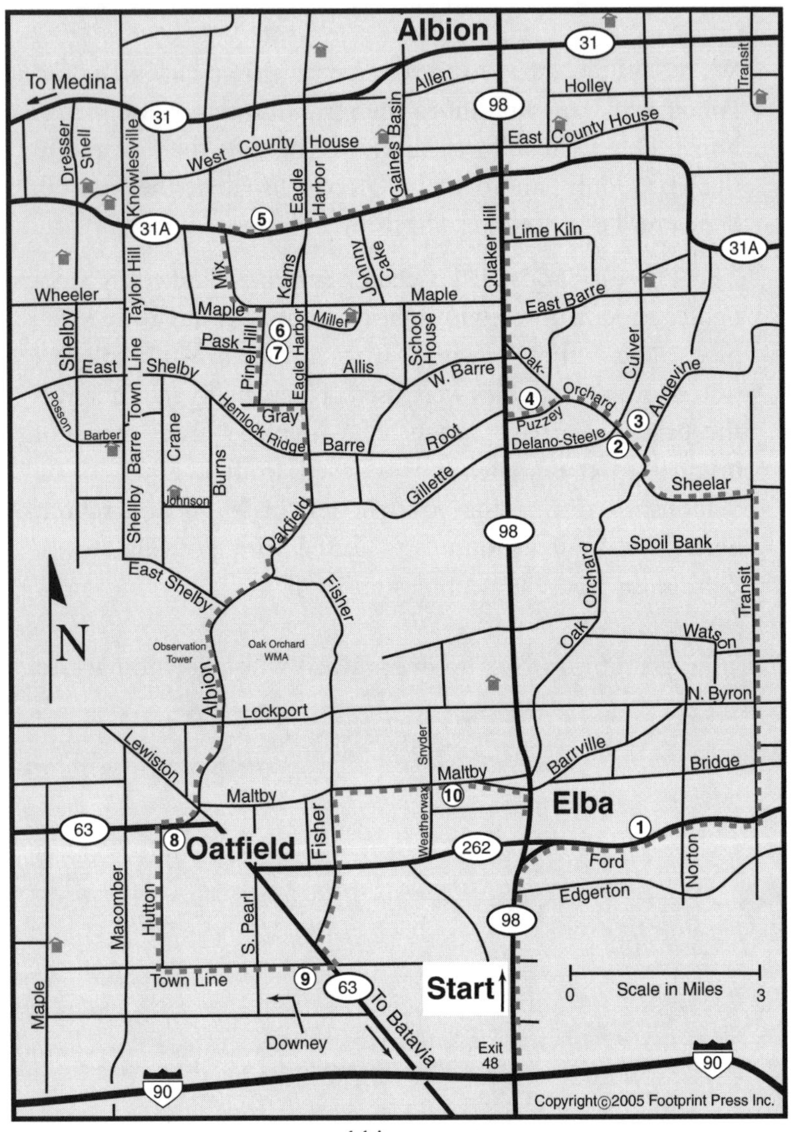

Cobblestone Tour 5

North of Batavia in Genesee and Orleans Counties
Total Distance: 52 miles
Approximate Time: 2 hours

Step back in history to pioneer days on this tour. The people who built these cobblestone homes migrated here as settlers, and lived in log cabins before becoming prosperous enough to build their cobblestone homes.

Begin the tour by heading north on Route 98 from Batavia (NYS Thruway exit 48). Turn right onto Route 262 (Ford Road) and watch left, 0.8 mile from the turn.

1. "Castleton" Ford House
Address: 4899 Ford Road (Route 262), Elba
Original Owner: Nathaniel Ford
Year Built: 1841
Style: Greek Revival entrance

Nathaniel Ford purchased his land from the Holland Land Company in 1833 and used natural rectangular field cobbles, set 4 courses per quoin, to build his home, which he called Castleton. He also used large, square-cut limestone lintels and quoins. The front door framed with engaged columns and sidelights, is classic Greek Revival. During a 20th century renovation a cobblestone walkway was uncovered. It was rare to use cobblestones to build structures other than buildings. This house remained in the Ford family until 1965. Today, it is beautifully preserved.

Continue east on Route 262. Pass Norton Road, and take the next left onto Transit Road. Continue north for 4.7 miles, then turn left onto Sheelar Road. At the end turn right onto Oak Orchard Road. Watch for two old barns with cobblestone foundations on your right as you drive. Pass Angevine Road and watch left, behind trees, shortly before Delano-Steele and Culver Roads.

2. Sears House
Address: 5306 Oak Orchard Road, Albion, Town of Barre
Original Owner: Ogden and Betsy Sears
Year Built: Late 1830s

Ogden Sears was a cooper in his native Connecticut and practiced his trade for a short while after emigrating to New York. In Barre, however, he was known simply as a farmer. *Landmarks of Orleans County* recounts "he picked up the stones on his own land, burned the lime used in erecting it, made the plaster and mortar and carried it to the workmen in a sap bucket." Eventually, Ogden and Betsy's daughter Betsey Ann married George Batchellor and lived in this house. Batchellor descendants have lived here ever since.

Sears House, 5306 Oak Orchard Road, Albion

The field cobbles are still in evidence on this 2-story home with a hip roof. Both horizontal and vertical mortar joints are Vs. Notice the mixed sandstones used as quoins. It has an aluminum sided addition on the left.

Continue northwest on Oak Orchard Road a short distance, and watch right at the next house.

3. Barre District #9 Schoolhouse
Address: 5283 Oak Orchard Road, Albion, Town of Barre
Year Built: 1845

Additions to the front and side of this 1-story schoolhouse converted it to a private residence but obscured most of the cobblestone structure. It was built with lake-washed cobbles laid horizontally, vertically and diagonally. The horizontal mortar joints are Vs but the vertical mortar joints are beaded. The door sill contains a benchmark (a survey indication of elevation).

Continue northwest on Oak Orchard Road past Delano-Steele/Culver Road. Turn left onto Puzzey Road (sometimes spelled Pusey or Puzey Road), and watch right.

4. Puzey House

Address: 14581 Puzzey Road, Barre, Town of Barre
Original Owner: James Puzey
Year Built: 1841
Period: Early

James Puzey came from England and married Eliza, who was born in New York. They were early settlers to the Town of Barre in the late 1830s.

The use of field and water-rounded cobbles of varied sizes, shapes and colors, without discernable lines, and flat mortar joints denotes an early period cobblestone building. The house has wooden lintels and sills, rough sandstone quoins, and a brick water table.

Continue west on Pusey Road (now spelled differently on the road sign). At the end, turn right onto Route 98 (Quaker Hill Road), and continue north to Route 31A. Turn left onto Route 31A at the blinking light. Pass Gaines Basin Road, Johnnie Cake Lane and Eagle Harbor Road, then watch for a red barn on the left, signaling the cobblestone home on the right.

5. Lee House

Address: 13121 West Lee Road (Route 31A), Albion, Town of Barre
Original Owner: Judge John Lee
Year Built: Late 1830s
Style: Greek Revival

Judge John Lee was born in Barre, MA, in 1763. He purchased this property in 1816 and moved his family into a log cabin in 1817. It wasn't until the late 1830s that he built his cobblestone house.

This 2-story home was built using the depressed hexagonal Gaines pattern without mortar rows between the water-rounded cobbles. The water table is only on the front of the building. The lintels in the front are cut gray sandstone, but stones set on edge in flat arches were used for the side lintels. The quoins are red and gray sandstone and the sills are red sandstone. It has flat mortar and an oval shaped gable decoration. Sidelights frame the front door.

Local folklore states that this house had "decoal" or carbide lights installed in the 1920s or 1930s — one of the first in the county. Carbide was purchased in white powder form and delivered in wooden kegs from Niagara Falls via horse and wagon. Water dripped over the carbide producing a vapor. The vapor traveled through pipes into the house to fixtures which could be lighted.

Continue west on Route 31A (West Lee Road). Notice the cobblestone foundations on the red barn across the street and the house next door. Take the first left onto Mix Road. After a sharp bend, turn right onto Pine Hill Road at the stop sign and watch left.

6. Finch House

Address: 4721 Pine Hill Road, Town of Barre

Mason: Probably the same mason who built the previous house (13121 West Lee Road) as evidenced by the similar construction.

Original Owner: Jacob Finch

Year Built: Mid-1830s

Jacob Finch was born in Columbia County, New York in 1797. He married Sarah Reynolds of Otsego County around 1813, and together they moved to Barre in 1826. They purchased the land on Pine Hill in 1832 and lived here the rest of their lives, raising 9 children.

This beautiful home is obscured by trees and partially covered in ivy. A large, modern addition was added to the back. The 2-story cobblestone structure has wide friezes on the sides, fine cut sandstone lintels, quoins and water table. It was built with small, water-rounded and oval field cobbles of varied colors set in mortar with V joints.

The next building is already in view. Continue south on Pine Hill Road, past Pask Road, and watch left.

7. Pine Hill District #6 Schoolhouse

Address: 4757 Pine Hill Road, Town of Barre

Year Built: The schoolhouse was in operation ~ 1835

This 1-room schoolhouse was constructed similar to the home you just viewed (4721 Pine Hill Road) with small, round, mixed-color field cobbles, rough cut red sandstone lintels and quoins, set in V-jointed mortar. The side has a frieze. Look closely at the quoins. It is unusual to find thin stones used as filler under alternate quoins. It served as a school for over 100 years and closed in the late 1850s due to centralization of the school district. Extra windows were added and the ceiling was lowered in the 1920s.

The original school black boards were just that — boards painted black. The formula was described in *3000 Useful Things Everyone Needs to Know* by R. R. Moore in 1884.

"Paint for Black Boards in Schools:

Common glue, 4 oz.

Flour of emery, 3 oz.
Just enough lampblack to give an inky color
Dissolve the glue in ¾ quart warm water, stir until there are no lumps. Apply to the board with a woolen rag, smoothly rolled. Three coats are sufficient."

Continue south on Pine Hill Road. At the end turn left onto Gray Road. At the end turn right onto Eagle Harbor Road. Continue straight as the road changes to Oakfield Road. Bear right onto Albion Road. Follow this as it winds to the end, passing through Oak Orchard Wildlife Management Area with swamp overlooks and an observation tower. Cross Lewiston Road and jog right to continue on Maltby Road, heading south. At the end, turn right onto Route 63, and watch left.

8. Calkins House

Address: 2810 Judge Road (Route 63), Oakfield
Mason: Daniel and Disbrow Calkins (They were stone masons on the Erie Canal.)
Year Built: 1830-1837
Style: Federal

The Calkins brothers came from Connecticut to work on the Erie Canal. They bought this land from the Holland Land Company. Now partially obscured by trees, this 2-story home was built slowly. In the spring and fall each year, oxen were driven to Lake Ontario to gather lake-washed cobbles. These were combined with field cobbles from the

Field cobbles with horizontal beaded joints,
4 courses per quoin, and chiseled limestone quoins.
(4892 West Swamp Road, Stanley, #8 on tour 16)

surrounding land to build the house. It has 4 courses per quoin on the front and 3 on the west wall. The quoins and lintels are gray limestone. Unusual are the brick around the front door, the larger stone foundation, then a bumped-out section of cobblestone around the base, and the small attached building.

Continue west on Route 63, and then take the next left onto Hutton Road. Take the first left onto Town Line Road. Pass Downey Road, and watch right.

9. Allen House
Address: 3328 Town Line Road, Batavia
Original Owner: Libbeus Allen
Year Built: 1840

In the fall of 1815, 22-year-old Libbeus Allen left his home in Otsego County, New York, and took a stagecoach from Syracuse to Canandaigua. He then continued on foot to the pioneer town of Batavia where he worked as a farm hand. In 1817 he moved to Dunham's Corners and married Esther Wright of Ogden in 1818. They eventually had four sons and three daughters.

In 1828 Libbeus Allen and William Walsh bought two lots at public auction. A year later, Allen acquired Walsh's lot and in 1840 built his cobblestone house. Esther died in 1864, but Libbeus lived on to the ripe old age of 94, dying in 1887.

This nice 2-story, field cobble farmhouse has paired, attached columns and sidelights at the front door, and cut gray limestone lintels, quoins and water table. The quoins are 12 inches high, 8 inches wide and 4.5 to 6 inches thick. The mason split many of the cobbles, giving them a flat appearance. They're set 4 courses per quoin on the front and left wall and 3 courses per quoin on the right wall.

Continue west on Town Line Road, and take the first left onto Route 63. Take the first right onto Fisher Road. Pass Route 262, then turn right onto Maltby Road. Pass Weatherwax Road, then look right, across from a red barn.

10. Cook House
Address: 4048 Maltby Road, Elba
Original Owner: Sheldon Cook
Year Built: 1828

Sheldon Cook purchased this land from the Holland Land Company in 1828 and quickly built his cobblestone home. How fitting to end this route with this gorgeous 2-story, home built with field cobbles of varied sizes, shapes and colors, set 2 courses per quoin. The lintels, sills and quoins are cut limestone. Look for the cobblestone wing out back (as well as the huge addition) and the small, attached building on the left. The porch, added in 1912, obscures the original etched datestone over the front door.

Continuing east on Maltby Road, bear right at the Y, and turn right at the stop sign to head south on Route 98 (Main Street, Elba). Continue south to the NYS Thruway (I-90) to complete the loop.

Cobblestone home owner Pete Consler stands in front of a deep window well, common in cobblestone houses. (956 Kent Road, Kent)

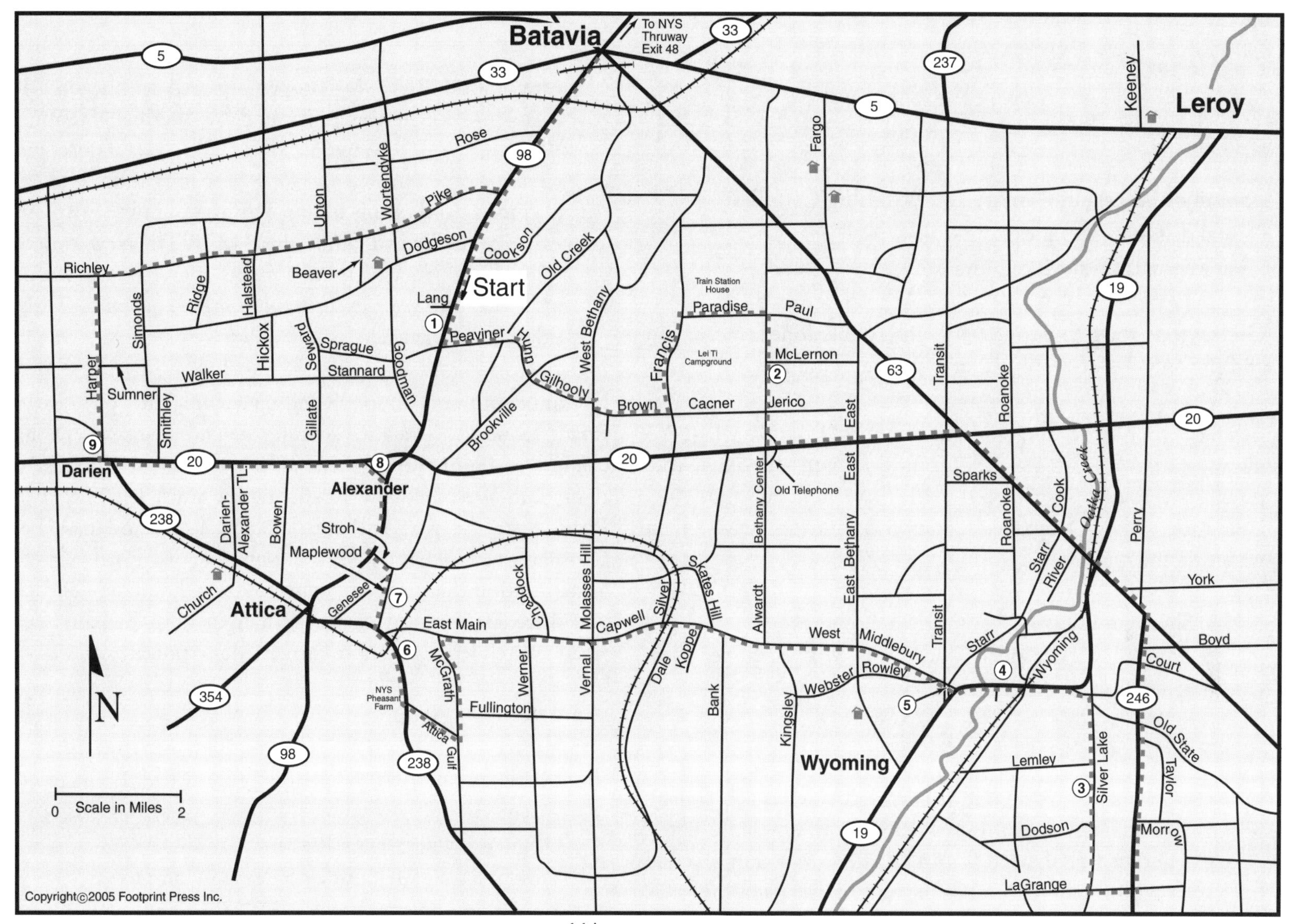

Cobblestone Tour 6

Cobblestone Tour 6

South of Batavia in Genesee and Wyoming Counties
Total distance: 69 miles
Approximate Time: 2.5 hours

On this tour you'll find some very early cobblestone construction and the only 3-story cobblestone building in the U.S.

Begin the tour by heading south on Route 98 from Batavia (NYS Thruway exit 48). It's 5.6 miles from the center of Batavia (the junction of Routes 98/33/5/63) to the first cobblestone building. Pass Rose, Pike, Dodgeson, Cookson and Lang Roads, then watch right.

1. Sherman House
Address: 9970 Alexander Road (Route 98), Alexander
Original Owner: Moses Page
Year Built: 1837
Style: 5-bay Federal

This two-story farmhouse has field cobbles laid 3 courses per quoin in straight rows. The cut gray limestone lintels and quoins were hauled from LeRoy by oxen. An inverted T-shaped ornament of limestone panels decorates the gable ends. The view is partially obscured by trees.

After Moses Page, this property passed to his son Albert Page. In 1866 it was purchased by Sherman Hammond. With the next change in ownership, this house would remain in the same family for a very long time. Notice the plaque in front of this house. This is a Century Farm, in the hands of the Brown family since 1877. The New York State Agricultural Society honors farms that have survived for more that 100 years in the hands of the same family with the title Century Farm.

Continue south on Route 98 and take a quick left onto Peaviner Road. Continue straight, crossing several roads as the name changes to Hunn Road, then Gilhooly Road. At the end turn right onto West Bethany Road, then a quick left onto Brown Road. Take the first left onto Francis Road and pass Lei-Ti Campground. Take the first right onto Paradise Road. Watch for a train station that has been converted to a home on your left as you drive. At the next corner turn right onto Bethany Center Road. Watch left at the next corner (McLernon Road).

2. Rumsey House
Address: 10051 McLernon Road, Bethany, Town of Bethany (or 10105 Bethany Center Road, Bethany Center)
Original Owner: Jessee Rumsey
Mason: Reputedly built by Sherman Hammond
Year Built: 1830

Period: Very early

In 1811 Jessee Rumsey purchased this land from the Holland Land Company. The cobblestone house and property stayed in the Rumsey family until 1897.

This large, 2-story farmhouse is a fine example of early period cobblestone construction with walls 17 to 18 inches thick. Sidelights frame the front door. Notice the large field cobbles laid 3 courses per quoin, and rough cut gray limestone lintels, quoins and sills. The front and back door thresholds are also limestone. A pump still sits in the side yard, in front of the porch. The side gable end has a round medallion.

Continue south on Bethany Center Road, past Cacner/Jerico Road, and follow the Route 20 East sign left onto Old Telephone Road, then another left onto Route 20. Pass East Road and Transit Road, then turn right onto Route 63 south at the signal light. Pass Route 19 then turn right (south) on Route 246. Take the third right onto LaGrange Road, then the first right onto Silver Lake Road at the stop sign. Pass Dodson Road, and watch to the left, across the street from a large red barn.

3. Fisher House
Address: 1132 Silver Lake Road, Town of Covington
Year Built: 1837

This 1.5-story house with green shutters was built with field cobbles and rough lintels and quoins. Notice the sandstone lintels set on edge. A small porch frames the front door.

Continue north on Silver Lake Road. Pass Lemley Road. At the end turn left onto Route 19 West. Pass Wyoming Road and railroad tracks, and then look right across from Markin Lane.

4. Gorton House
Address: 636 Route 19, Wyoming, Town of Covington
Original Owner: Samuel Gorton (sometimes spelled Cotton)
Mason: Alexander McFarland
Year Built: 1840

The datestone over the door is engraved with "Samuel Gorton 1840." Both the inset door and porch on the wing have columns. This house has field cobbles and cut gray sandstone lintels, quoins and water table. The horizontal and vertical V mortar joints are very straight and even. Notice the square stone foundation.

Continue west on Route 19, cross Oatka Creek, and take the next right onto W. Middlebury Road. Cross Starr Road and immediately look left.

5. Coefield House
Address: Starr Road (historically listed as Rowley Road), Town of Middlebury
Original Owner: Edward or Frank Coefield

What a shame. Here's an example of a large 2-story cobblestone house that needs some tender loving care. It was built with field cobbles and rough limestone quoins with lintels on edge. Roughly half of the vertical mortar joints are Vs, the rest are embellished.

Continue west on West Middlebury Road. After Koppe go straight over railroad tracks, onto Capwell Road, as West Middlebury bends left. Continue heading west, merging onto East Main Street. After passing Werner Road, turn left onto McGrath Road, then the first right onto Attica Gulf Road. At the end, turn right onto Route 238 north, and watch for a barn on the right, before railroad tracks.

The cobblestone barn at 513 Route 238, Attica

6. Cobblestone Barn
Address: 513 Route 238, Attica
Year Built: ~1841

Here's a barn built with large field cobbles and rough lintels and quoins.

Continue north on Route 238 over railroad tracks, pass East Main, and then turn right onto Maplewood Road, and watch to the right.

7. Cogswell House
Address: 11231 Maplewood Road, Attica
Original Owner: Thomas Cogswell
Period: Early

This L-shaped building (2 attached buildings) is unique in its rough construction. Notice the uneven sized cobbles, lack of straight lines, uneven limestone quoins and rough limestone frames around the windows and door. The lintels over the windows are wider at the top than at the bottom.

Continue north on Maplewood Road. At the end turn left on Stroh Road. At the end turn right onto Route 98 north. At the stop sign turn left onto Buffalo Street (unlabeled, but there's a Citgo, Yahama, and Clark Appliance at the corner), and watch right.

8. Alexander Classical School
Address: 3323 Church Street, Alexander
Mason: Hezekiah Barnard
Year Built: 1837

Alexander Classical School, 3323 Church Street, Alexander

Alexander Town Hall is the only 3-story cobblestone town hall in America. It was originally built for $7,000 in 1837 as a private school by the Literary Society of the Alexandrian Library. It was probably the largest cobblestone school ever built. Students boarded with local families. It became a public school after the Civil War. In the 1850s 300 students were enrolled. Classes were held here until 1938. The domed octagonal cupola with a balustrade (wooden fencing) originally housed the school bell. The quoins are rough cut gray limestone. Today the third floor houses the

A close-up of the field cobbles at Alexander Classical School, showing the horizontal V mortar joints and vertical pyramid joints

Alexander Town Museum of local history. It's open by appointment, so call ahead, (585) 591-1204.

Continue west on Buffalo Street, and turn left onto Route 20 at the end. Across from the Route 238 junction, turn right onto Harper Road, and look left shortly up from this corner.

9.

Address: 10554 Harper Road, Darien
Year Built: Early 1830s

Levi Harroun purchased this land from Holland Land Company sometime in the 1820s and may have had this cobblestone home built before deeding the land to Theda Carter in 1834. When Darien City Postmaster Squire Thomas Riddle acquired this house in 1838, he used it as the post office. It served as the post office again from 1914 through 1940. It has also been used as a town court and as a voting place.

This small 1-story house with brown trim can be easily seen. It was built with field cobbles and cut, painted gray limestone quoins and lintels 10 inches high.

To return to the start, continue north on Harper Road. When it ends, take a right on Richley. It will turn into Pike, then meet Route 98. A left onto Route 98 will lead north to Batavia.

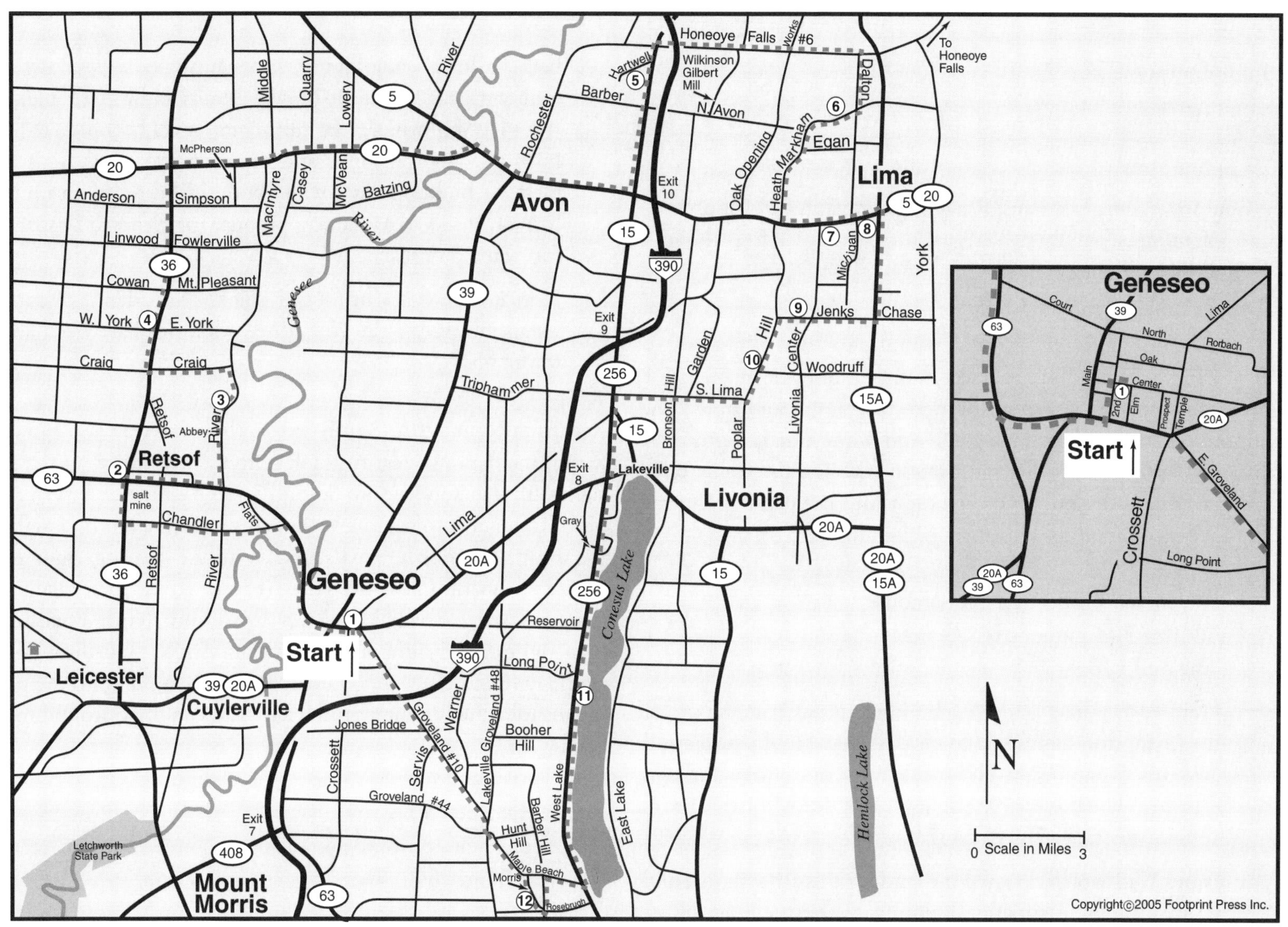

Cobblestone Tour 7

Cobblestone Tour 7

Geneseo, Avon, Lima and Rush in Livingston and Monroe Counties
Total Distance: 72 miles
Approximate Time: 3.5 hours

Begin in the village of Geneseo. (See the inset detail map for Geneseo on page 75.) From Route 39, turn east onto Route 20A. In one block, watch for the green and white library sign, then turn left (north) onto Second Street. Take the first right onto Center Street (no sign), and turn right into the parking area for the Livingston County Historical Museum.

1. Geneseo District #5 Schoolhouse
Address: 30 Center Street, Geneseo
Year Built: 1838

Feel free to walk around this building. It has been the site of the Livingston County Historical Society Headquarters and Museum since 1932. The museum is open May through October, Thursdays and Sundays, 2 to 5 PM or by special appointment, (585) 243-3457.

James Wadsworth donated the land for this schoolhouse and wanted to see a superior building constructed. It shows, because for a schoolhouse, it is unusually large and finely built with cut limestone lintels, quoins and water table. The front has uniform sized, multi-colored field cobbles, defined horizontal mortar joints and some vertical joints. This cobblestone building has 2 wings and hipped roofs, an unusual format. It served as the schoolhouse for Geneseo District #5 for nearly a century.

Notice the variety in mortar colors — evidence of various repair jobs. Over the years three additions have been added to the south side.

Return to Route 20A (South Street) the same way you came in. (From the parking area, turn left onto Center Street. At the stop sign, turn left (south) onto Second Street.) At the end, turn right onto Route 20A west. Follow the signs to Route 63. Bear right to the Route 63 north bypass and continue bearing right onto Route 63 north. Cross over the Genesee River, then take a left onto Chandler Road. Pass River Road and Retsof Road, then turn right onto Route 36 north (Main Street). Go through the traffic light at the Route 63 intersection, then pull into the parking area for the building on the left. You can drive around to the back.

2. Ramsdell Store
Address: 3678 Route 36, York
Year Built: 1840

This long, narrow building with wide windows and numerous doors has seen many uses and many additions. It was built as a village store using field cobbles. It has served as a post office and barbershop.

Go back to the traffic light and head left onto Route 63 east. Pass Retsof Road, then turn left onto River Road. Pass the Trappist Abbey of the Genesee. (Stop to visit their chapel and bookstore and buy some Monks Bread. www.geneseeabbey.org. Store hours are 8 - 11 AM, 1:30 - 3:30 PM and 5:30 - 6:30 PM. Baking is done Tuesday, Thursday and Saturday.) Then watch left at the top of a knoll.

3. Hayden House
Address: 3016 River Road, York
Year Built: ~1840

Moses Hayden, the first judge in Livingston County, built this home around 1840 using field cobbles. It is now part of the Abbey of the Genesee.

Four 2-story columns grace the large front porch. The main door is in the wall facing south. The twin chimneys and overhanging roof were later modifications. The front and basement windows and doors are all framed with cut limestone. The quoins and lintels are a tan color. Lintels are missing from the side windows. Notice the differing window sizes — tall on the first floor and small on the second floor. Also notice the oval window in the peak of the front portico.

Continue north on River Road, then take the first left onto Craig Road. Turn right onto Route 36 (Main Street) and head north to the next intersection with York Road (County Road 35) and look left.

4.
Address: 2682 Route 36, York
Year Built: 1830

This 2-story home was built with field cobbles and limestone lintels and quoins. The mortar has definitive horizontal V joints. A fanlight dresses up the front gable end. Notice two doors, one above the other, on the side of the building.

Continue north on Route 36, then turn right (east) onto Route 20 at the traffic light. Turn right as Route 20 merges with Route 5 at a flashing light. Cross the Genesee River, and pass through a roundabout in the village of Avon. Turn left onto Route 15 north at a traffic light. Pass Barber/N. Avon Road, then turn left onto gravel Hartwell Road. Watch to the left.

5.
Address: Hartwell Road, Rush, Town of Rush
Year Built: Mid-1830s

This 2-story home was built with field cobbles and limestone lintels, quoins and water table. In addition, the pair of narrow front doors are framed in cut limestone with a fan and arch of cut limestone over the top of the door. The mortar is in definitive horizontal rows.

Turn around and head back to Route 15. Turn left, heading north on Route 15. Take the next right onto Honeoye Falls #6 Road at the flashing light and cross over I-390. Take the third right onto Dalton Road. Take the next right at the stop sign onto Heath Markham Road. Pass a white silo on the right, then look right.

6.
Address: 6857 Heath Markam Road, Lima

Here's another 2-story field cobblestone home with limestone framing the windows as well as limestone quoins, lintels and water table, and V mortar joints.

Continue down Heath Markham Road to the end, then turn left onto Route 5 and 20. Pass Livonia Center Road and pull into the right shoulder at the next house.

7. Morgan Farmhouse
Address: 6870 West Main Street (Route 5 and 20), Lima
Year Built: 1832

Morgan Farmhouse, 6870 West Main Street, Lima

Does this look familiar? It's almost identical to house #5 (Hartwell Road), most likely built by the same builder. Notice the arched fan over the front door and the hitching post in the front yard.

Continue east on Route 5 and 20, into Lima. Pass Michigan Road, then watch right.

8.
Address: 7192 (Route 5 and 20), Lima

This 2-story field cobblestone building has a wooden shake roof and a fanlight in the front gable end. The ornate porch on the front and side are additions.

Continue east on Route 5 and 20, then turn right at the traffic light onto Route 15A in the center of Lima. South of the village, take a right onto Jenks Road. Pass Michigan Road and Livonia Center Road, then watch right.

9. Lima District #6 Schoolhouse
Address: 6679 Jenks Road, Lima
Year Built: 1843

Built as a schoolhouse, this field cobblestone building now serves as a home but still sports a bell on top. It was built rather crudely with no lines to the mortar. The cobblestones

Lima District #6 Schoolhouse, 6679 Jenks Road, Lima

vary in size on the side facing the road and are more uniform on the front. It has limestone lintels and quoins, but also notice the narrow limestone blocks framing the door.

Continue west on Jenks Road to the end. Turn left onto Poplar Hill Road, and watch right among a grove of trees.

10.
Address: 2798 Poplar Hill Road, Lima

Here's a pretty 2-story field cobblestone farmhouse with narrow windows. The lintels are set on edge, even over the basement windows. The mortar has horizontal V joints. There's a fanlight in the side gable end.

Continue south on Poplar Hill Road, and take the first right onto S. Lima Road. At Route 15 (Lakeville Road), turn left, then bear right onto Route 256 south. Pass Lima Road and several others, including Route 20A. After Long Point Road, watch left along the shore of Conesus Lake.

11. Wadsworth House
Address: 4907 West Lake Road (Route 256), Geneseo
Year Built: Early 1850s

The large 2-story Wadsworth House was built using large field cobbles and horizontal mortar joints. The second floor windows are rounded at the top and poke up into the dormer. Sidelights surround the front door. Notice the narrow panel bay window on the north side of the building.

Continue south on Route 256. Turn right on Maple Beach Road (County Road 45) to climb a hill. At the first intersection turn left on Barber Hill Road, then take a right on Morris Road, and watch left as the road bends.

12. Parks House

Address: 6054 Morris Road, Groveland

Original Owner: Morris Parks

Here's another 2-story farmhouse built with field cobbles and horizontal mortar joints. The lintels and quoins are different colors. A small porch frames the front door. Notice the repair job — evidenced by lighter mortar in the upper right.

Morris Parks was flooded out of his former house so he chose higher ground to build his cobblestone home; we're just not sure when. He is shown as owner of record on the 1872 atlas. The second owners were the Johnsons. Then the house was purchased by Kenyon Warner, who gutted the inside in 1918. In 1919 he moved in with his new bride and lived here for the next 50 years. Upon his death, his granddaughter, Mrs. Sebastian Loturco, moved in and lives here to this day. This is one of many examples of how cobblestone homes remain in a family for multiple generations.

Continue north on Morris Road to the end. Turn left, back onto Maple Beach Road. At the stop sign, turn right onto County Road 10. Bear left to follow County Road 10 (Groveland Road) when County Road 48 (Lakeville Groveland Road) bears right. Cross over I-390. This road ends at Route 20A. Turn left to return to Route 39 and the heart of Geneseo.

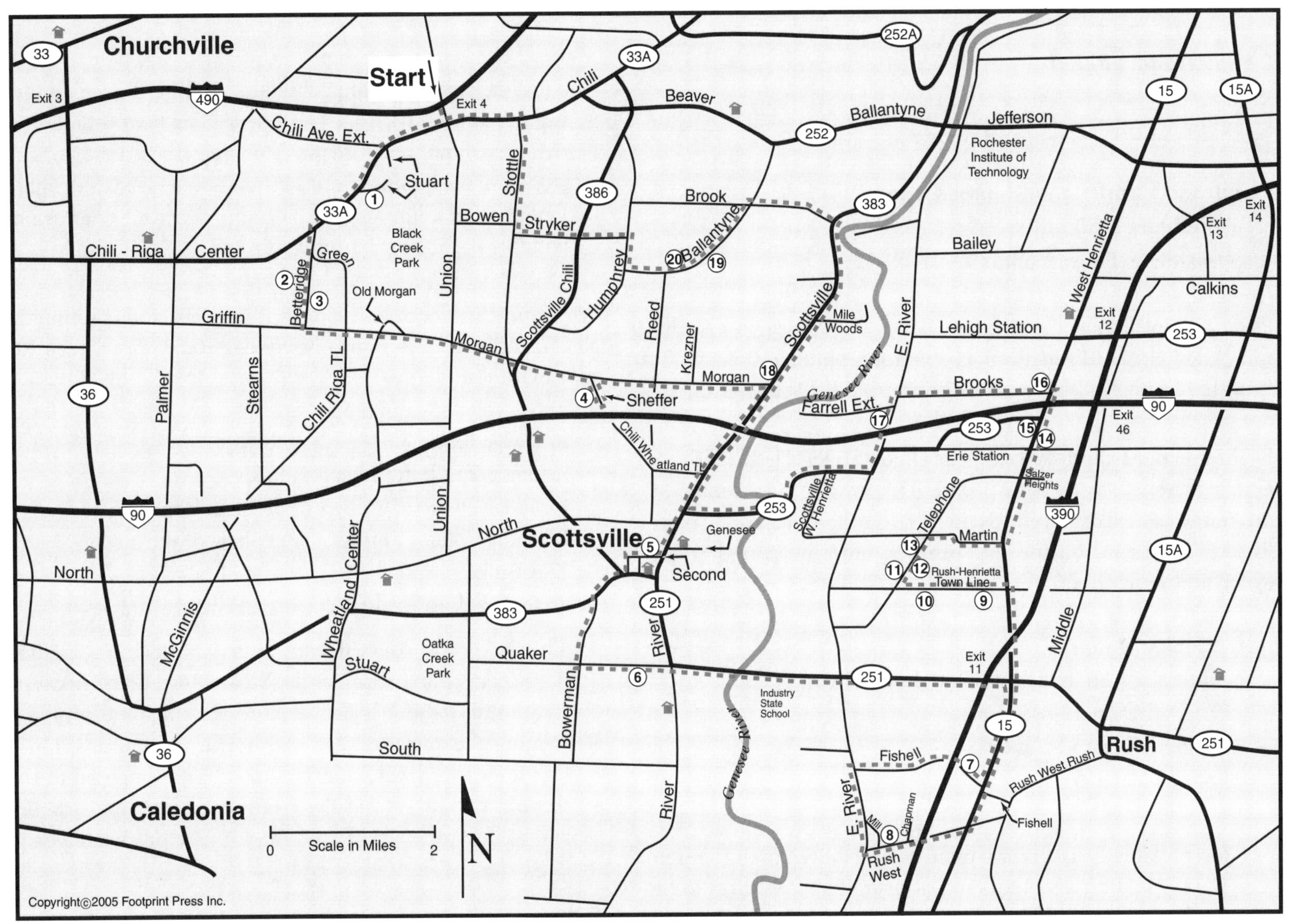

Cobblestone Tour 8

Cobblestone Tour 8

Chili and Henrietta in Monroe County
Total Distance: 50 miles
Approximate Time: 2 hours

From a simple Quaker meeting house, to large fancy homes, this tour highlights a diversity of cobblestone buildings. Being far from Lake Ontario, they were all built using field cobblestones.

Begin the tour from I-490 exit 4 at Union Street. Head south on Union Street, then right on Route 33A west (Chili Avenue) at the traffic light. Pass Chili Avenue Ext. to the right, then Stuart Road (a dead end) on the left. Turn left onto the second Stuart Road, and watch right.

1. Sibley House
Address: 61 Stuart Road, Churchville, Town of Chili
Original Owner: Joseph Sibley
Mason: William Emmons
Year Built: 1835
Style: Federal

Joseph Sibley was an early pioneer who moved to this area in 1811. He built a sawmill and flour mill and went on to be the first supervisor of Chili.

This is a large, 13-room cobblestone house. The main building is 2-stories, with a 1-story wing. The field cobbles are in definitive rows and laid flush on the front. Fine cut limestone lintels, quoins and water table were used. Sidelights, a fanlight and a limestone arch frame the front door. An oval window decorate the front gable end.

Turn around and head back out to Route 33A and continue west (left). Take the next left onto Betteridge Road. Pass Green Road and watch right.

2. Stowe House
Address: 253 Betteridge Road, Riga
Original Owner: William Betteridge, from England
Mason: William Emmons, a nephew of the owner
Year Built: ~1830s
Style: Greek Revival front with a Federal entrance

This 2-story, uncoursed lake-washed and field cobble home has similar construction as the Stuart Road house because of a common mason. It's unusual to see cut stone completely framing the entranceway. Also notice the shutters. On the first floor they have 3 louvered sections as opposed to the 2 sections on the second floor shutters. Sidelights, a fanlight and a limestone arch frame the front door. A fanlight also decorates the front gable end.

The carpenters were paid 50 cents per day to work on this house. The property contains a "brew house" built with uncoursed lake-washed cobbles and rough field cobbles.

Continue south on Betteridge Road, watching left.

3. Hale House
Address: 280 Betteridge Road, Town of Riga
Mason: William Emmons
Year Built: 1840
Style: Greek Revival

The walls on this home are 47-inches thick. It was built with jointed courses of cobblestones both above and below the water table and cut limestone lintels and quoins. The brick section on the back was a recent addition.

Continue south on Betteridge Road. At the end, turn left onto Griffin Road. Head east, passing several roads and crossing Route 386. Griffin Road becomes Morgan Road. Take the next right onto Sheffer Road and drive toward the end of this dead-end street and watch right. Beware of the dogs — stay in your vehicle.

4. Sheffer House
Address: 95 Sheffer Road, Chili, Town of Chili
Mason: Same unnamed mason as two homes on Route 386 (they're not on a tour)
Year Built: 1835-1840
Style: Greek Revival

The placement of the off-center door and center windows on this home were driven by floor plan requirements. The original exterior shutters have adjustable louvers with over 129 parts each. These were common on pre-Civil War buildings. This 2-story home was built using field cobbles and cut limestone quoins, lintels and water table.

Turn around in the loop at the end of Sheffer Road. Turn right, back onto Morgan Road. At the end of Morgan Road, ignore the cobblestone Chili Schoolhouse Museum near the corner for now (we'll return here later), and turn right onto Route 383 at a stop sign. In Scottsville, turn right onto Second Street and look right.

5. Slocum House
Address: 6 Second Street, Scottsville, Town of Wheatland
Mason: Osborn Filler
Year Built: 1838
Style: Queen Anne

This home was built with field cobblestones and cut limestone lintels, quoins and water table. Its second floor was added. Notice the wood shingle roof.

Continue west on Second Street. Pass a stop sign, and then the road bends to meet Main Street. Turn right onto Main Street (Route 383 west). Pass the Route 386 junction. Turn left onto

Bowerman Road then the first left onto Quaker Road, and watch right at the top of the second hill.

6. Quaker Meeting House
Address: 409 Quaker Road, Scottsville, Town of Wheatland
Original Owner: Orthodox Quakers
Year Built: 1834
Style: Federal

Orthodox Quakers used this 1-story, plain, rough field cobble building as a meeting house for 20 years. Then, the more liberal Hicksite Quakers used it from 1854 to 1873. Between 1937 and 1963 it was used as a Grange Hall and is now a private residence. The design is classic Quaker with two entrances (one for men and one for women) and a very simple architecture.

Continue east on Quaker Road, and it will turn into Route 251 east. Cross over I-390, then turn right onto Route 15 south. Turn right onto Fishell Road. Look right shortly before the I-390 overpass.

7. Fishell House
Address: 512 Fishell Road, West Rush
Original Owner: John Fishell
Year Built: 1838
Style: Federal

Henry Fishell, an early pioneer, moved to Rush in 1808 from Gettysburg, PA. His son John raised 21 children in this house.

For his 2-story home, Fishell (or his many children?) selected mainly small-sized field cobbles from their property but built their home very roughly. It has cut limestone lintels and quoins. The inset door has sidelights on both sides and is capped with a window fan and distinctive limestone arch.

Continue west on Fishell Road. At the end turn left onto East River Road. Take the 2nd left onto Rush West Road, and look left.

8. Winans House
Address: 42 Rush West Road, West Rush
Year Built: 1826
Style: Federal

This small 2-story home with an addition on the left was built using large, rough field cobbles. Notice the rough limestone quoins and limestone lintels set on edge. It was originally built into the side of a hill, possibly by the Winans family.

Continue east on Rush West Road, pass under I-390, then turn left at the stop sign onto Route 15 north. Pass Route 251 (traffic light) and cross over I-390 (2nd traffic light), then turn left onto Rush-Henrietta Town Line Road, and watch left.

9. Hoyt House
Address: 889 Town Line Road, Henrietta
Original Owner: Ebenezer Hoyt
Year Built: 1834
Period: Early
Style: Federal

This house was built with rough field cobbles and rough cut limestone quoins. The lintels are limestone set on edge. Look for a tie rod holding the structure together on the left side.

Continue west on Town Line Road, looking left.

10. Bushman House
Address: 791 Town Line Road, Henrietta
Original Owner: Abner Bushman
Year Built: 1846
Style: Federal

This 2-story box is set back from the road, so it's hard to see. It was built using rough fieldstones.

Continue west on Town Line Road, then turn right at the stop sign onto Telephone Road, and look left.

11. Jacob Bushman House
Address: 887 Telephone Road, Henrietta
Original Owner: Jacob Bushman and his wife Mary Snapp
Year Built: 1839, 1926 addition (plaque on house says 1830)
Style: Federal

This house stayed in the Bushman family until the early 2000s when Mrs. Bushman vacated the premises at the age of 96. The small 1.5-story house was built with field cobbles. Horizontal and vertical mortar joins are Vs.

Another cobblestone house used to stand across the field but its roof caved in. Henrietta, which once had 14 cobblestone buildings, now has 13.

Continue north on Telephone Road and look right.

12. Bullard House
Address: 830 Telephone Road, Henrietta
Original Owner: Leonard Bullard
Year Built: 1830s
Style: Federal

Leonard Bullard owned this land as of 1826 and built his home some time in the 1830s. Like the previous house, quoins and lintels are limestone, with the upper lintels set vertically over the windows to create a fan. The Federal entrance is more elaborate than most in the area with side-lights framing the door. The half-elliptical fanlight above the front door contains leaded glass.

Continue north on Telephone Road and look left at the corner of Martin Road.

13. Bushman House
Address: 633 Telephone Road, Henrietta
Original Owner: Andrew Bushman
Style: Federal with Italianate details

This field cobble house has three courses per quoin on the front and larger stones on the sides. Quoins and lintels are limestone, with the upper lintels set vertically over the windows to create a fan. The original home had 10 rooms but was modified when an oil furnace was installed. The cornice, entrance and center front gable were added in the late 19th century.

Turn right onto Martin Road, and then take the first left onto West Henrietta Road (Route 15 north). Pass Erie Station Road at a traffic light, and look right (across from Wheeler Road).

14. Post House
Address: 5582 West Henrietta Road, Henrietta
Original Owner: Abel Post, elected as Common School Commissioner in 1818
Year Built: 1832
Period: Early
Style: Federal

This house was built with field cobbles that vary in size, shape, color and texture. The mortar joints are uneven Vs. The quoins are rough limestone, and the limestone lintels are set on edge to form a fan like the other homes on this street. The walls are 24 to 30 inches thick as evidenced by the deeply recessed first floor windows. This house has a limestone keystone arch that was originally gilded. The large entrance with sidelights and leaded window fan are original.

Continue north on Route 15. Turn left into the Moose Lodge parking area before the next traffic light. You can walk around this building.

15. Carriage/Wagon Shop
Address: 5375 West Henrietta Road, Henrietta
Year Built: 1830s

Joseph and Alexander Williams were the earliest recorded owners of this blacksmith and wagon shop. Census records show that their 1865 production was 25 buggies, 50 lumber wagons, 13 plows and 25 sleighs. At one point, an extension at the north end (which no longer exists) housed a steam sawmill and a carriage construction area. Then it was used as a foundry. The first floor is built with rounded field cobbles and the second floor was an oak frame structure supported by 15-inch timbers. In 1970 fire consumed the top floor, and it was replaced by brick.

Wagon Shop, 5375 West Henrietta Road, Henrietta

At one time 100 people worked here. It has had a long, convoluted history. During World War II it was a garage, then the Carriage Stop Restaurant, followed by a Chinese restaurant and now it's a Moose Family Center.

On the Thruway Park (Route 253, north) side you'll find a rubble wall where the extension was once attached. On the front you can find a patched area where windows used to be. Look closely at the cobblestone area to see a good example of uneven, horizontal V-shaped mortar joints. The vertical mortar joints are either plain or V, depending on where you look.

Continue north on Route 15, pass over I-90, then take a quick left onto Brooks Road at the RIT Inn and Conference Center. The next cobblestone building is on the right at this corner, but it's hard to see due to the ivy covering.

16. Fenner House
Address: 5121 West Henrietta Road (west side), Henrietta
Original Owner: Daniel Fenner
Year Built: 1830s
Style: Federal

This house is obscured by ivy.

Continue west on Brooks Road. At the end, turn left onto East River Road, then look right at the corner of Ferrell Road Extension.

17.
Address: 5015 Ferrell Road Extension, Henrietta
Style: Federal

This 2-story house has a porch at the front door. It was built with rough field cobbles, rough limestone quoins and limestone lintels set on edge.

Continue south on East River Road, cross over I-90, and turn right onto Erie Station Road (Route 253 west) at the traffic light. Follow Route 253 over the Genesee River, then turn right onto Route 383 north at the traffic light. Cross under I-90, pass Morgan Road, and take the next left into the parking area for the Chili Schoolhouse Museum.

18. Chili District #4 Schoolhouse

Address: 2525 Scottsville Road (west side), Henrietta, Town of Chili
Year Built: 1848
Style: Greek Revival

Peter Sheffer, one of the first landowners in Chili, donated the land for this school. The 1-story Chili District #4 Schoolhouse operated for over 100 years, from 1848 until 1952. Today it is still outfitted as a school and became the Chili Schoolhouse Museum (operated by the Town of Chili) in 1965. Go ahead and peak inside the windows. To make an appointment to go inside, call the Chili Town Historian at (585) 889-6123. The schoolhouse was built with rough multi-color cobblestones and has wide friezes.

Continue north on Route 383. When the Genesee River is near the road on your right, turn left onto Brook Road. Take the first left onto Ballantyne Road at the stop sign, and watch left.

19. Krenzer House

Address: 745 Ballantyne Road, Henrietta, Town of Chili
Period: Early
Style: Federal

Look carefully at the cobblestones on this simple, 1.5-story building. They're unusually flat, resulting in an even appearance not normally associated with cobblestone buildings. Even the foundation is made from cobblestones. The lintels are limestone set on edge.

Continue west on Ballantyne Road and watch right, across from the Reed Road intersection.

20. Marshall House

Address: 860 Ballantyne Road, Henrietta, Town of Chili
Year Built: 1845
Style: Greek Revival

Large, multicolor cobblestones comprise this 1.5-story, 8-room house. The wide friezes have rectangular grills. Notice the small limestone blocks set on edge for lintels and the porch over the front door.

To return to I-490, continue west on Ballantyne Road. At the end, turn right onto Humphrey Road, then a left onto Stryker Road. At the end turn right onto Stottle Road. When it ends at Route 33A, turn left, then a right onto Union Street at a traffic light to find the entrance to I-490.

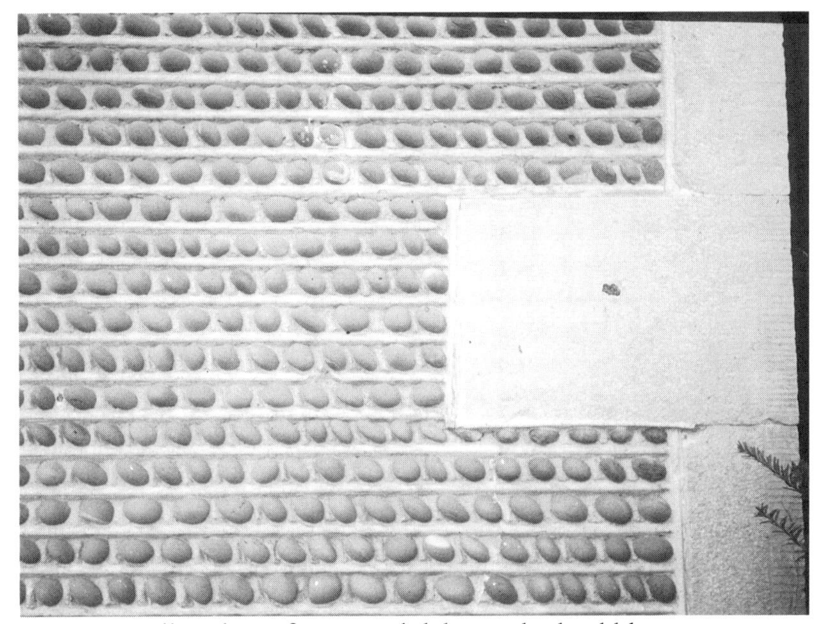

Small, red, uniform sized, lake-washed cobbles are a
common building material near Lake Ontario,
especially for later period homes.
(100 Old State Road, Penn Yan, house #4, Tour 16)

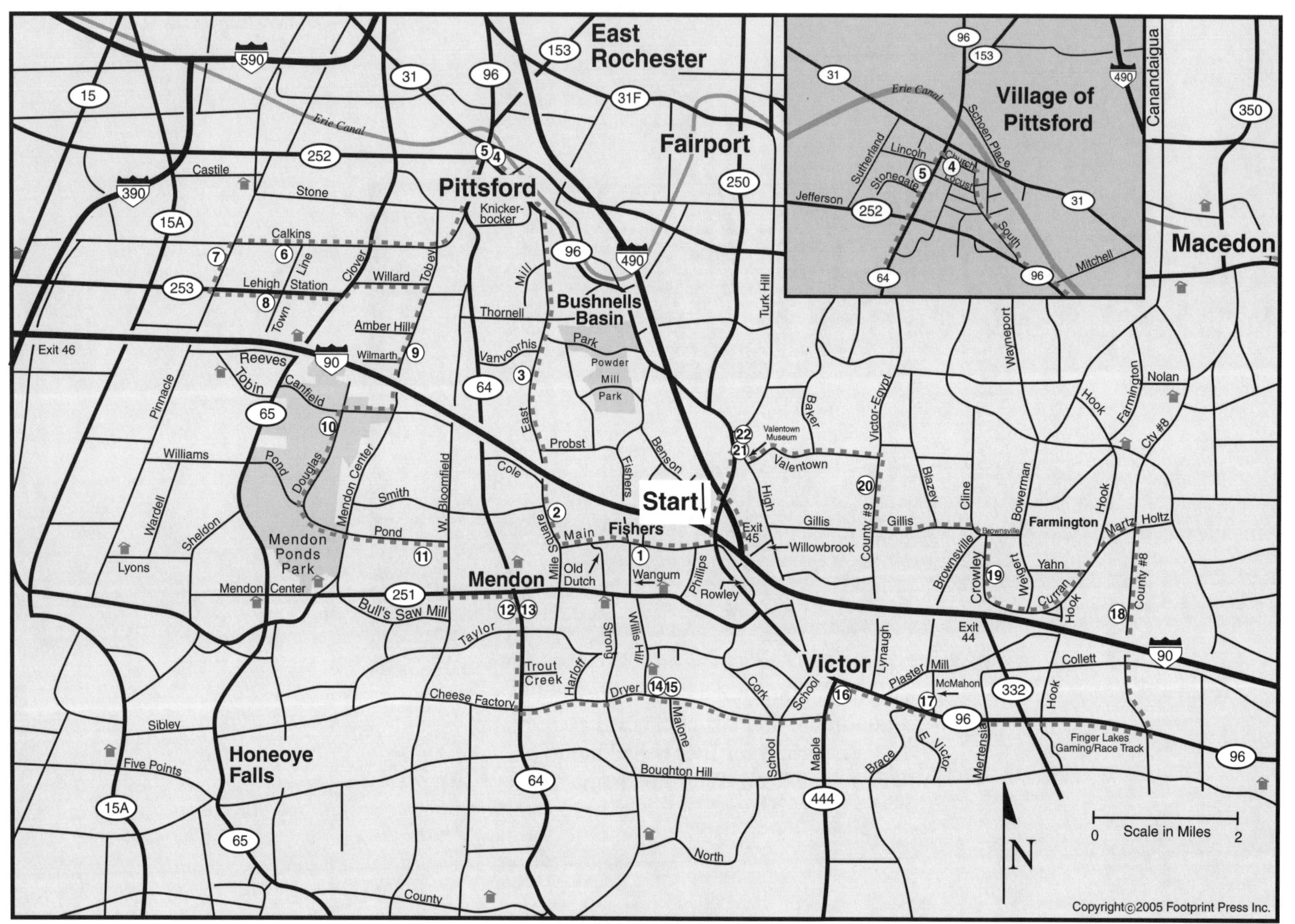

Cobblestone Tour 9

Cobblestone Tour 9

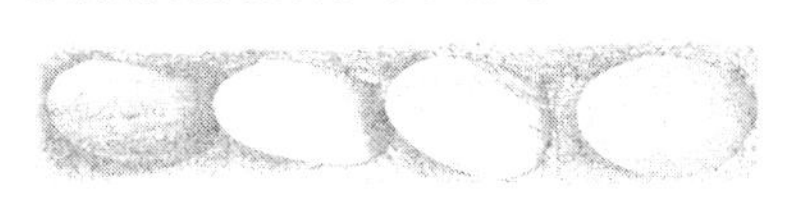

Pittsford, Mendon and Victor in Monroe and Ontario Counties
Total Distance: 57 miles
Approximate Time: 2.5 hours

Begin from Exit 45 off the NYS Thruway (I-90). After the toll gates, immediately bear right to the Victor exit, then turn left onto Route 96 south. At the next traffic light turn right onto Main Street, Fishers. Pass the Phillips Road traffic light, then Log Cabin Road. Watch left after the Fishers post office (before the firehouse) for a cobblestone pumphouse. You can park at the post office or behind the firehouse to get a close view.

1. Auburn and Rochester Railroad Pumphouse

Address: Main Street, Fishers, Town of Victor
Year Built: 1845

This pumphouse (a unique, tall, square building) was built beside the railroad tracks when steam locomotives needed to refuel with water. The first scheduled train of the Auburn and Rochester Railroad ran here September 10, 1840 with Charles (not Chester, as is often reported) Fisher as the agent. It is believed that the pumphouse was built somewhat later. A stream near the back may have been the source of the water used to "water" the trains.

Auburn and Rochester Railroad Pumphouse, Main Street, Fishers

The sign on the front claims this is the second oldest cobblestone pumphouse in existence. Actually, it is the second oldest railroad building in existence. The oldest railroad building is a brick structure in Ellicott City, MD. The pumphouse sits beside the Auburn and Rochester Railroad, which is now the Auburn Trail, a 7.5-mile multi-use rail-trail that runs between Fishers and Farmington, part of a network of trails developed and maintained by Victor Hiking Trails. www.victorhikingtrails.org

Continue west on Main Street to the end. Turn right onto Mile Square Road, and watch right.

2. Cole House
Address: 933 Mile Square Road, Pittsford
Original Owner: Mason Cole
Year Built: 1832 is stamped into an attic floorboard
Style: Federal

Mason Cole was the supervisor of Mendon when he built this 2-story house in 1832 using field cobblestones of various sizes and colors.

There is evidence that a house may have existed here before the cobblestone one was built. What is now the kitchen in the cobblestone house, may have been an older house, or part of one moved to this location. Also, the dining room was built with door casings and moldings like an outside door, and there is a slight difference in the level of the floors between the two rooms.

On the outside, the horizontal rows are uneven with V mortar joints. The vertical joints are plain or sometimes crude pyramids. The quoins are narrow limestone blocks, as is the framing around the front door, although shutters hide it. The front stairway is not original. Notice the casket door on the right side. The cellar walls are 22 inches thick. The walls are 18 inches thick on the first floor and 14 inches thick on the second floor.

A succession of owners had title to this property after Mr. Cole. Sometime after 1918, a barn fire scorched the windows of the house. The bank (Federal Land Bank of

Cole House, 933 Mile Square Road, Pittsford

Springfield) repossessed the house during the depression. David Canfield has owed this home for the past 20 years. It was placed on the State and National Register of Historic Places in 1997.

Continue north on Mile Square Road. Pass over the Thruway (I-90), and Mile Square Road becomes East Street. Watch to the left at the top of a hill.

3. Homer (or Hosmer) Williams House
Address: 563 East Street, Pittsford
Mason: Caleb Martin
Year Built: ~1815
Period: Early

Rough field cobbles were used to build this 2-story farm-house. It was still an operating farm in 1968. Horizontal mortar joints are irregular convex Vs and vertical mortar joints are irregular pyramids and Vs, both representative of early period cobblestone construction. Sidelights and white columns flank the central entrance. Inside the attic window contains original glass, and the fireplace is original, although it hasn't been used since 1916.

Continue north on East Street to the end. Turn left onto Route 96. Pass Mitchell Road on the right, and then take the next right at the traffic light, onto South Street. Take the forth left onto Church Street. (You can drive by the next 2 places for a quick glance or park somewhere along Church Street or Main Street, Pittsford to walk by them for a closer view.) Watch left on Church Street for the cobblestone Masonic Temple, set back from the road.

4. District School #6 (now the Northfield Masonic Temple)
Address: 15/17 Church Street, Pittsford
Mason: Samuel Lee Crump, an English stonemason, emigrated to Rochester from Hadlow County Kent, in 1842, and built several of the area's cobblestone buildings before he died in 1884. His descendants still live in the area.
Year Built: 1842
Style: Greek Revival

At least 50 schoolhouses were among the hundreds of cobblestone buildings erected in the middle third of the 19th century, but most were simple single-story buildings. The Masonic Lodge purchased this 2-story building in 1892. It was constructed with both fieldstones and water-rounded cobbles, with limestone quoins, lintels and water table. The narrow gable end faces the street with a door in its center. The horizontal mortar joints are finished with a convex V in most areas. The vertical joints are Vs and small pyramids. Inside, the main room still has tin ceilings. A basement was added but didn't exist when this building was originally built.

Walk around this building to get a good view of the varied cobble size from the front (4 courses per quoin) to the sides and back. The tan and gray colored cobbles are limestone. The multicolored stones are part of the Canadian Shield, brought south by the glaciers.

Leave your car here and walk to view the next house or drive by. Either way, follow Church Street north to Main Street, and turn left. Watch to the right after Lincoln Avenue.

5. Rand House
Address: 53/55 South Main Street, Pittsford
Year Built: 1830
Style: Blend of Greek Revival and Federal

This home was originally built as a 1.5-story cottage. The wood-framed second story was added in 1910. The cobblestones were laid four courses to the quoin on the front but notice the variety in size, color, shape, and texture. In 1830 when it was built, cobbles could be collected in the fields for free. Bricks cost a penny apiece. The horizontal mortar joints are flat Vs but vary around larger cobbles.

Continue south on Route 64, passing the junction of Routes 96 and 252. At the next traffic light, when Route 64 bends left, continue straight on Calkins Road (no sign). Pass Route 65 and Town Line Road on the left, then turn left at the sign "Tinker Nature Park" to park behind Tinker Homestead and Farm Museum.

Tinker House, 1585 Calkins Road, Henrietta

6. Tinker House (now the Tinker Homestead and Farm Museum located at Tinker Nature Park)
Address: 1585 Calkins Road, Henrietta
Original Owner: James and Rebecca Tinker
Mason: Michael McCanty (sometimes shown in records as McCarthy or McCarty)
Year Built: 1828-1830
Style: Federal/Adams style with some Greek Revival

James Tinker, his wife Rebecca, and their 6 children moved to what would become Henrietta from New Haven,

Detail on Tinker House, 1585 Calkins Road, Henrietta, showing a limestone arch over the gable window.

Connecticut, in 1812 and lived in two log cabins. The opening of the Erie Canal gave their farm access to new markets for their wheat and enabled them to build this cobblestone home. Their descendants occupied this home for six generations until 1991, when John and Carol Aldridge, descendants of the Tinkers, sold it to the Town of Henrietta.

Today, it's a museum (open every day except Monday, 9 AM to 4 PM, 585-359-7042) preserved to replicate the turn of the 20th century Victorian era, and open for all to tour. The 2-story cobblestone building is unique in that the red, brown, gray, tan and black field cobbles are of similar size on all four walls. The walls are 17 inches thick. The quoins are thin, split limestones with only the corners squared. Notice the roughly cut tapered stones forming a Federal style arch over the windows. Also note the original shutters at the door with the curved tops. These provided ventilation in summer before the invention of screens.

Continue west on Calkins Road. Take a left onto Pinnacle Road at the traffic light, and immediately look right.

7. Carriage House

Address: 593 Pinnacle Road, Henrietta

This carriage house near the road was built with rough fieldstones, wooden lintels and cut limestone quoins.

Continue south on Pinnacle Road, and take a left onto Lehigh Station Road (Route 253) at the traffic light, and watch right at the top of a knoll at the "Liberty Hill 2201" sign. It will be hard to see this home behind the bushes and trees.

8. Liberty Hill
Address: 2201 Lehigh Station Road, Pittsford
Original Owner: Liberty Ansel Hanks
Year Built: 1839

You're looking at the side of the residence of the President of Rochester Institute of Technology, currently Dr. Albert J. Simone. This building was donated to RIT. The front has 9 windows and a door. Each cobblestone on the front is slightly tipped forward at the top. The bottom quoin is red sandstone and the ones above it are limestone. The side has a coffin door. This building was once covered in ivy — a plant destructive to mortars. The ivy even grew inside the dark attic.

Continue east on Route 253. At the end turn left onto Clover Street (Route 65 north). Take the first right onto Willard Road. At the stop sign turn right onto Mendon Center Road. Watch to the left after Amber Hill Drive. Trees and bushes also obscure this house.

9. Acer House
Address: 476 Mendon Center Road, Pittsford
Original Owner: David Acer
Style: Federal

By 1800 William and Dorothy Acer migrated from Massachusetts to the area of south Pittsford that would become Northfield, built a log cabin, then a frame house, and raised their family. They bequeathed their land to their son David. David married Sarah Post and they raised 6 children. Records in 1855 showed the cobblestone house, which had been built earlier, was valued at $2,500.

David's son, John Adams Acer, lived next door in a frame house valued at $3,000 with his 5 children and 8 servants. David died in 1859. The cobblestone house was inherited by his daughter Mary J. who had married George Fisher. Because of its owners name and many occupants, neighbors joked that "the house covered ten acres."

This 2-story house has a porch at the front door. Notice the mortar ridges between the field cobbles. The quoins, lintels and sills are all limestone.

Continue south on Mendon Center Road under I-90. Take the next right onto Canfield Road and enter Mendon Ponds Park. Take the first left onto Douglas Road. Watch for the cobblestone building on the right then pull into the parking area, following the "one way" signs.

10. Stewart House
Address: Douglas Road, Mendon
Original Owner: Jeremiah Stewart
Year Built: ~1835
Style: Federal

Twenty-nine-year-old Jeremiah Stewart arrived here from Dutchess County in 1833. His wife and hired helper, 27-year-old Richard Canfield, arrived the next year. Jeremiah purchased the land (80 acres, including the pond) from Elijah Ferris in 1834. According to the 1855 census, Richard Canfield was still living with them. By 1872 Mr. Stewart must have died, since a map shows Mrs. Stewart as owner. The 1887 map shows a Mrs. Canfield as the owner.

The Stewart House has been owned by Monroe County Parks since 1928 (sold by Stewart Canfield). A succession of park superintendents lived here. In 2004 the Parks Department completed major repairs to fix sections of the cobblestone walls that had sustained significant water damage, particularly in the back.

The limestone quoins are probably Onondaga limestone hauled by oxcart from a Scottsville quarry. The field cobblestones are "hardheads" gathered from the surrounding hills. The mortar has more gravel than usual, which has led to significant weathering. The horizontal mortar joints are wide and flat, wavy Vs. The vertical joints are pyramid shaped. This is characteristic of early cobblestone masonry when masons were experimenting with decoration between the stones.

Notice how much cruder the workmanship is in the back of the building. One key is that the mortar is flush with the cobblestones on the sides and back as opposed to the front, which has more depth to the stones. The quality of the quoins also varies from front to back. The far left (south) side of the building is the smokehouse. Between the two, was originally an open area for carriage storage.

This house is framed with oak and tamarack from the surrounding forests. Inside is a massive fireplace, exposed framing timbers and a hand-hewn stair rail. It was placed on the State and National Register of Historic Places in 1997.

Continue south on Douglas Road. Turn left onto Pond Road. Pass Pittsford Mendon Center Road, then watch right in 1.2 miles.

11. Whitcomb House
Address: 437 Pond Road, Mendon
Original Owner: Roswell Whitcomb
Year Built: Mid-1840s
Style: Federal

Sixty-four-year-old Roswell Whitcomb bought 52 acres of land in 1847 for $2,800 and built his cobblestone home. The 1855 census valued the home at $600.

Henry Hamlin and his wife purchased this 1.5-story house in 1957. They renovated it to its original state with the help of renowned cobblestone expert Carl Schmidt. The front door (wide enough to fit a casket through) is not original, but the 8-inch-wide jambs and 10-inch-high lintel over the door are both original and unusual in cobblestone houses of this period. This cobblestone gem was also placed on the State and National Register of Historic Places in 1997.

Continue east on Pond Road. At the end, turn right (south) onto West Bloomfield Road. At the next intersection, turn left onto Route 251 east. In Mendon, turn right onto Route 64 south at the traffic light and watch right.

Mendon Academy, 16 Mendon-Ionia Road, Mendon

12. Mendon Academy - Mendon District School #2, (now Golden Lynx Art Gallery)

Address: 16 Mendon-Ionia Road, Mendon
Year Built: 1835
Style: Federal

The original 2-story building was constructed as Mendon Academy — students had to pay to attend. Elementary students paid $3 per quarter and higher students paid $4 - $5 per quarter. Records state that in 1839 this school had two departments, two teachers, and 93 students. During that year, the school was acquired by Mendon School District #2. By 1945 grades 1 through 6 were taught in the two-room schoolhouse. Classes ceased June 23, 1950 and the building was sold to Mendon Fire District. They added the one-story addition with a cobblestone façade. Since 1995 the building has housed the Golden Lynx Art Gallery and private residence.

Cobblestones for the schoolhouse were gathered from area farms and vary in size, shape, color and texture. The original building is an example of dark mortar where local dirt was added to the mortar mix as a darkening agent. Both horizontal and vertical joints are Vs. The gable ends sport elliptical fans. The quoins, sills, lintels, water table and keystone arch over the front door are all limestone. Notice how the quoin pattern also frames the windows and front entrance. It was placed on the State and National Register of Historic Places in 1997.

Details of Mendon Academy (16 Mendon-Ionia Road, Mendon) showing a limestone arch over the door, limestone blocks around the windows and S-shaped tie bars.

Kitty-corner, across the street, is the next cobblestone building.

13. Sheldon House
Address: 21 Mendon-Ionia Road, Mendon
Original Owner: Milton Sheldon
Year Built: 1833
Period: Federal

The white wooden portion of this home predates the cobblestone portion. Written in pencil on an upstairs door (and left unpainted over the years) are the words "the wooden part of the house was built in 1820; the stone part 1833 by a man named Sheldon." The inscription is signed by D. Allen and Maude Tomlinson and dated 1898. Since only the partial name Sheldon is given, it's uncertain which Mr. Sheldon was the builder, although it is assumed to be Dr. Milton Sheldon. The community had Sheldon's who were doctors, gristmill owners and tavern keepers. This home has had many owners over the years.

What's unusual about this cobblestone construction is that the fieldstones were placed flush with the mortar. The stones below the water table have horizontal V mortar joints, which suggests the flush mortar was the result of repairs made over the years. Notice the coffin door on the north sidewall.

Look to the east side to find a small detached, gabled, brick smokehouse in the Greek-Revival style. This house was also added to the State and National Register of Historic Places in 1997.

Continue south on Route 64. Take the third left onto Dryer/Cheese Factory Road. Pass Strong and Willis Hill Roads and watch left.

14. District #10 School (now a private residence)
Address: 7728 Dryer Road, Victor
Year Built: The obituary of Mr. Dryer published in the *Victor Herald* on May 8, 1925 says this cobblestone schoolhouse was built in 1842 to replace a log school, but there is some doubt about the date.

This small, 1-story school operated until 1941. It is now a private residence.

Its construction is similar to the previous building. The school was built with varied field cobbles set 3 courses per quoin. The mortar has been extensively repointed on the west wall. The east wall, which was originally an exterior wall, is now inside the house.

Continuing east on Dryer Road, the next house, opposite Malone Drive, is also a cobblestone, but it's hard to see behind a row of trees.

15. Dryer House
Address: Dryer Road, Victor
Original Owner: Otis Dryer
Year Built: 1833
Style: Greek Revival

Here's another similar construction home. This one has 2 stories and has a fanlight in the gable end. (Please respect this and all homeowners' privacy, and stay on the road.)

Continue east on Dryer Road to the end. Turn left onto Route 444 North. The next building is at the corner of Route 444 (Maple Avenue) and Route 96 in the Village of Victor. You can drive past it or turn right after the railroad tracks to park in the municipal parking lot behind the shops in Victor and walk to the corner for a close viewing. To drive by, continue north on Route 444, then turn right onto Route 96. The cobblestone building is on this corner to your right.

16. Jenks Store and A. Simonds & Sons General Store (now a vacant Mahar Business Forms)
Address: 2 East Main Street, Victor
Original Owner: Nathan Jenks
Year Built: 1834
Style: Greek Revival

This building was originally built by Nathan Jenks as a village general store called Jenks Dry Goods Store. Albert Simonds began as a clerk in Jenks Store, then became a partner in 1837. When Nathan Jenks retired, Simonds took over the store and changed the name to A. Simonds & Sons Dry Goods. It remained in the Simonds family for 133 years, until it was sold in 1967. This building sustained damage in the great Victor fire of 1981. The building has been converted to offices and apartments.

Look for the keyed fanlight in the gable end facing East Main Street. An unusual aspect of this building is that all four sides were constructed with similarly sized cobbles, set 4 courses per quoin.

Drive east on Route 96 through the village of Victor, passing Lynaugh, Plaster Mill, Brace and East Victor Roads. The next cobblestone building is on the left at the corner of McMahon Road.

17. Felt Cobblestone General Store (now Cobblestone Antiques)

Address: 6452 Victor-Manchester Road (Route 96), Victor
Year Built: ~1836
Style: Greek Revival

Built as a store, this building was sold in 1841 to Samuel Rawson to settle debts, upon the death of Charles S. Felt. The settlement mentions "the cobblestone store, the two old stores occupied as dwelling houses, a tailor shop and ashery and the dwelling house occupied by Jabez Felt."

It was bought in 1905 by Barney Goldfarb and was operated by the Goldfarb family as a general store until the mid-1970s. In 1923 a cider mill was started here. The building continued to house a succession of businesses and remains a commercial building today.

This store was built with field cobbles, with a fanlight in the gable end. The original structure had wooden front steps and a wooden landing. Notice the recessed first floor windows with wooden panels below them. This building is on the National Register of Historic Places.

Continue east on Route 96, past Route 332 and Finger Lakes Gaming and Race Track, and take a left onto County Road 8. Cross over the Thruway (I-90), then watch left.

18. Herendeen House

Address: 880 County Road 8, Farmington, Town of Farmington
Original Owner: James Herendeen
Year Built: 1832 (datestone over the front door)
Period: Early
Style: Five-Bay Farmhouse

This 2-story farmhouse was one of the earliest cobblestone buildings built in Ontario County and is still owned within the family, now by Harold Herendeen. It was built with large field cobbles and roughly squared limestone quoins of varying sizes. See if you can see the "plugging holes" on the front where scaffolding was attached during construction. In 1932, Josephine Herendeen made this one of two known Ontario County sites where cobblestone construction was done in the 20th century. She added a cobblestone arcade to the south side where the basement (containing the original kitchen) is exposed, and added the entrance porch and stone piers on the front landing.

Continue north on County Road 8, and take the next left onto Martz Road. At the end, turn left onto Hook Road. Go straight on Curran when Hook Road bends left (the road sign is turned around). At the stop sign, turn right onto Crowley Road. Look right, to the top of a hill after a big bend in Crowley Road.

19. Crowley House (see photo on back cover, 4th insert)
Address: 751 Crowley Road, Farmington,
Town of Farmington
Period: Early

Here's another fine example of an early period cobblestone farmhouse, built high on a hill in drumlin country. This one is part of a working dairy farm. The 2-story building has big, rough field cobblestones. The number of courses per quoin varies. The cobblestone foundation juts out from the walls above it. The two top windows (upper left on the front) still have their original 6 panes of glass. The front porch was added in 2003 to replicate the original design (only it's 1.5 feet shallower than the original).

The current owners, Harold and Beatrice Weigert, have lived here for the past 58 years.

Continue north on Crowley Road. At the end, turn left onto Brownsville Road. Continue straight toward Cline, then take the next left onto Gillis Road. Pass Blazey Road, then turn right onto County Road 9, and watch left.

Rowley House, 422 County Road 9, Victor

20. Rowley House (currently Hackers Bar and Grille)
Address: 422 County Road 9,Victor
Original Owner: Andrew Rowley and his wife
Year Built: 1831
Period: Early
Style: Federal

Here's another early period cobblestone house built with large quoins and large glacial field cobbles set 4 courses per quoin. In typical Federal style, it has a central 2-story section with a 1-story wing on each side with pillared porches. Notice the fanlight in the front gable end.

Built by the Rowleys, this home was owed for many years by the Keefe family. Today, it is owned by Cobblestone Creek Golf Club and is operated as Hackers Bar and Grille in the summer to serve golfers on this private course.

Continue north on County Road 9, then take the first left onto Valentown Road. At the end turn right onto High Street. (Notice Valentown Museum at the corner of Valentown Road and High Street. This was the first shopping mall in the U.S.) Take the next right onto High Street Extension, and watch left.

21. District #7 Cobblestone Schoolhouse
Address: 236 High Street Extension, Victor
Mason: David Fowler
Year Built: 1845
Style: Greek Revival

According to district meeting minutes, the #7 School was completed in the spring of 1845 with a "$50.33 balance due to the estate of David Fowler for building schoolhouse for district, assumed to widow Sophronia Fowler."

Currently it's an ivy-covered private home with a fieldstone wing added to the south side. School children may have planted the rows of maple trees on the grounds during Arbor Day ceremonies.

Look out back to see if you can spot the four-holer cobblestone privy. District minutes recorded "1845 — M.S.

Wilcox, $1.50 for digging privy." The privy has 2 doors — one for boys and one for girls.

Continue to the end of High Street Extension.

22. Bonesteel House (currently vacant)
Address: 953 High Street Extension, Victor
Original Owner: Philip S. (or P.?) Bonesteel
Year Built: 1835
Period: Middle
Style: Greek Revival with Italianate porch

Here's another building with an undetermined future, caught up in development plans. This was the home of Cobblestone Arts Center until 1993. However, it currently sits vacant and untended and is being eyed by developers.

"In 1835 I built me a house of cobblestones, of the following description; front 45 x 83 feet, 2 stories, forming an L in rear of 65 x 23 feet, single story for kitchen, washroom and wood shed. My plan for the thickness of wall was: the cellar wall 20 in. thick to first floor, drop off two in. to second floor, then drop off two in. and extend out to top. Sort your stones so as to have the outside course three or four in., with straight lines for cement. Take the coarsest of sand for the stone, and a fine sand for brick. I used the common stone lime, one bushel of lime to seven of sand for stone, and the same kind of lime one bushel to two of sand for brick. Furnished all materials on the ground, and paid my masons

$3.75 per hundred feet. He furnished his own tenders and made his own mortar, built his own scaffolds and tended themselves. I boarded them. I think I have as good a house as can be made of the same materials. There is not a crack on the walls that you can stick a pin in as yet. The stone, I do not consider any expense as it frees the land of them. There is no painting to be done to it, as is required of brick or wood, it makes the strongest of walls, and I think the neatest and cheapest building that can be made. You may calculate the expense of the building at so much a perch, according to the size you wish to build. I did not keep an exact account of my building, as the stone, sand and lime were bought at leisure spells."

P. P. Bonesteel, Victor, Ontario County
From *The Cultivator,* 1842, No. 7

When Mr. Bonesteel built his home it was more modest than what you see today. Some time between 1845 and 1850, an Italianate front porch was added. By 1878 the eves had been expanded and a wooden second floor was added to the rear wing. Notice the terne (leaded iron) roof.

Turn around and return down High Street Extension. Turn right onto Valentown Road. At the traffic light, turn left onto Route 96 south. Watch the signs to make a left turn to return to the Thruway (I-90).

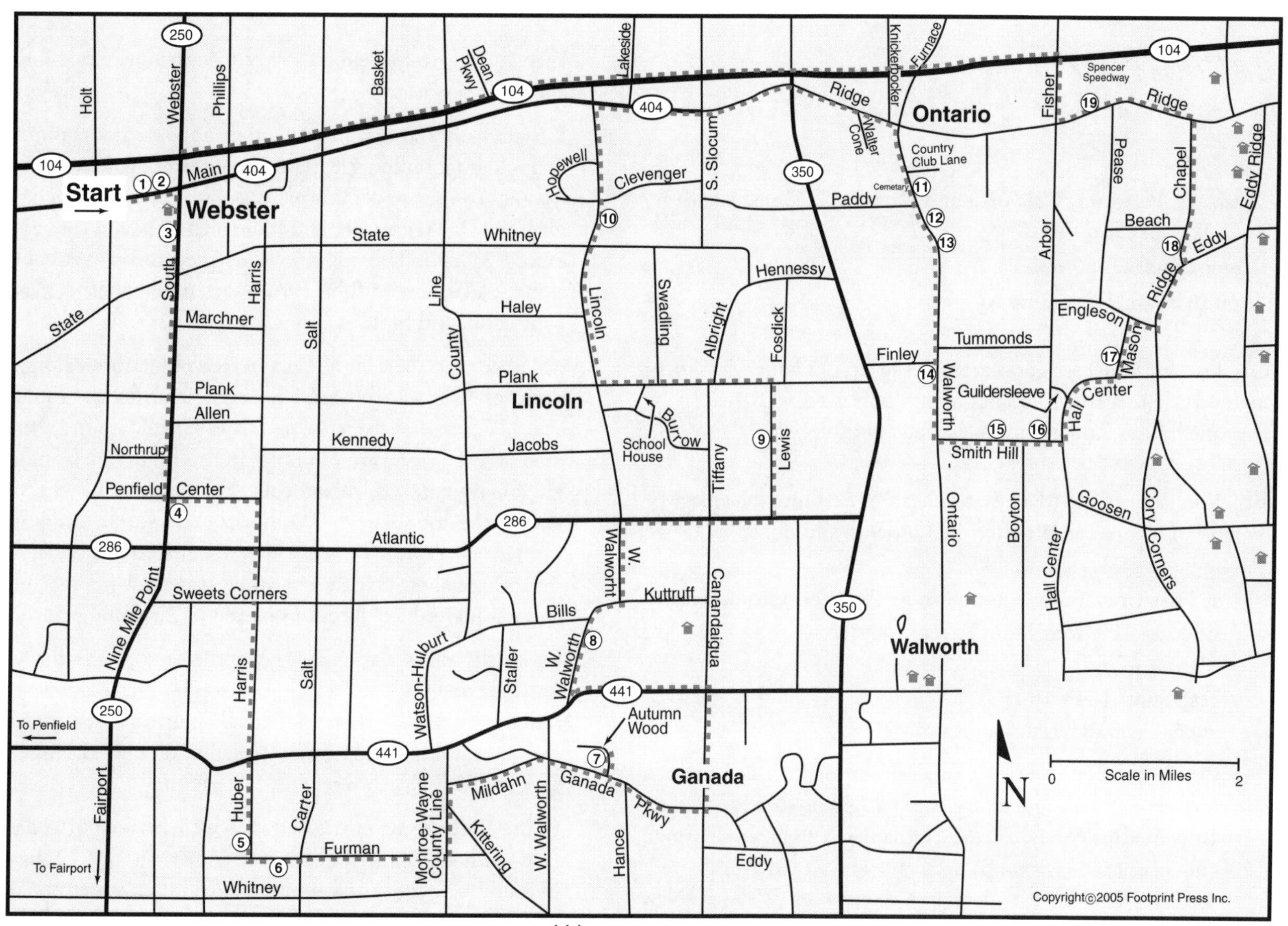

Cobblestone Tour 10

Cobblestone Tour 10

Webster, Perinton, Walworth and Ontario in Monroe and Wayne Counties
Total Distance: 50 miles
Approximate Time: 2 hours

On this tour you'll see good examples of houses built with finely matched, lake-washed cobblestones, contrasted with field cobblestone houses, and even some striped houses.

Begin on Route 404 (Main Street) heading east into the village of Webster. Look to the left after the Lutheran church.

1. First Universalist Church (now Webster Automotive)
Address: 109 West Main Street, Webster
Mason: John Farr
Year Built: 1843-1845
Style: Greek Revival

On September 2, 1843 a small group of men and women met in a schoolhouse to organize a religious society based on Universalism. They elected Nathaniel Knight as chairman and Ebenezer Dayton as secretary and voted to call their society "The First Universalist Society of Webster, New York." The group held monthly meetings in schoolhouses and members homes.

But after only several months, they appointed a committee to look into building a permanent meeting location. On May 4, 1844, the committee was authorized to purchase a lot from Dr. A. Crocker and build a church, at a cost not to exceed $1,200. The committee decided to build a cobblestone structure with John Farr, a society member, as mason, contractor, and builder.

Members and their families gathered cobblestones along the shore of Lake Ontario and brought them to the building site. The stones were sorted and small, round, finely matched, red sandstone cobbles were used on the front, and less finely matched, mixed-color cobblestones on the sides and as the foundation. The horizontal mortar joints were formed as convex Vs and the vertical joints as triangular pyramid shapes. Finely cut stone was used for the lintels and quoins. A medallion was placed in the front gable end.

Originally there was a square wood tower on the top with louvered openings and a solid balustrade. The windows were framed by long, 3-part louvered shutters. The finished church was dedicated during a celebration on November 12 and 13, 1845, by Reverend L. L. Spaulding.

In the 1920s some of the windows were bricked in and covered with a cobblestone veneer. Then, in the 1970s the building was converted to commercial use. Storefront windows were installed, the east and west windows were filled in with concrete blocks and the wood louvered shutters were removed.

Continue east on Main Street (Route 404) looking at the next building on the left.

2. Dean House
Address: 93 West Main Street, Webster
Year Built: Before 1839
Style: Greek Revival

The first deed for this property appeared when Lewis Stratton purchased an 84-acre plot from the Phelps and Gorham Tract in 1832. The land was then sold in 1835 to Oliver Reynolds, a pioneer doctor and inventor. In 1839 Aaron Van Wormer was deeded the 1-acre lot on which this cobblestone house sits, with the provision that "a proper fence" must be maintained around it. The deed describes the land only, but the mention of the fence may indicate the cobblestone house was already there.

It's possible that this house was later used as a parsonage for the Universalist Church. A map from 1852 shows a parsonage just east of the church. In 1868 Fawni A. Smith deeded the house to Eugene and Ednah Dean. The Dean family owned it for over 70 years so it became known as the Dean House.

This house has a 2-story main building with a 1-story wing off the rear. It was built with large fieldstones of varied sizes and colors. The mortar joints are unusual. Both the horizontal and vertical joints are flush with the cobbles protuding only 1/2 to 1 inch on the front. To embellish the joints, the mason used a metal tool to strike a depressed V into the horizontal joints and made a smaller indent in the vertical joints, making sure it didn't touch the horizontal Vs. The mason used brick for the quoins and lintels, a detail more commonly used in English flint houses. The open porch with Colonial Revival detailing was added around 1900. The rear porch and brick chimneys were added in the 20th century.

Continue east on Main Street. At the traffic light turn right onto South Avenue. Pass a cobblestone house on the right (19 South Avenue) that is mostly obscured by additions (and is in danger of being torn down), then pull into the church on the right.

3. Webster Baptist Church
Address: 59 South Avenue, Webster
Year Built: 1855-1857
Style: Greek Revival

Two men were contracted to supply the cobblestones for this church at a grand total of $150. They, with the help of church members, gathered the stones along the shore of Lake Ontario, using the dark red, water-rounded stones on the front and mixed colors on the other sides. Of about 20 cobblestone churches built, this was the largest. The open

Webster Baptist Church, 59 South Avenue, Webster

cupola on top, with eight Ionic columns supporting a dome, houses a bell that remains in use today and is rung weekly before worship service. The church bell rang in the early years of the village every time there was a fire because it was the only building in the village that could alert a call to the whole village. The day the Civil War ended in 1865, the bell was rung by two young boys for several hours which caused the bell to crack. The stained glass windows date to the early 20th century.

The Webster Baptist Church is the only cobblestone structure that was built during this period that is still used today for its original purpose by the same continuous organization. The Webster Baptist Church was formed in 1830 by a few members of the First Baptist Church in Penfield to establish a Baptist presence in the Webster village. In 2005, the church celebrated its 175th year of continuous ministry in Webster.

Continue south on South Avenue as it becomes Nine Mile Point Road. Turn left onto Penfield Center Road, and look right at the corner.

4. Penfield District #11 Schoolhouse
Address: 1586 Fairport-Webster Road, Penfield
Year Built: 1849
Style: Greek Revival

In contrast to the church you just viewed, here's a 1-story schoolhouse built with multi-colored field cobbles and sandstone lintels and quoins. It functioned as a school until at least 1949 and is now a private residence. In typical Greek Revival fashion, it sports a wide frieze. This is the only cobblestone building that was built in the town of Penfield.

Continue east on Penfield Center Road. At the end, turn right (south) on Harris Road. Cross Route 286, then Route 441.

Harris Road will become Huber Road. Look right just before the end.

5.
Address: 2543 Huber Road, Fairport, Town of Perinton
Original Owner: Myron Palmer
Year Built: ~1840

This 2-story home sports large, uniform cobblestones and a wide frieze with belly windows. Notice the herringbone pattern on the wall under the porch and on the side.

Turn left onto Furman Road, and watch right at the corner of Fieldston Grove.

6.
Address: 1 Fieldston Grove, Fairport, Town of Perinton
Year Built: 1852
Original Owner: Jacob Conklin

Here's a gorgeous example of herringbone pattern. The 2-story building of large, lake-washed cobblestones was nicely preserved when the large addition was added to the rear. The building has a cobblestone foundation and cut limestone lintels and quoins.

Continue east on Furman Road, then turn left onto Monroe-Wayne County Line Road at the stop sign. Take the second right onto Mildahn Road. Turn right at the end onto Ganada Parkway at the stop sign. Cross West Walworth Road, then take the third left onto Autumn Wood Drive in the Wood Hill development. The house sits to the left, near this corner. Turn left onto Cobblestone Trail to view the back of this house.

7.
Address: 3347 Autumn Wood Drive, Walworth

A new housing tract now surrounds this historic 2-story field cobblestone house, but at least it wasn't torn down. Vines, with their mortar busting roots, were recently removed from most of the house, but are still growing on the back wall. It's an unusual example of brick use in a cobblestone building. Bricks are used in the quoins and to totally surround the windows. Brick is also used to form an arch over the first floor windows.

Return to Gananda Parkway, and turn left to head east. Turn left onto Canandaigua Road at the flashing light, then left onto Route 441 at the stop sign. Take the next right onto West Walworth Road, and watch right for a church, in half a mile.

8. Zion United Methodist Church
Address: 3960 West Walworth Road, West Walworth

This church was built with small multi-colored stones, 5 to 6 courses per quoin. The lintels are sandstone, and the quoins are limestone. The front sports a white bell tower.

Continue north on West Walworth Road. Turn left to stay on West Walworth Road, then turn right onto Atlantic Avenue, Route 286, at the stop sign. Take the second left onto Lewis Road, and watch left in 0.3 mile.

9.
Address: 4625 Lewis Road, Walworth
Year Built: 1835

This 1.5-story home with a 1-story wing, was built using field cobbles, 5 courses per quoin. The limestone lintels are set on edge. The quoins are sharply cut limestone.

Continue north on Lewis Road to the stop sign at the end. Turn left onto Plank Road. Take the third right onto Lincoln Road at the flashing light. Pass Haley and Whitney Roads, then watch right.

10. Whitney-Raymor House
Address: 5668 Lincoln Road, Ontario
Style: Colonial

In contrast to the previous home, this 2-story house has rough-cut limestone quoins and large field cobbles set in flat mortar, 3 courses per quoin. The lintels are bricks set on edge. A fan decorates the gable end. A small building is attached.

Continue north on Lincoln Road, then turn right onto Ridge Road (Route 404) at the stop sign. Pass Route 350, then, in the village of Ontario, turn right onto Walworth-Ontario Road at the traffic light. After Country Club Lane watch left, across from a cemetery.

11. Freeman-Buck House
Address: 5820 Walworth-Ontario Road, Ontario
Year Built: 1838

Small red cobblestones adorn the front, with rougher stones on the sides. The home is 2-stories with a 1-story wing. Note the unusual shape of the lintels — wider at the top than at the bottom.

Continue south on Walworth-Ontario Road, watching left.

12. Casey-Bebernitz House
Address: 5708 Walworth-Ontario Road, Ontario
Period: Early

Here's an early period, 1.5-story home, as evidenced by the rough-cut gray limestone quoins. Various colored lake-washed cobblestones were used, with a predominance of gray color. The limestone lintels are set on edge.

Continue south on Walworth-Ontario Road, looking left at the third house.

13. Camp-Scully House
Address: 5656 Walworth-Ontario Road, Ontario
Year Built: 1834
Style: Colonial

Here's a beautiful 2-story home built with a mixture of lake-washed and fieldstone cobbles and limestone lintels set on edge, like the previous home. Again the quoins are rough-cut. The front door is framed in sidelights and transom windows, and notice the arch in the gable end.

Continue south on Walworth-Ontario Road, and watch right at the corner of Finley Road.

14.
Address: 5097 Walworth-Ontario Road, Walworth
Style: Colonial

Built of multi-colored field cobbles, this 2-story home has cut limestone lintels set on edge, including over the basement windows. The gable sports a fan and the front door is framed in sidelight and transom windows with a fanned lintel over it. Behind the house is a cut-stone smokehouse.

Continue south on Walworth-Ontario Road, and take the next left onto Smith Hill Road. Watch left.

15.
Address: 2427 Smith Hill Road, Walworth

This stately 2-story home has large cobbles, 4 courses per quoin. The design is quite similar to the previous homes with cut limestone lintels set on edge and a fan in the side gable. The front door is framed in sidelight and transom windows. Notice that cut limestone was used in the foundation on the front and rougher stones on the sides. Similarly, larger cobbles were used on the side peaks.

Continue east on Smith Hill Road, watching left after Boynton Road, at the corner of Arbor Road.

16.
Address: 2677 Smith Hill Road, Walworth

Here's a smaller 1-story building with a major addition built above it. It appears that similar sized stones were used on all sides. The sandstone lintels are set on edge. Cracks have developed on the sides. You can get a good look at them from Arbor Road.

Continue east on Smith Hill Road to the stop sign at the end. Turn left onto Hall Center Road. At the T, turn right to stay on Hall Center Road. Take the next left onto Mason Road, and watch left.

17. Wells House (most likely)
Address: 5137 Mason Road, Marion
Year Built: Prior to 1833

Wells House, 5137 Mason Road, Marion

Here's a 1.5-story home with limestone quoins and lintels set on edge. It was built on a cobblestone foundation. Look carefully at the middle section of the side facing Mason Road — it's striped with bands of white, red and brown cobbles! Also notice the cobbles on the wing that increase in size as they progress to the back and culminate in field boulders. This house was built in stages. The walls of the earliest part are 16 inches thick and those of the later section are 19 inches thick. The mortar is red and pebbly with V horizontal joints and a mixture of Vs and pyramids for vertical joints.

Going back in history, from Ervin Duste, the owner in 1955, it is surmised that someone in the Wells family built this house. Before Mr. Duste, his uncle owned the house for 38 years, before that Wally Morris for 7 years, Alvert Wells for 40 years, and Wells' father before him.

Continue north to the end of Mason Road, and turn right onto Engleson Road at the stop sign. At the end turn left onto Ridge Eddy Road. Continue straight, past Eddy Road, and watch left.

18.

Address: 5621 Ridge Chapel Road, Williamson
Year Built: 1830

This 2-story home has a 1.5-story wing that's now faced in clapboard. The cobbles are lake-washed, red sandstone. The quoins are finely cut limestone, whereas the lintels are sandstone set on edge. There's a fan in the gable end.

Continue north on Ridge Chapel Road, then turn left onto Ridge Road at the stop sign. Pass Pease Road, then watch right.

19. Adams-Grabowski House

Address: 2871 Ridge Road, Williamson

The small red cobblestones face the current driveway. The other sides have large, mixed-color stones. The cobblestone wing was added about 20 years after the original building by a mason named Adams. The quoins are a mix of limestone and sandstone, with lintels of limestone set on edge.

Continuing west on Ridge Road. Take the first right onto Fisher Road, then a left onto Route 104 to return to Webster.

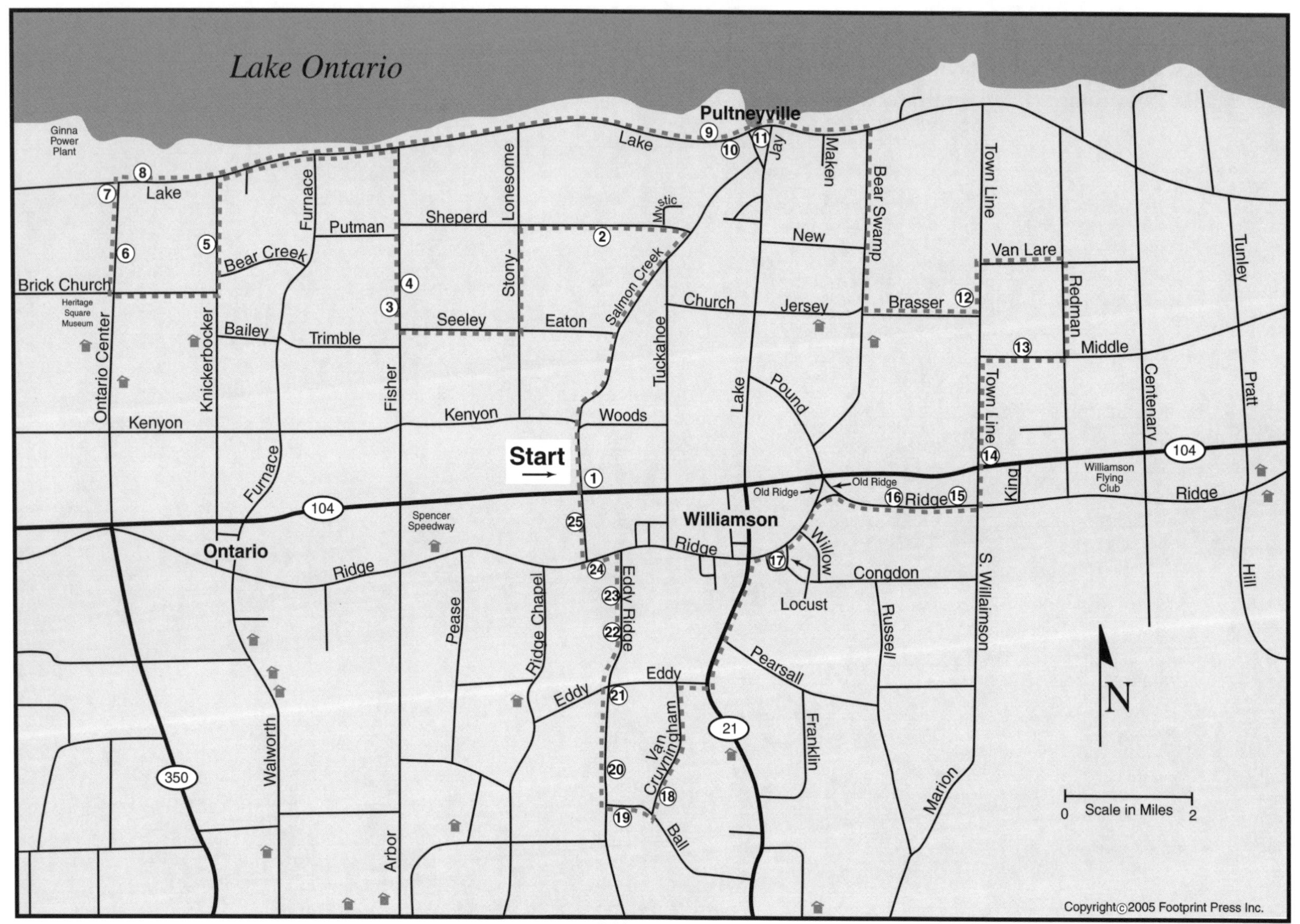

Cobblestone Tour 11

Cobblestone Tour 11

Williamson, Ontario and Pultneyville in Wayne County
Total Distance: 38 miles
Approximate Time: 1.5 hours

You know you're physically near Lake Ontario when you see the multitude of tiny, red, uniform cobbles used to build these homes. It's a sight repeated throughout this northern route because the builders didn't have to haul the lake cobbles very far.

Begin by heading north on Salmon Creek Road off Route 104 (between Ontario and Williamson), and watch right.

1. Fisher-Calus House
Address: 6554 Salmon Creek Road, Williamson

Here's the first of many homes built with tiny, red, uniform cobbles. Note the belly windows in the wide frieze and the medallion in the gable end on the side. The lintels have an unusual shape — almost an inverted T shape. The lintels and quoins have been painted and there's a white house addition. The foundation and lintels over the basement windows are cut limestone.

Continue north on Salmon Creek Road, and take the third left onto Shepherd Road, heading west. Watch to the left.

2.
Address: 3530 Shepherd Road, Williamson
Year Built: 1834

These lake cobbles are multi-colored. The home was set on a sandstone foundation and used sandstone quoins and lintels set on edge. The front of this T-shaped house faces east.

Continue west on Shepherd Road, and take the first left at the stop sign onto Stony-Lonesome Road. Take the first right onto Seeley Road. At the end, turn right onto Fisher Road, and watch left.

3. Jobse-VanEnwyck House
Address: 7105 Fisher Road, Ontario

This 2-story home was probably built earlier than the previous ones. It used mixed-color, squarish stones and rough-cut quoins that are mixed limestone and sandstone. It has huge lintels, and a death door is visible on the south side.

Continue north on Fisher Road, watching right in a grove of pines.

4.
Address: 7227 Fisher Road, Williamson

This 2-story home is set back from the road making it hard to see. It's also in disrepair. It was made with small, red cobbles, cut limestone lintels and quoins and a wide frieze with 5 belly windows.

Continue north on Fisher Road to the end and turn left onto Lake Road at a stop sign. Take the a left onto Knickerbocker Road, and watch right.

Riker-Enderling House, 7325 Knickerbocker Road, Ontario

5. Riker-Enderling House
Address: 7325 Knickerbocker Road, Ontario
Mason: Trimble (wing added in 1868 by Potter)
Year Built: 1840s

Here's another home built with small, red cobbles, 5 courses per quoin on the front, and mixed color cobbles on the sides. The sandstone lintels are set on edge, even for the basement windows. The inset front door gives you an idea of how deep the walls are.

Continue south on Knickerbocker Road, and take the first right onto Brick Church Road, then the next right onto Ontario Center Road at a stop sign, and watch right.

6. Hodges-Peterson House
Address: 7272 Ontario Center Road, Ontario
Mason: Clark
Year Built: ~1840s

This large, 2-story home was set on a sandstone foundation but used limestone for the quoins and lintels. Look for the herringbone pattern on the south side of the wing.

Continue north on Ontario Center Road, and look left at the corner of Lake Road. Don't dally here, however. This area is monitored closely because of its proximity to the Ginna Nuclear Power Plant. You'll be turning right onto Lake Road at the stop sign.

7. Motley-Loomis House
Address: 1556 Lake Road, Ontario
Year Built: ~1835

This is a brick house. The cobblestone addition was added in the late 1830s as a woodshed. Today, part of the front and a side wall facing east, are the visible parts of the cobblestone addition.

You're heading east on Lake Road. Watch left.

8. Brewer-Wilson House
Address: 1695 Lake Road, Ontario

Small, red cobbles grace the front and even predominate on the sides. The corners are white pilasters instead of quoins. This building has a sandstone foundation and lintels. The wide frieze sports grill work.

Continue east on Lake Road for 5.3 miles. Watch left as you approach Pultneyville, just past the cemetery.

9. Waters-Dunning House
Address: 4025 West Lake Road, Pultneyville
Original Owner: Zimri Waters
Mason: Philip Wemesfelder or Cotrell (records conflict)
Carpenter: Rufus Moses was employed 1851-1852 (sometimes he's listed as the mason)
Year Built: 1850-1852
Period: Late
Style: Greek Revival

Zimri Waters paid $350 plus some farm produce to have his home built. His ledger states that he paid three men to draw stone. One of these was Jacob DeWine who was paid for "one cord stone blocks, too, from the canal" presumably used for quoins or corner blocks. Rufus Moses was paid for the collection of sand and lime as well as for his labor.

The porch on the wing is original, but the porch on the main house with white columns was added in the 20th century. Sidelights and a transom frame the front door and the wide frieze sports original cast iron grills on the front. The water-rounded red sandstone cobbles on the front and sides came from the Sodus area. They're set 6 courses between each cut limestone quoin on the front.

Continue east on Lake Road, and watch right.

10. Pultneyville Schoolhouse
Address: 4092 Lake Road, Pultneyville
Year Built: 1845
Period: Late

According to the Pultneyville Historical Society, the first school, a small crude building, was built on this site in 1808. It burned in 1816 and was replaced by a larger schoolhouse. The cobblestone building was built in 1845 and served as a school until 1943 when the Williamson School District centralized.

It is now a private residence. Ivy, which partially concealed the building, is being removed. Notice the cobbles set at an angle. A metal bar circles the building as reinforcement — a modern addition.

Bear left at the stop sign, onto Mill Street. Mill Street takes a sharp bend at Lake Ontario and becomes Washington Street. Look right.

11. Throop-Graeper House
Address: 4184 Washington Street, Pultneyville, Town of Williamson
Original Owner: Captain Horatio Nelson Throop
Mason: Washington Throop
Year Built: 1832
Period: Early

Washington Throop built this home for his brother, Captain Horatio Nelson Throop, the first person to be born in Pultneyville. It was completed in time for his marriage to Mary F. Ledyard. Captain Throop became a prominent citizen of Pultneyville, an inventor, ship builder and lake captain. A museum featuring Captain Throop and his inventions is maintained by the Pultneyville Historical Society at 4130 Mill Street, open weekends, 2 - 4 PM.

Throop House is now a bed & breakfast called Captain Throop. It was built with sandstone quoins, including those framing the front door. There's a transom window over the front door, a wide frieze, and a crescent window in the gable end. The cobbles are mixed colors and large for the area; especially since this house sits on the Lake Ontario shore. Notice that the 2 front windows are longer than the side ones. Legend has it that they were built low so Mary could sit in a low chair and look out the window.

Continue east as Washington Street turns to Lake Road, then turn right onto Bear Swamp Road. Take the first left onto Brasser Road, then a left onto Town Line Road at the end. Look left at this corner. The house is set back a bit but is visible from both roads.

12.
Address: 7127 Town Line Road, Williamson

This large, 2-story home was built with small, red cobbles, cut limestone quoins and lintels, but a sandstone block foundation. The wide frieze on the side has grills, and there's a white medallion in the gable.

Continue north on Town Line Road, and take the first right onto Van Lare Road. Take the next right onto Redman Road at a stop sign, and right again onto Middle Road at a stop sign. Watch right at the top of a knoll.

13.
Address: 5149 Middle Road, Williamson
Period: Late

This home is very similar to the one on Town Line Road. Here you get a closer view. Notice the stones are all angled in the same direction.

Continue west on Middle Road, and turn left onto Town Line Road at the stop sign. You will be continuing straight across Route 104, but before you do, pause at the corner and look left.

14. Willard House
Address: 6520 Town Line Road, Williamson (at the corner of Route 104)
Original Owner: J. R. Willard
Year Built: 1848

This home is from an earlier period than the previous one. A datestone in the gable end reads "J.R. Willard 1848." The limestone quoins and block foundation are rough cut. The back corner uses a mixture of limestone and sandstone quoins. Like others in the area, it used small, red lake cobblestones in neat rows.

Willard House, 6520 Town Line Road, Williamson

Continue south across Route 104, onto South Williamson Road. Take the next right onto Ridge Road at the stop sign and watch right at the third house from the corner.

15.
Address: 4965 Ridge Road, Williamson

This house has some differences from other area homes. The cobbles are light colored, and the lintels may be wooden. Notice the angled piece at the top of each lintel. Also notice

Cobbles form a decorative arch over the front door at 4540 Millville-E. Shelby Road, Stanley (not on a tour)

the three tie rods on the front of the house, near the roof line.

Continue west on Ridge Road for 1 mile, and watch right.

16.
Address: 4535 Ridge Road, Williamson

This home was built with multicolored cobbles, brick quoins, and brick lintels set on edge.

Continue west on Ridge Road for 0.9 mile into Williamson. Pass Locust Street and watch left or pull into the church parking lot to walk around.

17. 1st Baptist Church of Williamson
Address: 4214 Ridge Road, Williamson
Year Built: 1843

Square pilasters grace the corners of this church, but no quoins. The pilasters are brick with a stucco covering. The church was built on a large rock foundation. Small, red cobbles were used on the front, and multi-colored cobbles on the sides. The lintels are wood, painted white. A wide frieze surrounds the building.

Continue west on Ridge Road, then turn left (south) on Route 21 at the traffic light. Leave the village of Williamson, pass

Pearsall Street, then turn right onto Eddy Road. Take the first left onto Van Cruyningham Road and watch left.

18.
Address: 5336 VanCruyningham Road, Williamson

This 2-story home with a 1-story wing was built with multi-colored field cobblestones. The quoins are cut limestone. The lintels on the first floor of the front are cut sandstone. All other lintels are cut limestone set on edge. The two square attic windows are unusual. Notice the rows of angled cobbles on the main house, near the roof line. Also, reddish stones were used on the first floor and lighter color stones on the second floor. The wing has rows of cobbles at an odd angle making it appear that this house was built in stages. The south facing sides used limestone blocks.

At the end, turn right onto Ball Road (unlabeled), and look left.

19.
Address: 3624 Ball Road, Marion

Here's a simple 1.5-story farmhouse with a 1-story wing. The front was built with multicolored lake-washed cobbles. Like the previous house, there's cut limestone on the south side, but this house has cobblestones in the gable end. The quoins are rough cut limestone and the lintels are limestone blocks set on edge.

At the end, turn right onto Eddy Ridge Road, and watch right.

20.
Address: 5330 Eddy Ridge Road, Marion
Style: Greek Revival

This two-story farmhouse with a side wing was built using small, multi-colored cobbles, many with a brownish hue. The front foundation is limestone blocks, but the sides of the foundation are large fieldstones. It has rough-cut limestone quoins and lintels set on edge. A small porch with pillars frames the front door.

Continue north on Eddy Ridge Road, and look right at the stop sign on the corner of Eddy Road. You will be continuing straight after viewing this house.

21.
Address: 3520 Eddy Road, Williamson

Another 2-story farmhouse, this one built with large, multi-colored cobbles, rough-cut limestone quoins and limestone lintels set on edge.

Continue north on Eddy Ridge Road, and watch left.

22.
Address: 5810 Eddy Ridge Road, Williamson

This small cobblestone building is now the back of a cut limestone home.

Continue north. Pass one house on the left, and watch for the second house.

23.
Address: 5875 Eddy Ridge Road, Williamson

Here's a 2-story home built mostly with red cobblestones on the front and mixed colors on the sides. The quoins are cut limestone and the lintels are cut limestone set on edge. Notice the two windows on the left with brick between the lintels and windows, perhaps due to window replacements. The house sits on a cut limestone foundation. There's a small attached cobblestone building and a much larger recent white house addition on the right.

Continue north on Eddy Ridge Road to the end, and turn left onto Ridge Road. You will be taking the first right onto Salmon Creek Road, but before turning, look left.

24. Ridge Chapel
Address: 3424 Ridge Road, Williamson
Year Built: 1839

In poor shape today, this building began life as the First Methodist Church of Williamson. It was built using multi-colored cobbles, rough-cut limestone quoins, limestone lintels on edge, and mixed fieldstones for the foundation. The datestone in the middle front reads "Ridge Chapel 1839."

Turn right onto Salmon Creek Road, and watch left.

25. Adams-Demyda House
Address: 6405 Salmon Creek Road, Williamson
Original Owner: C. B. Adams
Year Built: 1850
Period: Late
Style: Greek Revival

Here's a good example of late period work in a 2-story farmhouse. A datestone is inscribed "C. B. Adams 1850." It was built with small, red cobblestones with a wide frieze and medallions in the gable ends (missing from the north side.) Also note the herringbone pattern on the north side with small oval cobbles (1 to 1.5 inches) set at the diagonal.

Continuing north completes the loop to Route 104.

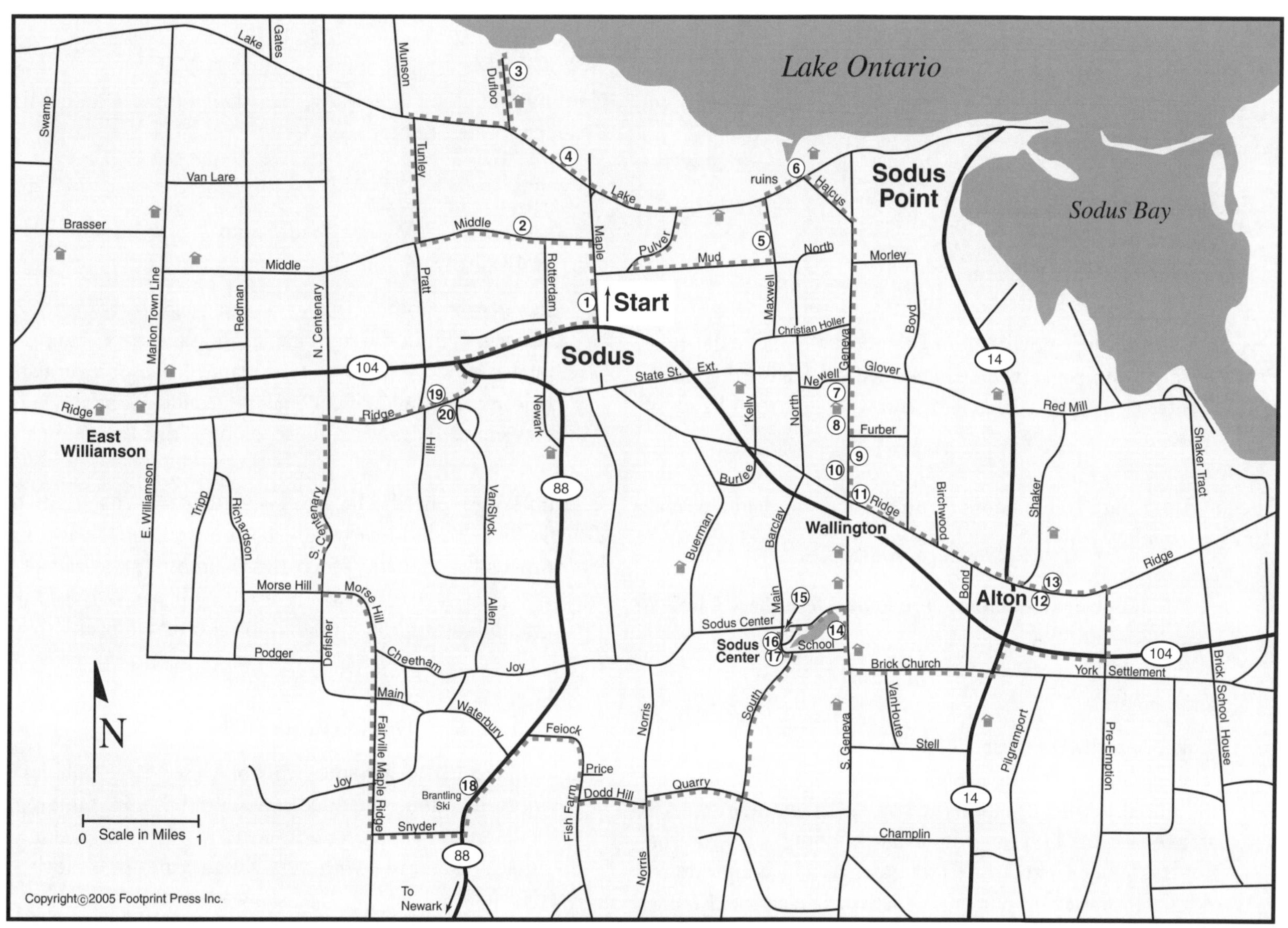

Cobblestone Tour 12

Cobblestone Tour 12

Sodus area in Wayne County
Total Distance: 36 miles
Approximate Time: 1.5 hour

As a result of to their proximity to Lake Ontario, the majority of the houses on this route utilized small, red, lake-washed cobbles. Watch for the effect of a creative mason who alternated bands of red and white cobblestones.

Begin from Route 104 in Sodus. Turn north onto Maple Avenue, and watch left.

1. Feller-Pulver House (now the Sodus Veterinary Clinic in the back)
Address: 6813 Maple Avenue, Sodus
Period: Late

This house had a mason with creativity. Every 6th row of lake-washed cobbles is a row of white instead of the usual small, red cobbles. As in many houses, larger, multi-colored stones were used on the sides of the building. The front has sandstone quoins and lintels set on edge. The quoins on the sides are a variety of cut rocks. Narrow friezes line the sides of the building.

Continue north on Maple Avenue, then turn left onto Middle Road, and watch right.

2.
Address: 6499 Middle Road, Sodus
Year Built: 1846

This 2-story home, built with small, red, lake-washed cobbles, has a fan in the front gable, and sandstone quoins. The lintels are oddly shaped — a square central portion flanked by lower rectangles. They may be wooden. These same lintels were used on other houses along Ridge Road.

Continue west on Middle Road and take the first right onto Tunley Road. Take the next right onto Lake Road, then the first left onto Duffloo Road. Watch right, almost at the end of this dead-end, dirt road. (Along the way you'll pass 7570 Duffloo Road, a cobblestone house that has been mudded over.)

3.
Address: 7752 Duffloo Road, Sodus

Unlike other area homes, this one used large cobbles and sandstone quoins of varied sizes. The 1.5-story building has a wide frieze containing belly windows. Its back, facing Lake Ontario, was built with very rough sandstone blocks and large quoins.

Continue to the turnaround at the end of the street. Here you'll find a cut sandstone home. Return to Lake Road, turn left and watch left.

4. Swales-Burns House
Address: 6543 Lake Road, Sodus
Original Owner: William Swales Sr.
Period: Late

William Swales Sr. built several homes in this area. This later period, 2-story cobblestone home has small, red lake-washed cobbles and rough limestone quoins, but cut limestone lintels on edge.

Continue east on Lake Road, pass Maple Avenue, then turn right onto Pulver Road. At the end, turn left onto Mud Lane, then take the next left onto Maxwell Road at a stop sign, and watch left.

5.
Address: 7147 Maxwell Road, Sodus

A red Japanese maple in the front yard sets off this beautiful 2-story home. The house was built with small cobbles, rough-cut quoins and an inset porch with 2 square columns. Frieze windows extend into the cobblestone courses, which is unusual.

Continue north on Maxwell Road to the end. Turn right onto Lake Road. Immediately to the left, hidden under trees and brush are the ruins of a cobblestone house now on the property of Beechwood State Park. You can park in the parking area for Beechwood State Park and hike back to see the ruins up close. Or, continue driving east and watch left.

6. Preston House (now Maxwell Creek Inn Bed & Breakfast)
Address: 7563 Lake Road, Sodus
Original Owner: John and Elizabeth Preston
Year Built: 1846
Style: Federal cornice

Beautifully preserved, here's another mason who used small, water-rounded cobbles. They're predominately red with some gray and black cobbles mixed in. The sandstone lintels are angled or tapered and are set in a flat arch. Behind the house sits a barn built with large, round cobbles, set with the flat side out.

Schooners sailed into Maxwell Bay to trade wheat for the flour that was made at the gristmill that was built here in 1794. The first gristmill was destroyed by a freshet (flood) in 1807. A second gristmill was built by Captain John Maxwell, which later became known as Preston's Mill. This mill stood until about 1920, before being torn down.

William Swales Sr. built this home in 1846 for his daughter Elizabeth and her husband John Preston as a wedding gift.

The house once served as a way station on the Underground Railroad.

Turn right onto Halcus Road across from the B&B. At the end, turn right onto Geneva Road. After Glover and Newell Roads, watch right.

7.
Address: 6563 North Geneva Road, Sodus

Don't dawdle here, the basic cobblestone building is lost among additions.

Chase House, 6387 North Geneva Road, Sodus

Continue south on Geneva Road, watching right.

8. Chase House
Address: 6387 North Geneva Road, Sodus

Here's a 2-story home that has been maintained as a cobblestone home should. It was built with small, red cobbles. A wing was added to the right. Notice the unusual shape of the lintels with a square piece above the rectangular block.

Continue south on Geneva Road, watching left after Furber.

9. Cunningham House
Address: 6242 North Geneva Road, Sodus

Now we're back to rectangular lintels, but still unusual — the lintels protrude with recessed centers. This 1.5-story home was built with small, red cobbles and limestone quoins. There's a wide frieze across the front. Notice the copper gutters and downspouts and the wood shingle roof.

Continue south on Geneva Road, watching right. Pull into the parking area for the Wallington Schoolhouse.

10. Wallington Schoolhouse, District #8
Address: 6135 North Geneva Road, Wallington, Town of Sodus
Year Built: 1826-1828

Wallington was originally known as Arms Crossroads, named after its founder Daniel Arms, who donated the land for the schoolhouse. It was built between 1826 and 1828 and operated as a schoolhouse until 1950. Today the Wallington Community Center Association owns the Wallington Schoolhouse. Students from all over the area visit and experience "a day in a country school," complete with a pump in the side yard and an outhouse out back. The stone building on the north side was the coal shed. Peer in the windows to get a peek at a 1-room schoolhouse. For a tour, call (315) 483-9791 or (315) 483-8454.

Wallington Schoolhouse, District #8
6135 North Geneva Road, Wallington

This building has unusual construction, which appears to be opportunistic. Rough field cobbles and gray sandstone quoins were used. The quoins got more refined as the building progressed. Look at the northeast corner to see large limestone blocks around the quoins. The sills and lintels may be wooden. There's a fan in the gable end, over the front door. Notice the metal brackets and bar added to hold the building together (a later addition).

Continue south on Geneva Road, then turn left onto Ridge Road East at the stop sign. Near the corner, turn left into the Wallington Fire Department parking lot to view the building you passed at the corner.

11. Wallington Tavern
Address: 7851 Ridge Road East, Wallington, Town of Sodus
Original Owner: William Walling
Year Built: 1834
Period: Early

Wallington Tavern was built as a 2-story tavern and inn near the midpoint between Rochester and Oswego on the Oswego-Lewiston stage route. It's now a private residence.

Built with field cobbles and rough limestone quoins, it's obviously early construction for this area. The lintels are wider at the top than at the bottom. The wrap-around porch was a later addition.

8524 Ridge Road, Alton

Continue east on Ridge Road East, crossing Route 14 into Alton, and watch right.

12.
Address: 8524 Ridge Road, Alton, Town of Sodus
Year Built: 1840

This 2-story home was built with mixed-color field cobbles laid in neat rows with raised mortar. A fan can be found in the side gable end. This house is more refined than other area cobblestone buildings.

Continue east, and pull into the church parking lot on the left.

13. United Methodist Church
Address: 8575 Ridge Road, Alton, Town of Sodus
Period: Late

What a contrast to the previous home. The church was built using small, lake-washed cobbles, collected by the congregation in bushel barrels and hauled using oxen. On the front the cobblestones alternate with 4 rows of red cobbles then 4 rows of white cobbles. The corners are massive cement structures, not quoins. Walk around to see the mixed color sides and rougher stone back. Look up to see the white bell tower with a copper roof.

Continue east on Ridge Road and take the next right onto Pre-Emption Road. Turn right onto Route 104 at the stop sign, heading west. Turn left at the traffic light, onto Route 14, heading south. Take the first right onto Brick Church Road. At the end, turn right onto South Geneva Road, and look left after School Street. (Pass a cobblestone building — 5502 South Geneva Road — obscured by a mustard-colored house.)

14.
Address: 5577 South Geneva Road, Wallington,
Town of Sodus
Period: Late
Style: Greek Revival

Here's a good contrast with the previous building. This one used very small, red lake cobbles and fine cut quoins and lintels. It sits on a cut block foundation and has a water table. There's a wide frieze across the front with belly windows, and a porch with pillars at the front door. Look closely at the cobbles over the lintels on the front windows to see the herringbone pattern. Then look out back at the end of the driveway to see a barn built with mixed-color cobblestones.

Continue north on South Geneva Road, and take the next left onto Sodus Center Road. Pass Metz Pond, and take the second left onto Main Street. Look left at this corner.

15.
Address: 5584 Main Street, Sodus Center, Town of Sodus

Here's another contrast — a crudely built home that used field cobbles, rough quoins, and wooden lintels.

Continue south on Main Street, and watch right.

16.
Address: 5549 Main Street, Sodus Center, Town of Sodus

We're back to small, red cobbles on this 2-story home. The wooden lintels have a raised segment in the middle of the top. Repairs to the mortar are evidenced by lighter colors and filled-in cracks.

Continue south on Main Street, watching right at the next house.

17.
Address: 5539 Main Street, Sodus Center, Town of Sodus

We're back to an early period 2-story home like #15 (5584 Main Street). There are no rows to the mortar. The back wing and wrap-around porch are later additions. The front gable end has a medallion.

Continue south on Main Street, which bends to the left, and take the next right onto South Street. Turn right at the stop sign onto Quarry Road. At the end turn left, then take a quick right onto Dodd Hill Road. At the end turn right onto Fish Farm Road. At the bend, bear left onto Feiock Road, then take a

16967 Route 18, Kendall (not on a tour)

left onto Route 88 (Newark-Sodus Road) heading south. Pass Waterbury Road and watch right for an out building between a large white house and a red barn.

18.
Address: 4917 Newark-Sodus Road (Route 88), Sodus

Behind this home is a small outbuilding built with small, red, lake-washed cobbles and brick quoins on a sandstone block foundation. Notice the slate roof.

Continue south on Route 88, then take the next right onto Snyder Road. At the end turn right onto Fairville Maple Ridge Road. After several cross roads, turn right onto South Centenary Road at a stop sign. Take the next right at a stop sign onto Ridge Road. Pass Pratt Road and Hill Road, and watch left.

19.
Address: 6123 Ridge Road, Sodus
Style: Greek Revival

This home is missing the lintel over the front door. It was built with small, red, lake-washed cobbles. The lintels have the same shape as house #16 (5549 Main Street).

Continue east on Ridge Road, watching right.

20.
Address: 6172 Ridge Road, Sodus
Style: Greek Revival

This house most likely had the same builder as the previous house using the same style and materials. Small cobbles were used on the front and sides. The corners are pilasters rather than quoins. The lintels again have a raised segment in the middle of the top.

Continue east on Ridge Road. A left turn onto Route 88 north will complete the loop back to Route 104.

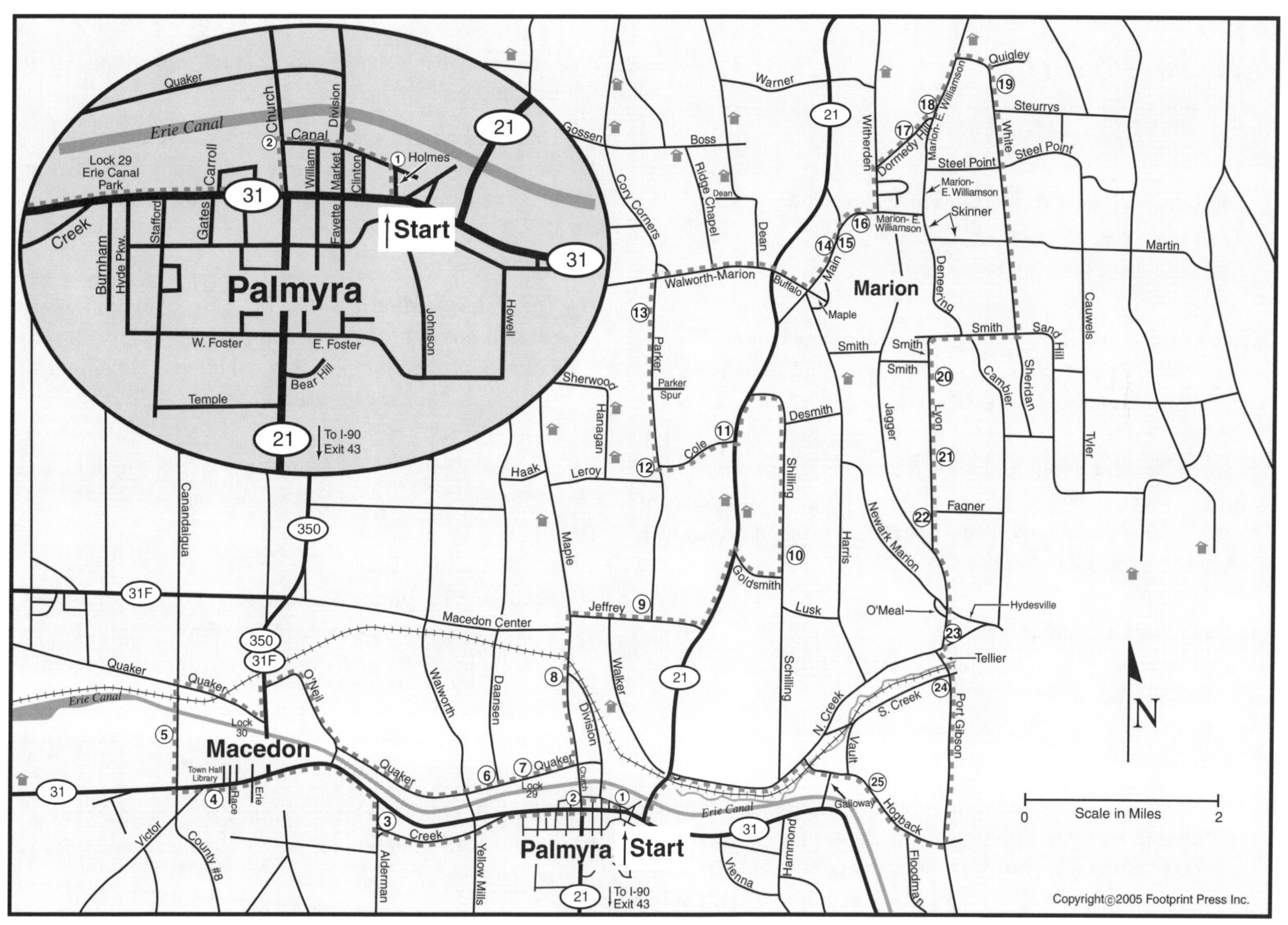

Cobblestone Tour 13

Cobblestone Tour 13

Palmyra, Macedon and Marion in Wayne County
Total Distance: 45 miles
Approximate Time: 2.5 hours

On this route you'll see some basic cobblestone homes. They're not as ornate as ones found on other routes, but a common feature will be cut limestone lintels set on edge over the windows.

Begin in Palmyra. From Route 31 (Main Street), turn north onto Holmes Street. Pull over in front of the stop sign to view the cobblestone warehouse across Canal Street. Or, turn left onto Canal Street and park along the street.

1. Newton Warehouse
(currently owned by John S. Blazey, Inc.)
Address: Canal Street, Palmyra
Original Owner: Butler Newton
Year Built: 1845

This warehouse was built to store apples and potatoes awaiting shipment via the original Erie Canal which ran behind this building. The Erie Canal was enlarged and rerouted several times over the years as freight demands increased. Today the Erie Canal is slightly north of its original route near this warehouse.

Lake-washed, red sandstone cobbles were used on the west, north, east and portions of the south walls. Large fieldstones and even some brick was used for the south wall, facing Canal Street. Brick was also used to construct part of the east wall.

Today the warehouse is used by John S. Blazey, Inc., a tractor and pump dealer, as it has since the 1930s. It's a good example of deterioration in a cobblestone building, with a major crack in the east wall.

Turn left and drive west on Canal Street. At the end, look across Church Street.

2. McKachnie House
Address: 151 Church Street, Palmyra
Original Owner: Alexander McKachnie
Year Built: 1830s

Alexander McKachnie, a native of Scotland, built this house along with a brewery and malt house in the rear. Only the house remains.

The 2-story house with a narrow front, was built using lake-washed, red, round sandstone cobbles. The limestone lintels are set on edge.

Turn left onto Church Street then right onto Route 31 at the traffic light. Turn left onto Creek Road across from the "Town of Macedon" sign and Lock 29 Erie Canal Park. At the end, follow the Y to the right. Turn right onto Alderman Road, and watch right.

3. Jordon House
Address: 1484 Alderman Road, Macedon
Year Built: 1834

This is a pretty 2-story house with a 1.5-story wing fronted by a porch. It was built with multi-colored cobbles, cut limestone quoins, and lintels set on edge. Look for the repaired cracks in the mortar.

The woodwork inside is chestnut, as was common on cobblestone houses. This is a rare wood today because of the blight that wiped out our chestnut trees in the early 1900s.

Continue north on Alderman Road, and turn left onto Route 31 at the stop sign, heading west through the village of Macedon. At the far side of the village, just past the new Town Hall and Library buildings, pull into the right shoulder, and watch left.

4.
Address: 5 West Main Street, Macedon
Period: Middle

You won't want to dawdle here. This 2-story home is only in fair shape and sits on a busy highway. It's an L-shaped building with a medium width frieze and a fan in the front eve. The field cobbles are set 4 courses per quoin on the front.

Continue west on Route 31, and turn right (north) onto Canandaigua Road at the traffic light. Watch left in 0.3 mile.

5. Baker House
Address: 1727 Canandaigua Road, Macedon
Original Owner: J. Baker
Mason: Jacob Terry
Year Built: 1850

J. Baker hired Jacob Terry to build his home. Terry considered this to be his best work. It's a slightly smaller version of the Hawks House (#2 on Tour 14). Terry used bricks for the quoins and lintels, with the bricks set on edge. Sidelights and a transom surround the front door. A fan window decorates each gable end.

Continue north on Canandaigua Road, over the Erie Canal. Turn right onto Quaker Road at the flashing light. At the end, turn left onto Route 31F north. Turn right onto O'Neil Road. At the end, turn left onto Quaker Road. Cross Walworth Road, and watch left.

Chapman House, 2631 Quaker Road, Palmyra

6. Chapman House
Address: 2631 Quaker Road, Palmyra
Original Owner: William Chapman
Year Built: 1827-1830

This 2-story home sits across from Lock 29 on the Erie Canal. Beside it is a big red barn labeled "Tamerlayne 1827" in large white letters. The house took 3 years to complete, using multi-colored cobbles gathered from the lake shore, and cut limestone lintels, quoins and sills. The walls are 28 inches thick. Two additions were added in the mid-1800s. In the mid-1960s, the Nusbaum family made major renovations to what they called "Tickertape Farm." Frederic Nusbaum was the president of a stockbrokerage firm.

Continue east on Quaker Road, watching left shortly after Daansen Road.

7. Lakey House
Address: 2799 Quaker Road, Palmyra
Year Built: 1837

The history of this building is sketchy. According to Carl Schmidt, Nelson Drake built it, but Thomas L. Cook attributed the building to Franklin Lakey.

Compare this with the fine workmanship you saw at 2631 Quaker Road. This one is a roughly built house; built with field cobbles. The quoins are brick on the back corners and uncut limestone on the front corners. The death door on the side has been stoned in. A fire in the 1950s destroyed the east side, which was replaced with a stucco-faced structure.

Continue east on Quaker Road, then turn left onto Maple Avenue and pull into the parking area of the Martin Harris Farm on the left in 1 mile.

8. Chapman-Harris House (currently the Martin Harris Farm)
Address: 2095 Maple Avenue, Palmyra
Mason: Robert Johnson

Year Built: 1849-1850

Martin Harris was a leading figure in the Church of Jesus Christ of Latter-day Saints, who mortgaged his farm for $3,000 to pay for the first printing of the book of Mormon in 1829. Harris owned this land in the 1820s and built a white frame house on this site, but it burned in 1849. Joseph Smith, founder of the Church of Jesus Christ of Latter-day Saints, is said to have dug the well. Mrs. Harris left her husband because of his devout church following. He sold the farm, moved west, and remarried.

William Chapman bought the property and had multi-colored cobbles hauled on 2 to 3 day trips from Lake Ontario on wagons to build his home. The 2-story, center entrance house has a 1.5-story wing on the north end. The cobbles are laid on a diagonal. It has wide friezes and chiseled limestone lintels and quoins that are now painted white. Notice the cobblestone chimney with limestone quoins on the parking lot side.

The home was purchased by the Church of Jesus Christ of Latter-day Saints in 1937 and is rented to its missionaries. The public parking area has restrooms.

Continue north on Maple Avenue over railroad tracks and turn right (east) onto Jeffrey Road. Pass Walker Road and watch left at the corner of Parker Road.

Thomas House, 3313 Jeffrey Road, Palmyra

9. Thomas Home
Address: 3313 Jeffrey Road, Palmyra

Thomas built his home with field cobbles of varying sizes and colors and even included some round and oval lake-washed stones. It has a porch across the front and another on the side. It sports rough limestone quoins and lintels set on edge. The eve has an arched window. Unusual is the cupola on top. David Jeffrey owned the home when the road was named.

Continue east on Jeffrey Road to the end. Turn left at the stop sign onto Route 21 north and take the next right onto Goldsmith Road. At the end, turn left onto Shilling Road, and watch right.

10. Luce House
Address: 2792 Shilling Road, Palmyra
Original Owner: William Luce
Year Built: 1839

William Luce had "W. L., 1839" inscribed over the entrance of his stately 2-story home. He used multi-colored, oval, lake-washed cobbles and arranged them diagonally in a herringbone design. Limestone set on edge forms the lintels over the windows and the front door. In 1970 Mr. and Mrs. Eugene East purchased this home. Among the many improvements they made was to add a wooden mantle for the kitchen fireplace that was hand-carved by 80-year-old artist, Michael Corbitt, to depict an Erie Canal scene.

Luce House, 2792 Shilling Road, Palmyra

Continue north on Shilling Road to the end. Turn left (south) on Route 21, then take the first right onto Cole Road. Stop at this corner to view the house on the right.

11. Durfee House
Address: 3175 Palmyra-Marion Road (Route 21), Palmyra
Original Owner: Job Durfee
Year Built: 1840
Style: Greek Revival

Small, red, lake-washed cobbles were used on the front. Notice how the colors became mixed as the mason progressed up the sidewalls and that the sidewall stones are ovals laid diagonally. In fact, each side on this house is different. The 2-story main building has a 1-story wing. The house has a wide frieze with belly windows and cut limestone lintels, quoins and sills. Notice the basement windows (but not the others) have limestone lintels set on edge. The house sits on a fieldstone foundation.

Continue to the end of Cole Road. At the end, look across Parker Road.

12. Avery House (currently Cobble Ridge Antiques)
Address: 3049 Parker Road, Palmyra
Original Owner: Galeb Avery
Year Built: ~1840

Galeb Avery built his 2-story, center entrance home, with a 1-story wing at the rear. He used field cobbles of varying sizes and colors and set the limestone lintels on edge.

Turn right onto Parker Road. Pass Parker Road Spur (also pass a cut fieldstone house at 3541 Parker Road), and watch left.

13. Sanford House
Address: 3713 Parker Road, Marion
Original Owner: Stephen Sanford
Mason: Stephen and Peleg Sanford
Year Built: 1822

Here's a home with similar construction as the previous one, just smaller. It was built with multi-color cobbles with an air space between the cobblestones and inside walls, The limestone lintels are set on edge, and the house sits on a cut limestone foundation.

Stephen Sanford lived for many years in a log cabin south of this building. When his sons were old enough to help, they gathered stones and built their cobblestone house. His son Peleg was a mason by trade. His other sons Harvey and Riley assisted with the carpentry work.

Continue north on Parker Road to the stop sign. Turn right onto Walworth-Marion Road (County Road 207). Cross Route 21 at the flashing light. Take the next left onto Main Street at the traffic light, and head into the village of Marion. Watch left.

14. Christian Church Parsonage
Address: 4057 North Main Street, Marion
Year Built: 1833

This simple, 2-story house was originally built as a parsonage to house the pastor of the Christian Church. The congregation was budget conscious, so they used field cobbles, rough-cut limestone quoins and lintels set on edge. Notice there is no separate foundation. Inside, the ceiling heights were kept to an absolute minimum. The exterior walls were built with an air space to provide insulation and reduce heating costs. The stairway inside resembles the design often seen in English cottages where there is no landing outside the doors at the top of the stairs.

Continue north on Main Street a short distance, and look right.

15. Blacksmith Shop
Address: 4110 North Main Street, Marion
Year Built: Most likely early 1850s

This 2-story home is partly hidden behind a hedge row, but well worth looking for. The corners are rough-cut limestone piers — not quoins. The front has small, red water-washed cobbles and the sides have mixed color cobbles. The vertical mortar joints are pyramids and the horizontal joints are Vs. A cut limestone water table separates the cobblestone house from the cut stone foundation. It has a fan in the gable end and a death door on the side. A porch once spanned the front.

It serves as a private residence today, but it began life as a blacksmith shop.

Continue north on Main Street and turn right onto Marion-E. Williamson Road, and watch right for a cobblestone barn behind a tan farmhouse with green shutters.

16. Cobblestone Barn
Address: 4154 Marion-E. Williamson Road, Marion
Year Built: 1840

This barn was built using multicolored fieldstones and limestone quoins. It has small windows with white painted, wooden lintels.

Take the next left onto Witherden Road, then turn right onto Dormedy Hill Road, and watch left at the top of the hill.

17. Green House
Address: 4471 Dormedy Hill Road, Marion
Original Owner: J. C. Green
Year Built: 1849

J. C. Green had his red, lake-washed cobbles hauled from Sodus Point on Lake Ontario for his L-shaped farmhouse. The stones were laid in a herringbone pattern on the two sides, but not on the front, and on the first floor only. This indicates the left portion of the house was built slightly later than the less ornate section. He placed a marble datestone inscribed "J. C. Green Erected A.D. 1849" between the second floor windows on the front.

The ornate porch on the front dates from the 1870s and may have replaced an earlier Greek Revival style porch. The foundation is cut limestone in the front but regular rocks on the sides. The limestone quoins are chiseled. On the back, east corner, the quoins start halfway up the wall. Multi-colored fieldstones were used on the back. A stoned-in archway on the wing in the back used to be the carriage house entrance.

This house was known for nearly a century as the Dormody House but John Dormody didn't buy it until 1874. He purchased it from John Barrett.

Continue north on Dormedy Hill Road to the stop sign at the end. Turn left onto Marion-E. Williamsville Road and immediately look left.

18. Barrett House
Address: 4685 Marion-E. Williamson Road, Marion
Original Owner: Samuel Barrett
Year Built: 1840

This 2-story, center entrance house has a 1-story wing. It was built with mixed color water-washed cobblestones and cut limestone lintels, quoins and sills. Atypical for cobblestone buildings, the smaller stones were used on the side walls rather than the front. The horizontal mortar joints are flat Vs and the vertical joints are roughly formed Vs or triangular pyramids. Mr. Barrett had a marble datestone inscribed "S.B. 1840," installed high above the front door on the front wall. There's a small frieze across the front, and the front door is framed with a transom and sidelights.

This was home to several generations of Barretts, one of whom invented the first non-refillable "throwaway" bottle. By the time Mr. and Mrs. Sydney Welch purchased the property, it was virtually a ruin with a caved-in roof and missing quoins. They spent 2 years renovating the house to return it to showplace condition. They replaced the missing quoins with concrete blocks which blend in remarkably well. The rebuilt roof was covered in painted metal which was often used 100+ years ago, but is rarely used today.

Continue north on Marion-E. Williamson Road, and turn right onto White Road. Pass Quigley Road, and watch left.

19. Smith House
Address: 4676 White Road, Marion
Original Owner: Samuel Smith
Year Built: 1830-1832

Multi-color field cobblestones were used to build this simple 2-story farmhouse. It was built as a double, with many small rooms. It has rough-cut quoins and limestone lintels set on edge for the first floor windows but brick set on edge as lintels on the second floor.

In 1880 James White, his wife and 5 children purchased this cobblestone house and 65-acre farm for $2,675. The house was surrounded by an apple orchard. For years the house was rented out and used for farm tenants. From 1918 to

Smith House, 4676 White Road, Marion

1948 Mr. William J. White used the building to store potatoes and let the grounds grow wild.

In 1948, James and Carrie White and their 4 children began a multi-year process of gutting the house and performing major renovations. These included installing the fireplace and external chimney, which was built with fieldstones to match the house. James custom made windows and sills to replace the originals, since each was originally handcrafted to different measurements. The Whites lived here until 1971, when once again the house was rented, then stood vacant.

In 1981 Tom & Cindy Ikewood (current owners) and their 2 children purchased the home. They continued the renovations but made the conscious decision not to add any wings onto the house. This makes it unusual among cobblestone homes.

Continue on White Road, past Steurrys, Steel Point and Skinner Roads. Then take a right onto Smith Road at the stop sign. Smith Road will take a sharp left turn. Continue straight as Smith Road turns into Lyon Road, and look left.

20.
Address: 3458 Lyon Road, Palmyra

This 1.5-story home was built with small, mixed color cobbles. It has a cut stone foundation and a frieze across the front. The limestone lintels are set on edge.

Continue south on Lyon Road, watching left.

21. Paul Jagger House
Address: 3142 Lyon Road, Palmyra
Original Owner: Paul Jagger
Year Built: ~1840

This 1.5-story home is turned sideways with the frieze, containing belly windows, across the sides. It was also built with small, mixed color cobbles, but what is unusual is the position of the front door — set at the front, right corner. Above the door is a wide lintel, supporting a drip edge lintel that reaches from the bottom of the top floor window.

Daniel and Abigail Jagger were pioneers of the Palmyra area, building their first homestead on Jagger Road in 1792. This land was part of their 1,000-acre tract. Their son, Paul Jagger, built this house around 1840.

Continue south on Lyon Road, watching right, just after Fagner Road.

22. Jagger House
Address: 2799 Lyon Road, Palmyra
Year Built: ~1840

Here's another 2-story home built with small, mixed-color cobbles and cut limestone lintels, quoins and sills. Like the previous house, it has a wide lintel over the door and a drip edge lintel above that. The front door is framed in a transom and sidelights. The house sits on a cut stone foundation. Those similarities are a clue that this home was probably built by another Jagger, near the same time as the previous house.

Continue south on Lyon Road, passing Hydesville/Newark Marion Road, to the stop sign at the corner of North Creek Road, and look left.

23. Cobblestone District #7 Schoolhouse
Address: Corner of Lyon Road & North Creek Road, East Palmyra
Year Built: 1846

A log schoolhouse first sat on this location, built before 1805. While the cobblestone schoolhouse was being built in 1846, classes may have been held in the Clark House (next on the tour). Stone school benches can still be found in the Clark House, and the original owner, Maltby Clark, was a schoolteacher.

The schoolhouse was built mainly with small, red cobbles on a fieldstone foundation. A plaque on the front reads "Jacob B. O'Meal Jr. 1946." He was the owner (a farm equipment dealer) who enlarged the front door to allow for machinery storage. The schoolhouse is showing wear with cracks and crumbling stone sections. But, it has new wooden gutters and a wood shingle roof. The side windows are now shuttered. Notice the old cemetery across Lyon Road.

Turn right onto North Creek Road then left onto Tellier Road. Cross Ganargua Creek and railroad tracks to the stop sign. Continue straight onto Port Gibson Road, and look right.

24. Clark House
Address: 4698 Port Gibson Road, East Palmyra
Original Owner: Maltby Clark

Mr. Clark built his home in three sections, beginning with the two-story main part. The 1-story section was added later as evidenced by the thickness of the walls where these two sections meet. It's the third, wooden section that was once used as a schoolroom. But still, it was built at an early date using hewn beams and wooden pegs.

This house looks different from other area cobblestones. It was built with large field cobbles and rough-cut limestone quoins and lintels set on edge. The foundation is made of large fieldstones. The lintels on the 1-story later addition are brick. The windows have an unusual placement, perhaps because of the staged building.

A small cobblestone house in the backyard can be seen from S. Creek Street. It contains a window, so it probably wasn't a smokehouse. Notice the herringbone pattern at the peak.

Continue south on Port Gibson Road, and turn right onto Hogback Road. Pass Floodman Road, and watch right.

25. Rogers House
Address: 4441 Hogback Road, Palmyra

This 2-story home was built with small red cobbles on the front and mixed-color cobbles on the sides. It has cut limestone lintels, quoins and sills but look closely at the side windows under the porch. They're the only ones with lintels set on edge. There's a field cobble foundation. The porch was added in 2005.

Continue west on Hogback Road to the end. Turn left onto North Creek Road. At a stop sign, turn left onto Route 21 south. At a traffic light, turn right onto Route 31 to return to Palmyra.

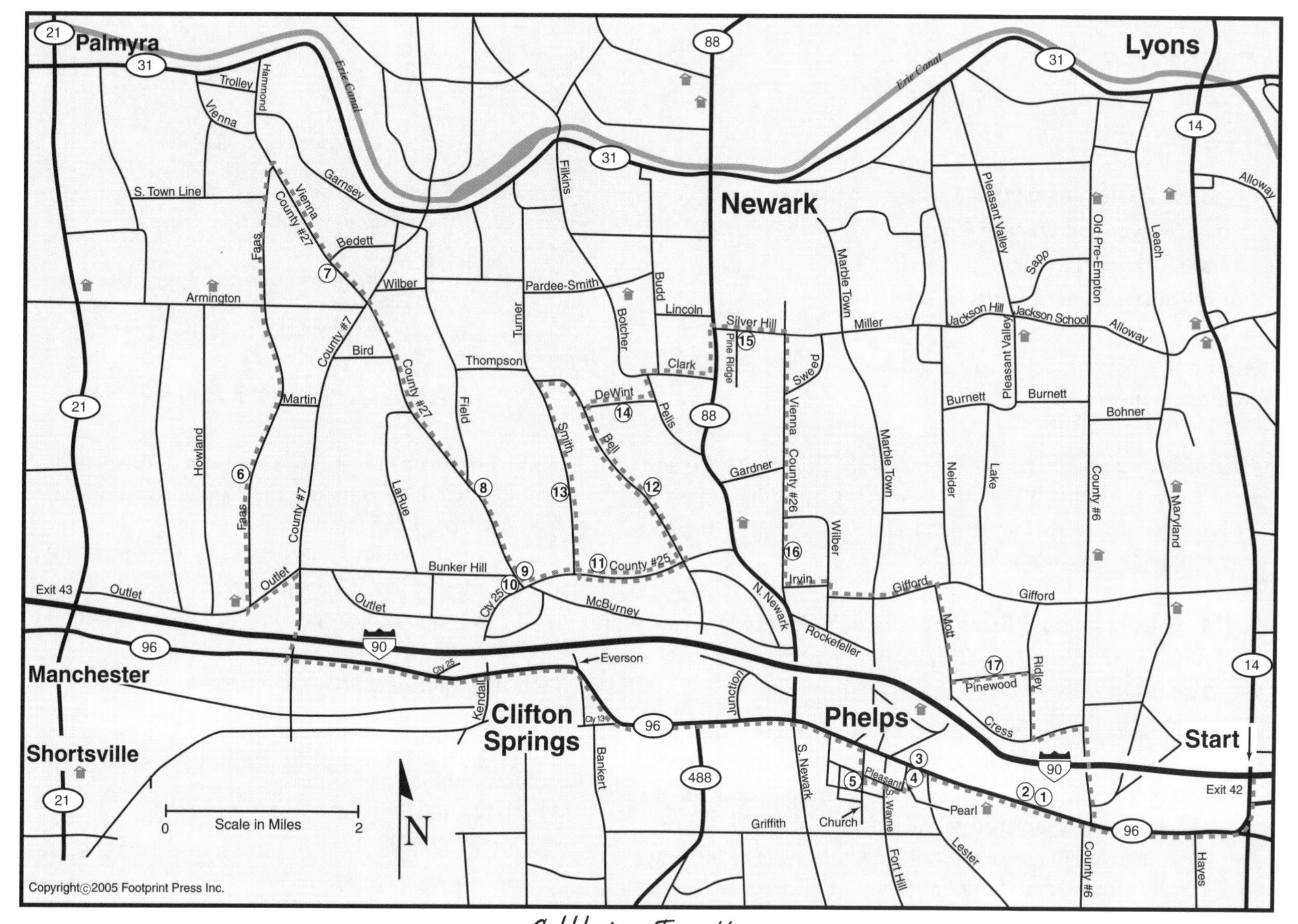

Cobblestone Tour 14

Cobblestone Tour 14

Newark, Phelps and Clifton Springs
in Wayne and Ontario Counties
Total Distance: 44 miles
Approximate Time: 2 hours

A great diversity of architectural styles and unique cobblestone features await you on this tour.

Begin from exit 42 (Geneva) off the NYS Thruway (I-90) and head right on Route 14 south. Bear right onto the ramp for Route 96 north. Pass Hayes Road and County Road 6, then watch right after a cut block house.

1. Swift House and Barns (now Stone Acre Farms)
Address: 928 Route 96, Phelps
Year Built: Early 1840s

This beautiful 2-story home and barn complex was built using large glacial field cobbles. It remains a prosperous working farm. One of the two cobblestone barns on the property is now attached to the house. In the mid-20th century these buildings were restored by the owner at the time, Henry Gleason, of Gleason Works in Rochester. In the 1960s concrete buttresses were added to support the barn walls. The main house has a transom and sidelights with unusual detail surrounding the front door and millstones were used as the steps at the front entrance. Notice the wood shake roof. Two pairs of obelisk markers can be found at the ends of the circular driveway. Between them is an old windmill. The property also contains a cobblestone wellhouse.

Swift House and Barns, 928 Route 96, Phelps

Continue west on Route 96, watching right at the next house.

2. Hawks House
Address: 988 Route 96, Phelps
Year Built: 1848
Style: Gothic Revival with a gable in the center over the door

This basic 1.5-story cottage was built for A. Hawks with small, dark red sandstone, water-rounded cobbles from the Sodus area, laid diagonally. They were set 6 rows per quoin on the front. The pointed tops on the first floor windows are emphasized by three pointed rows of cobbles. This house has louvered shutters that echo this same pointed line. The limestone quoins have hammered centers and tooled edges. There's also a limestone water table. Notice the hitching post and carriage step in the front yard.

Continue west on Route 96. On the left, pass a brick house at 1127 Route 96. In the back yard is a small cobblestone smoke-house built with irregular quoins and, therefore, irregular courses. Unfortunately, it's difficult to see from the road.

Pass Lester Road, and enter the village of Phelps. Turn left onto Pearl Street, and stop at this corner. You may want to park here and walk around. One house is behind you, on Main Street. The second is to your left at the corner of Main and Pearl Streets.

3. Bannister House
Address: 38 Main Street (Route 96), Phelps (on the north side of Route 96)
Year Built: 1830 and 1840
Period: Late

C. Bannister was an early Phelps physician. A stone in the east wing is engraved "C. Bannister — 1840." However, it is believed that the west section may have been built around 1830. There is clear evidence in the mortar that several masons worked on the building. It is jokingly said that the "apprentices practiced on this house, then went across the street to build a cobblestone house properly."

Peck House, 41 Main Street, Phelps

The front windows are framed with large limestone blocks and an oval cobblestone decoration is set in the gable end of the west section. This ornament is similar to the one built into the house on Maryland Street in Phelps (Smith House, #18 on Tour 15.) Look closely at the walls to see some wavy rows.

4. Peck House

Address: 41 Main Street (Route 96), Phelps (on the corner of Route 96 and Pearl Street)

Year Built: 1837

This pretty home has more sophisticated masonry than the one across the street. Notice that some rows of the cobbles are angled and that the gable end sports a fanlight. Some windows contain original glass. The basement retains original stone floors and a fireplace with an oven.

Continue south on Pearl Street. Follow it to the right as it becomes Pleasant Avenue. Take the second left onto Church Street at the second stop sign, and pull into the parking area for the First Baptist Church on the right.

5. Baptist Church of Vienna (later renamed Phelps)

Address: 30 Church Street, Phelps

Architects: John Skinner and Stephen Trumbull of Wayne County

Year Built: 1845

Style: Greek Revival with Gothic columns at the front

Here you can stretch your legs and get an up close look at cobblestone construction. The front was built with small, red sandstone, water-rounded cobbles set at an angle, five courses per quoin. The two sides used multi-colored cobbles, set four courses to the quoin. The rear wall is made of rougher field cobbles set three courses per quoin. Notice the finely chiseled limestone quoins, lintels and water table. The stone quoins around the front door are unusual.

This building was originally called Baptist Chapel and Phelps was once called Vienna, as evidenced by the plaque over the door that reads "Baptist Chapel Vienna Erected AD 1845." The windows are not original — they were changed to stained glass after the Civil War.

This is one of three cobblestone churches in Ontario County, but the only one still used as a church. The Second Baptist Church in Gypsum (Manchester) is now a private residence and The First Universalist Church of Bristol was destroyed. This building is listed on the National Register of Historic Places.

Return to Church Street, and turn left (north) toward the village. Turn left onto Route 96 west at the traffic light. Follow Route 96 west for 6.6 miles, then take a right onto County Road 7 at a flashing light. Cross the thruway, and take the first left onto Outlet Road. Turn right onto Faas Road, and watch left in 0.8 mile.

6. Short House
Address: 844 Faas Road, Manchester

This small 5-bay cobblestone house was built with small, predominately dark, mixed-color cobbles of various sizes and shapes. The gray limestone lintels and quoins have been painted.

Continue north on Faas Road to the end. Turn right onto Vienna Road. Pass Bedett Road, and watch right.

7.
Address: 228 County Road 27, Manchester

This small, simple house was built with multi-colored field cobbles and has a wrap-around porch on 3 sides. Note that the lintels vary in size. The wall facing the street has straight horizontal mortar lines about 2 inches apart. The variously shaped stones were set at different angles to make them fit in the 2-inch space.

Continue southeast on County Road 27. Pass County Road 7, Bird, LaRue and Field Roads, then watch left.

8. John Reed House
Address: 835 County Road 27, Manchester

John and his brother Albert had their cobblestone houses built on County Road 27 in Manchester at about the same time. Only John's house survives.

This house is plain but unique in several ways. The mixture of glacial field cobbles and lake-washed cobbles are set in a herringbone pattern on the front. The chiseled, gray limestone quoins stick out — not set flush like on all other cobblestone buildings. There's a cut limestone foundation on the front only.

Continue southeast on County Road 27, and view both sides of the road at the intersection of Bunker Hill Road.

This community was originally called Plainsville, but the name had to be changed when they got a post office, since there was already a Plainsville, NY. So, they chose the name Gypsum after the Gypsum deposits that were discovered along Canandaigua Outlet just south of town in 1812.

9. School at Plainsville (east side of the road)
Address: 1061 County Road 27, Gypsum,
Town of Manchester
Period: Late

This former schoolhouse is hard to see from the road, but look closely. It was built with small, red, lake-washed sandstone cobbles and tall windows. It was used as a school from

1853 to 1941. The recessed doorway has sidelights and a transom. There is a triangular window in the gable peak over the front door. Contrast this to the early period former church across the street.

10. Second Baptist Church (west side of the road)
Address: 1070 County Road 27, Gypsum,
Town of Manchester
Year Built: 1835
Period: Early

This early church was converted to a residential structure in 1954. The building is very rough with narrow quoins of varied sizes. The cobblestones are a mixture of glacial fieldstones and lake-washed cobbles. The window placement (which originally was twelve over twelve panes) is a clue that this was not built as a house. Records show that the community raised funds for this social and religious center in 1834. According to a 20th century owner, "the building was built by the parishioners with the help of a mason. The mason showed the amateur builders how to lay cobblestones in the parts of the wall framing the front door, where the joints are relatively straight and horizontal. As the distance from the door increases and amateurs took over, the joints bob and weave like drunken sailors." There's no way to verify or refute this claim. A major remodel occurred in 1851.

Continue southeast on County Road 27, and turn left onto County Road 25 at the end. Pass McBurney and Smith Roads (you'll loop back to here later), and look left.

11.
Address: 2450 County Road 25, Clifton Springs

This 1.5-story farmhouse is missing lintels. It's a simple design with big quoins of varied sizes. The small field cobblestones are set in straight rows.

Continue east on County Road 25, then take the first left onto Bell Road, and watch right in 0.8 mile.

Bell House, 905 Bell Road, Clifton Springs

12. Bell House
Address: 905 Bell Road, Clifton Springs
Style: Five-bay Federal Style

How's this for gorgeous? Rough, mixed cobbles were used, along with finely cut limestone lintels, quoins and sills. The gable end on the north side has a fanlight outlined by a row of cobbles. The front door has a sidelight on one side only. The house sits on a field stone foundation.

This house had a rough life. It stood open to the weather for many years and had its roof and interior walls damaged beyond repair. Rehabilitation began in 1977, building a new interior within the cobblestone shell, imitating the original design as closely as possible. See if you can spot the hole in the north side wall, part way up to the second floor windows, that supported scaffolding for construction.

Continue north on Bell Road. Pass DeWint Road (you'll return here later), then turn left onto Smith Road at the stop sign. Watch left in 1.6 miles.

13. Charles Harmon House
Address: 983 Smith Road, Clifton Springs
Year Built: 1842
Style: Greek Revival

The beauty continues ... the front and sides of this pretty house were built with small, red, lake-washed sandstone cobbles set at an angle. The 2-story main building has 2 wings. Large field cobbles were used on the wing that now connects to a garage. The lintels, quoins and water table are all uniform gray limestone with tooled borders and hammered center panels. The gable end has a limestone fanlight. Keep looking to find the smokehouse, also built with small, red, lake-washed sandstone cobbles. This house is on the National Register of Historic Places.

Charles Harmon House, 983 Smith Road, Clifton Springs

We're now going to complete a loop, passing 2 houses we've already seen. Continue south on Smith Road. At the end, turn left on County Road 25, and pass house #11. Take the next left on Bell Road, and pass house #12. This time turn right onto DeWint Road, and watch right in 0.5 mile.

14.
Address: 2269 DeWint Road, Clifton Springs
Style: Greek Revival

Here's an unusual design. The 2-story center building has wings on each side. Limestone pillars adorn the front and wide friezes adorn the sides. The area between the pillars is clapboard, while the second floor over the lintels and the 2 wings are cobblestone. The cobbles are small red, lake-washed sandstone. The bay windows are obviously a later addition.

Continue east on DeWint Road to the end. Turn left onto Pelis Road, and then take a right onto Clark Road at the stop sign. At the end, turn left onto Route 88 north, then take the first right onto Silver Hill Road, and watch right just after Pine Ridge.

15.
Address: 301 Silver Hill Road, Newark
Original Owner: George Howland
Year Built: Early ~1835-1845
Style: Greek Revival

Here's another large, 2-story house built with small, red, elliptical, lake-washed cobblestones on the front and sides, and fieldstones on the back. Sidelights and transom surround the front door. The limestone lintels, quoins and water table are precisely chiseled. There's a huge lintel over the front door. The frieze sports grills. Columns adorn the front porch, which was a later addition. The bay window was also a much later addition.

Continue east on Silver Hill Road and take the next right onto Vienna Road at the stop sign. Past Wilber the road name changes to County Road 26; watch left.

16.
Address: 989 County Road 26, Phelps
Period: Early

This 2-story house is simpler — a common farmhouse — that sits on a cobblestone foundation. It was built with rough field cobbles with V-shaped mortar joints. The brick quoins and lintels were plastered over and painted. The gutters collect water to feed into a basement cistern. The porch on the front was a later addition.

Continue south on County Road 26, and take the next left onto Irvin Road. At the end, turn right onto Wilber Road, then take a quick left onto Gifford Road. Cross Marble Town Road, then turn right onto Mott Road. Take the next left onto Pinewood Road and watch left.

17.

Address: 1092 Pinewood Road, Phelps
Year Built: Early 1830s (sometimes listed as 1837)
Style: Five-bay Federal

This 2-story home was built with rectangular field cobbles and rough quoins and lintels. The lintels are small blocks of limestone set on edge. The Federal entrance indicates that the home was built in the early 1830s. The roof was extended to overhang to keep up with late 19th century (post-Civil War) fashion. The gable ends each contain two small, square windows.

Continue east to the end of Pinewood Road, and turn right onto Ridley Road. At the end, turn left onto Cress Road. At the end turn right onto County Road 6. This will take you over the thruway to Route 96.

Millville Academy, 12405 West Lee Road, Millville
(not on a tour)

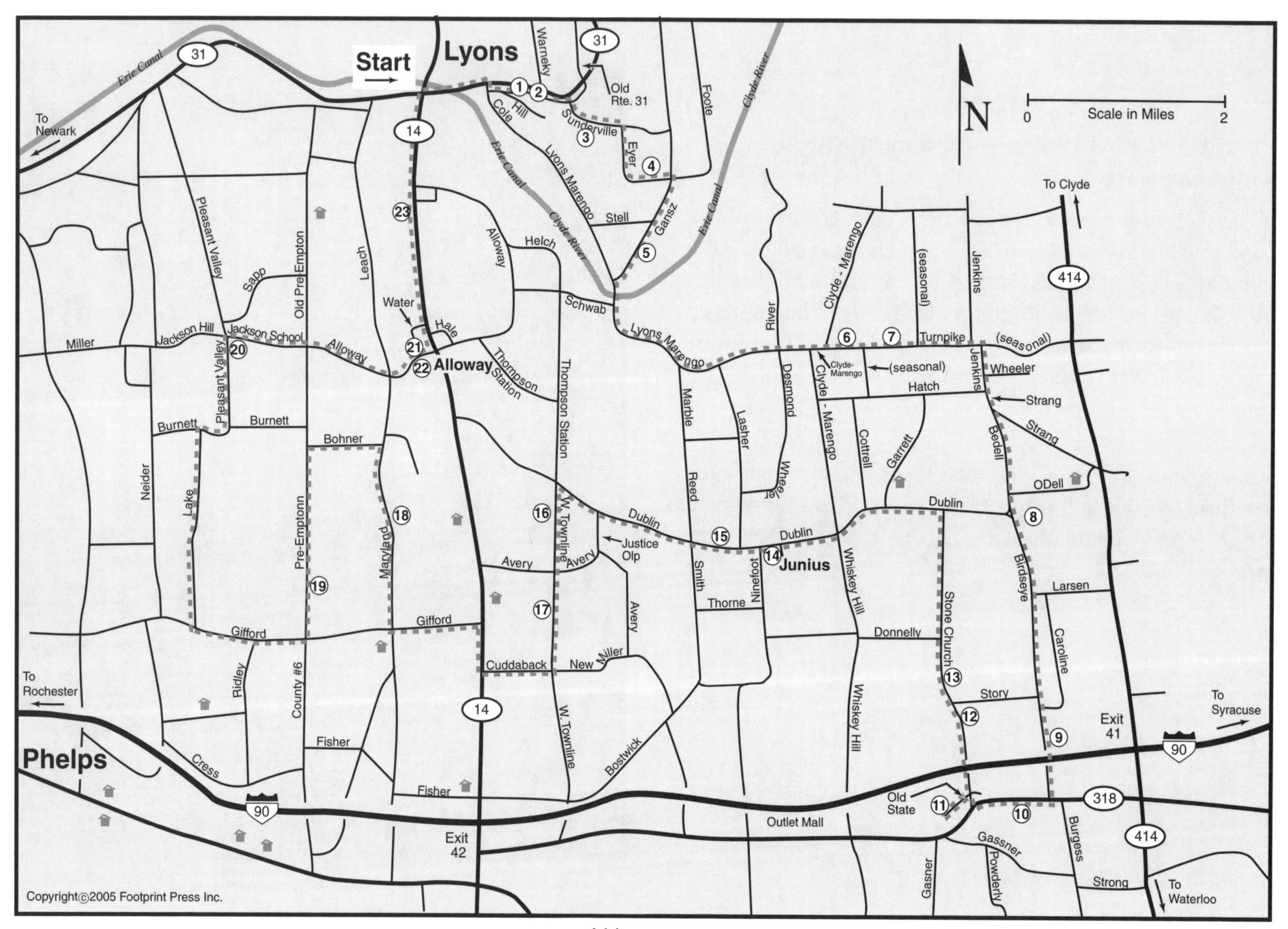

Cobblestone Tour 15

Cobblestone Tour 15

Sodus, Lyons, Alloway and Junius in Wayne, Ontario and Seneca Counties
Total Distance: 47 miles
Approximate Time: 2.5 hours

Follow this tour through the fields of glacial drumlins and you'll understand why most of the cobblestone homes in this area were built using field cobblestones.

Begin in Lyons, heading east on Route 31. Cross over the Erie Canal, then turn right onto Cole Road, and take a very quick left onto Old Route 31. Pass Hill Road, then watch to the left at the first bend, behind a row of arborvitae.

1. Teachout House
Address: Route 31, Lyons
Year Built: Somewhere between1826 and the early1830s

This is a 2-story building with a 1.5-story wing built with mixed-color field cobbles. It may have been built in stages. The main house has rough cut limestone lintels and quoins, whereas the wing used finer cut limestone. The house has 5 fireplaces, wide floor boards, and 2-feet-thick walls. Doric columns support porches on both the main house and wing.

The original owner is unknown, but this house is called Teachout House because the Teachout family lived here from 1847 until 1943, almost 100 years. As a young girl on her way to visit relatives with her father, Minerva Croul saw this house being built and dreamed of one day living here. Minerva married a tanner named Henry Teachout. They moved to Lyons, built a tannery, and purchased this cobblestone house and its 212-acre farm. The land was heavily wooded and stony at the time, and took a tremendous effort to clear for farming. Eventually tobacco became one of their major crops. Minerva lived here until she died in 1912 at the age of 90, fulfilling a childhood dream.

The front of this 5-bay house faces Old Route 31, originally called Montezuma Turnpike, but now has its driveway off new Route 31. When built, it faced the Erie Canal, which opened in 1825. Henry Teachout sold a right of way across his farm when the canal was first enlarged. (The route of the original Erie Canal and the enlarged Erie Canal is a trail today called Canal Park Trailway that is described in the guidebook *Take Your Bike - Family Rides in the Finger Lakes and Genesee Valley Region*. The current Erie Canal was moved to the south a bit to follow the bed of the Clyde River.)

Henry Teachout was respected within the community and would skate to town in winter to lead the choir in the Presbyterian Church, where he was an elder. When the Rochester & Southern Railroad was built in 1851, he sold a right of way across the south end of his farm for $500.

In 1906 Minerva was paid for an interurban trolley right of way. From this house, Minerva had a prime view of transportation history in the making.

Years later, Martha, a great granddaughter of Minerva and Henry Teachout, was living in this house. One September afternoon, a mail carrier named Earl Martin called on Martha and asked her to go for a ride. She refused, and he took out a revolver and shot her, then turned the gun on himself. He died instantly, and Martha died later that night in the hospital. No one could explain this odd behavior of a normally quiet, well behaved young man who routinely carried a gun in his truck on his route to the trains where he delivered mail.

Continue east on Old Route 31, watching left.

2. Richmond House
Address: 8729 Old Route 31, Lyons
Original Owner: Elias Richmond
Year Built: Original building ~1826, kitchen extension added 1834
Period: Early

This early period house was built with large field cobbles, rough-cut limestone quoins that are slightly smaller than those used in later buildings, and wooden lintels. A transom is over the inset front door. The house is set on a large stone foundation. The quoins on the wing are mixed stone. The front has some patches of mortar over the cobbles.

In 1883 Elias Richmond purchased 87.5 acres of land from his neighbor Henry Teachout. For many years this home was owned by a bachelor named George Richmond.

Continue east on Old Route 31, take the first right onto Sunderville Road, and watch right.

3.
Address: 8880 Sunderville Road, Lyons

This 2-story house with a porch across the front, was built later than the previous houses, using squarish field cobbles and cut limestone lintels and quoins. Look for the triangular vent in the gable end and the field stone foundation. The wing on the back was built with larger stones.

The Laster family owned this home from the early 1920s until 1973.

Continue east on Sunderville Road, then turn right onto Eyer Road. After a sharp bend, watch left.

4. Romyen House (now the Kyburg Black Angus Farm)
Address: 1018 Eyer Road, Lyons
Year Built: 1841

Similar to the previous home, this 2-story farmhouse used squarish field cobbles and cut limestone quoins, lintels and a water table on the front only. "T. T. Romyen 1841" is etched in the lintel over the front door and sidelights frame its sides. It has the same triangular vent in the gable end as the previous house. Look up to see the wood shake roof and at the end of the driveway to see the smokehouse out back.

Continue east on Eyer Road, then take the first right onto Gansz Road at the stop sign. Pass Stell Road, then watch left.

5.
Address: 790 Gansz Road, Lyons
Original Owner: a Gansz brother
Year Built: Probably ~late 1860s
Period: Late

Built on a large stone foundation, this house also used large field cobbles and limestone lintels and quoins, and water table again on the front only. It's a 2-story building with a single story wing, and bay windows on the front (an obvious upgrade). This may be the only cobblestone building in the area with a mansard roof.

The Gansz brothers built three mansions on Gansz Road.

Continue south on Gansz Road. At the end, turn left onto Lyons-Marengo Road and cross the Erie Canal. Continue straight on Lyons-Marengo Road (which changes to Turnpike Road). Watch left after passing Clyde-Marengo Road (2 off-set roads) for a small house far from the road.

6.
Address: 10065 Turnpike Road, Clyde

This small, plain house is set back from the road and is hard to see. It's a 2-story house with a 1-story wing, built with field cobbles and limestone lintels and quoins.

Continue east on Turnpike Road, watching left.

7. (now Thorn Farms)
Address: 10297 Turnpike Road, Clyde

Vines partially cover this 2-story home that was built with large cobbles, 4 courses per quoin. Notice the triangular window in the side gable end and the finely cut limestone quoins, lintels, sills and water table.

Continue east on Turnpike Road. Turn right (south) onto Jenkins Road. It will turn into Strang Road. Turn right onto Bedell Road. Look left at the stop sign.

8.
Address: 543 Birdseye Road, Waterloo

Don't dawdle here. This 1.5-story cobblestone home is set back from the road and hidden under additions. You can see it better from around the corner, on Birdseye Road. It was built with field cobbles and cut limestone lintels and quoins.

If you haven't already done so, turn left onto Birdseye Road. Pass Larsen, Story and Caroline Roads, then watch left.

9.
Address: 1229 Birdseye Road, Junius
Period: Early
Style: 5-bay Federal

This early period, 2-story building has an ornate front porch and white painted lintels, quoins and water table.

Continue south on Birdseye Road. Cross the NYS Thruway (I-90), and turn right onto Route 318 west at the end, and watch left.

10.
Address: 1370 Route 318, Junius

The house sits near the road but is obscured by pine trees. It's a 2-story home built with large cobbles, 4 courses per quoin, set on a fieldstone foundation. The front door is off-set to the right corner of the house and is framed in side-lights. Look for the rows of brick over the arch in the gable end. A white addition was added to the side.

Continue west on Route 318. Turn right onto Stone Church Road, then turn left onto Old State Road Extension, and look right at the dead end.

11. First Methodist Episcopal Church (now a private home)
Address: 1434 Old State Road Extension, Junius
Year Built: 1839

This church was built with field cobbles in 1839, as stated on a datestone between the front doors, which is obscured by bushes. It's unusual for a Christian church to have two doors. The original building had a wooden porch that covered the entire front, with wooden steps on 3 sides. Notice the oval stained glass window in the front.

Turn around, and head back out Old State Road Extension, and turn left (north) onto Stone Church Road. Cross the NYS Thruway (I-90), and watch right.

12.
Address: 1111 Stone Church Road, Waterloo, Town of Junius
Year Built: 1825

Large, rough field cobbles are set 4 courses per quoin on this pretty 2-story home. The attached cobblestone barn is now part of the house. It was built with chiseled limestone lintels and quoins.

1111 Stone Church Road, Waterloo

Continue north on Stone Church Road, and bear left to stay on Stone Church Road, then watch right.

13.
Address: 1027 Stone Church Road, Waterloo, Town of Junius

On this field cobblestone home, a 2-story main building has a 1-story wing forming an L-shape. The lintels, quoins and water table have all been painted white. It sits on a cut limestone foundation.

Continue north on Stone Church Road. At the end, turn left onto Dublin Road. Watch left at the corner of Town Barn Road in the hamlet of Junius.

14.
Address: 630 Dublin Road, Waterloo, Town of Junius

This 1.5-story house was built with field cobbles set at an angle in each row. The lintels and sills are wood and some have been removed. The quoins are cut limestone, and the foundation is field stone.

Continue west on Dublin, past Ninefoot and Lasher Roads, then look right.

15.
Address: 533 Dublin Road, Waterloo, Town of Junius
Style: Greek Revival

This home is still part of an active farm. The large 2-story farmhouse has 4 white columns supporting an overhanging roof in the front. A modern segment now connects the main building and a smaller 1-story side cobblestone building. The original front door is now in the east wall.

Continue west on Dublin. Turn left onto West Townline Road, and watch right.

16. Toll House
Address: 782 Townline Road, Phelps
Style: 5-bay Federal

This 2-story field cobblestone home has cut limestone quoins, lintels, sills and water table. The front door is framed in sidelights and a transom. The mortar is formed in definitive V joints. It's set on a field stone foundation and has a fan in the gable end.

Continue south on Townline Road. Pass Avery, and watch right for a house set back from the road and obscured by trees.

17. Huffman House (sometimes spelled Hoffman)
Address: 1064 West Townline Road (Ontario-Seneca County Line Road), Phelps
Year Built: 1845
Style: Greek Revival

William Huffman hauled the water-rounded cobbles for his home from Lake Ontario. The upper cobbles on the front are a darker brown — perhaps from a different beach? The L-shaped building has a 2.5-story main section and a 1.5-story wing, which is typical of a New York State farmhouse. Sidelights and cut stone surround the front door. In fact, the entrance, including the front steps and platform are all of cut stone, which is unusual. The builder had his initials and the date (W.H. 1845) carved into the frieze over the door. The lintels are wide and a triangular fanlight in the gable end lights the attic. This house is on the National Register of Historic Places.

Continue south on Townline Road, and take the next right onto Cuddaback Road. At the end, turn right onto Route 14 north. Take the next left onto Gifford Road. Turn right onto Maryland Street, and watch right.

18. Smith House
Address: 921 Maryland Street, Phelps
Year Built: 1841
Style: Greek Revival

The building date of "1841" is etched in a datestone above the front door. The front sports oval field cobbles set in a herringbone pattern about three quarters of the way up, then continues with standard cobblestone courses. It's capped with a herringbone course at the cornice line. The lintels, quoins and water table are all limestone, now painted white. An unusual circular ornament done in cobblestones can be seen in the gable end on the side wall. A similar ornament on the north gable end has a cobblestone star in it. This ornament is similar to the one built into the house on Main Street in Phelps (Bannister House, #3 on Tour 14.) This house has a cobblestone foundation.

Continue north on Maryland Street, and take the next left onto Bohner Road (unlabeled). At the end, turn left onto Pre-Emption Road, and watch left in 1.3 mile.

19. Reppard-Westfall House
Address: 957 County Pre-Emption Road, Phelps

Here's another L-shaped farmhouse, but this one is unique. Small red cobbles were used on the front, but white cobbles were saved for the frieze area. Mixed color field cobbles were used on the wing in the back. The side wing has grills in the frieze. A triangular window is in the gable end of the main building.

Continue south on Pre-Emption Road, and turn right onto Gifford Road. Take the next right onto Lake Road. At the end, turn right onto Burnett Road, then continue straight onto Pleasant Valley Road. Watch right before the stop sign.

20. Jackson Schoolhouse (now Peppermint Cottage and Jackson Schoolhouse Bed & Breakfast)
Address: 336 Pleasant Valley Road, Lyons
Year Built: 1831
Period: Early

This one-room schoolhouse was built using rough field cobbles and rough stone quoins at a cost of $187. The finished dimensions were 24 x 28 feet. It had an entry area when children left their coats and lunch pails. For desks, the students used shelves attached to the outside walls with benches for seats. The children sat with their backs to the teacher. When reciting, they moved to benches in front of the teacher.

The school was named after President Andrew Jackson, a distant relative of a local Jackson family. Clark Mason was the first teacher. For tuition, families in the district furnished 1/2 cord of wood, split and ready to burn, per child.

It served as a school until 1948, when it was sold to Judson and Isabel Rice. It is now owned by Mr. and Mrs. Mark DeCracker who live in one part and operate it as a Bed & Breakfast (888-997-1988).

Turn right onto Jackson School Road. Continue straight across Old Pre-Emption Road. Pass Leach/Maryland Roads. The road you're on is now called Alloway Road. Cross over Canandaigua Outlet, and look both left and right. To the left is an octagonal cobblestone barn. To the right is a cobblestone home.

21. Hale Blacksmith Shop
Address: Corner of Alloway and Water Streets, Alloway, Town of Lyons
Original Owner: Alfred S. Hale
Year Built: 1832 (1827 is also quoted)

Alfred Hale, a farmer, carpenter and blacksmith, settled in Alloway in 1823 and had this unusual building built for his blacksmith shop. Mr. Hale lived in a room over the shop for a short time. He was one of the first area farmers to grow mint and helped the area become famous for its peppermint. The blacksmith shop was eventually sold to a man named Fisher. Mr. Fisher painted the building red, white and blue after loosing an election bet. After Mr. Fisher's death it was sold to Cleve Frind. Mr. Frind operated his blacksmith shop here for over 40 years. Its current owners are Ralph and Helen Frind.

The 2-story field cobblestone building has eight sides, each 12.5 feet long and a segmented, conical roof. Notice the absence of quoins and the wood timber lintels.

22. Hale House

Address: 8272 Alloway Road (corner of Route 14), Alloway, Town of Lyons
Year Built: 1827

This 2-story house was built by blacksmith, Alfred Hale, with field cobbles and rough limestone quoins of varied sizes. The lintels in the house are wood planks while those in the blacksmith shop are wood timbers. Notice how narrow the lintels are. The mortar joints of the house and shop do not match, suggesting different building dates and masons.

Continue to the stop sign and turn left onto Route 14, heading north. Watch left, across from Westphal Parkway Drive.

23.

Address: 937 Route 14, Lyons
Year Built: 1830-34

This 2-story box home was built with large field cobbles and cut limestone lintels and quoins.

It's not known who the original owner was. Clarence Dunn sold it to Albert Westphal, who owned for many years. It is currently owned by Atty. John Gibbons.

Continue north on Route 14 to return to the heart of Lyons.

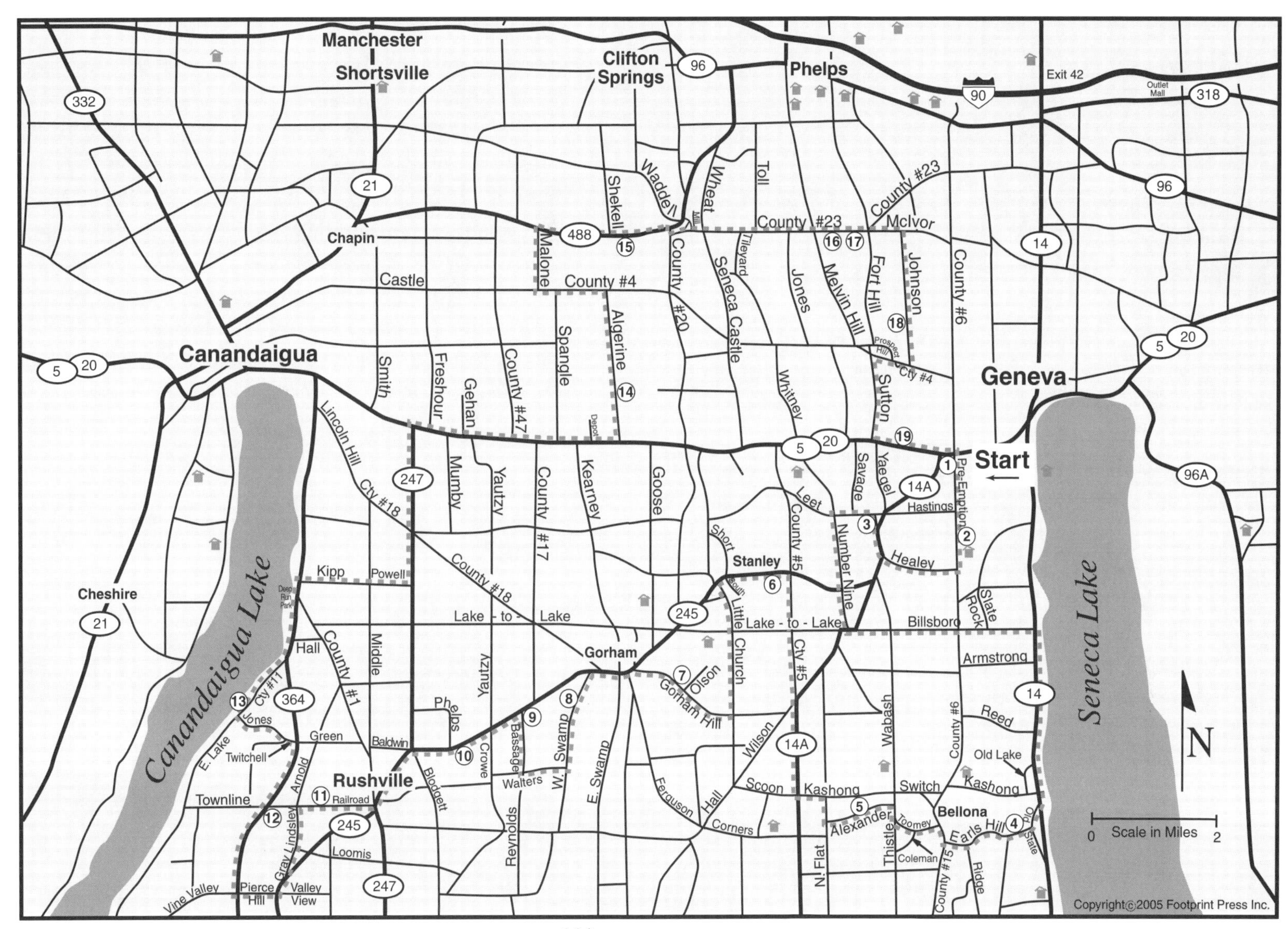

Cobblestone Tour 16

Cobblestone Tour 16

Geneva, Seneca and Gorham in Ontario and Yates Counties
Total Distance: 83 miles
Approximate Time: 3 hours

This route offers beautiful scenery on country roads between two Finger Lakes, as well as a diversity of cobblestone construction to admire.

Begin west of the city of Geneva, heading west on Route 5 & 20. At the traffic light, turn left onto Pre-Emption Road and pull into the parking lot of The Cobblestone Restaurant at the corner.

1. Tuttle-Fordon House (now The Cobblestone Restaurant)
Address: 3610 Pre-Emption Road, Geneva
Original Owner: Lt. Colonel Joseph Hammond Tuttle
Mason: Clark Morison, Amos Siglee and Samuel B. Coddington
Year Built: 1838

Route 5 & 20 came into existence as an Indian trail, then developed into a main thoroughfare for stagecoaches called the Genesee Turnpike. From 1790 until 1833 the Tuttle family operated Tuttle's Tavern in a log building on this spot. From March through November 1838, Lt. Colonel Joseph Hammond Tuttle replaced it with a 1-story cobblestone building that measured 52 feet by 29 feet. He built it over a 7-foot deep cellar with 1.5-feet-thick walls, using irregularly sized, mixed-color cobbles gathered from surrounding fields. The building had 10-inch-thick walls.

The hand-written building contract for the Tuttle House, stated: "*Article of Agreement made this third day of March in the year of our Lord one thousand, eight hundred and thirty-eight between Clark Morison, Amos Siglee and Samuel B. Coddington of the village of Geneva ... and Joseph H. Tuttle ... to build for the said party of the second part... a dwelling of the*

Tuttle-Fordon House, 3610 Pre-Emption Road, Geneva

kind ... hereinafter specified — that is to say... the said building to be built of cobble or feild (sic) stone the basement walls to be 1 1/2 feet thick, and ... to have a projection with 4 Grecian columns and a pediment with a raking cornice ... the six front and three north end windows to have Boston Crown glass of first quality and the rest Clyde glass. . . ." At the end of the contract there are the four signatures and the agreement that the cost of $1,550 was paid in full in 1838.

The building passed through several owners. Then in 1907 William F. Fordon purchased the tavern and added a second story. In 1915 he removed the south wing, added the east portico, and moved the original "Grecian columns" to the east side. Today, the building operates as The Cobblestone Restaurant with an exquisitely restored and decorated interior. Stop in for lunch or dinner ($11 - $20 meals, 315-789-8498) to experience the interior of a cobblestone building.

From the parking lot, head right (south) on Pre-Emption Road for 1.6 miles and look left for cobblestone gates.

2. Tucker-Lewis House, Bellwood Farm
Address: 4119 Pre-Emption Road, Geneva
Original Owner: Silas Tucker
Year Built: 1838

The mansion is hidden from view on a 600-acre estate, so all you can see are the gates made of field cobbles. Silas Tucker cleared the land, built a cobblestone farmhouse with a distinctive double porch on the south end, and farmed 150 acres. Two successive generations of Tuckers lived here. Katherine Belle Lewis, whose wealth came from Pennsylvania oil and gas fields, purchased it in 1905. She doubled the size of the house, being careful to match the field cobbles, lime mortar, and limestone lintels and quoins to the original structure. She added an extension to the north and a large porch on the east side. She also added two new cobblestone structures — a gatehouse that was destroyed by fire in the 1940s and a garden house with a second story porch.

Continue south on Pre-Emption Road, and take the next right onto Healey Road. At the end, turn right onto Route 245/14A. When Route 245/14A bends sharply, continue straight, and watch left.

3. Rippey-Banfield House
Address: 1227 Leet Road, Seneca
Mason: Workmen who built this home may also have worked on the Barron-Gracey House (#19 on this tour).
Year Built: 1854
Period: Late
Style: Italianate (reached height of popularity in late 1850s)

John Rippey Jr. and his wife Mary built this beautiful house in 1854 as evidenced by the inscription in the lintel over the front door. He styled it after 15th and 16th century Italian villas of the Tuscan region and used uniform, red, water-rounded sandstone cobbles from the Sodus area, carefully matched in size and uniformity, and set six courses per quoin. The paired windows have rounded, arch tops with a single arch of oval cobbles connecting the top of both. On the front gable end, the round window looks like an unblinking eye with the white made from mortar. The acorn-shaped wooden pendants in the heavy eves are hand carved. The living room has elaborate acorn molding that matches that of the exterior. On the wing, a band of field cobbles can be seen above the windows. From Leet Road you can see a field cobble wing on the back.

In 1965 Mr. and Mrs. Bruce Banfield purchased this property. Their renovations included peeling off 23 layers of wallpaper.

Turn left (west) onto Leet Road. Take the first left on Number Nine Road and cross Route 245. At the end, turn left onto Lake-to-Lake Road. Continue east as it becomes Billsboro Road. At the end, turn right (south) onto Route 14. Take the fifth right onto Old State Road. Look right just before the stop sign at Earls Hill Road.

4. Earl House
Address: 100 Old State Road, Penn Yan, Town of Benton
Original Owner: Jephtha Earl
Year Built: 1850 (or late 1840s)

Style: Eclectic; although regarded as Italianate — the cornices are Greek Revival but the eves project too far. The brackets are too close together and differ in shape from standard Italianate. The porch columns have flutes and shafts similar to Egyptian Revival. The interior is more Greek Revival.

Jephtha Earl (the father-in-law of Silas Tucker, the original owner of house #2 on this tour) had uniform, red, rounded sandstone cobbles hauled from Sodus for his home, a distance of 45 miles. They were set 6 courses per quoin on the front and 5 courses per quoin on the south wing. The architecture shows the changing tastes of the 19th century with Greek Revival giving way to Italian Villa. Notice the limestone ridge under the second story windows.

Turn right at the stop sign onto Earls Hill Road (County Road 6). At the end, turn right onto County Road 15 (Pre-Emption Road) into Bellona. Take a left onto Toomey Road. Bear right as the road becomes Thistle Street, then turn left onto Alexander Road, and watch to the right after a red barn.

5. Nichols House
Address: 1980 Alexander Road, Penn Yan, Town of Benton
Original Owner: William Nichols and Elizabeth Barden
Mason: Purton Grow (sometimes listed as Elmer Grow)
Year Built: 1838
Style: Greek Revival

Purton Grow was an engineer on the Erie Canal project, then turned to house building. The cobbles were hauled by ox team from Lake Ontario and sorted for size and color by the ladies. It took 3 years to accumulate enough stone. Only the small red ones were used on the front of the house, set 6 courses per quoin. The sides were set 5 courses per quoin and field cobbles were used on the back. The front entrance is unique. Instead of the usual Doric or Ionic columns, Mr. Grow devised a variation with fluted tops. The wide frieze across the front is set with grills. Notice the angled window on the west side. The lintels and quoins are limestone.

West of the house is a contemporary cobblestone smoke-house with field cobbles laid in a crude herringbone pattern.

Continue west on Alexander to the end. Turn right onto North Flat Street, and then take the first left onto Kashong Switch Road at the stop sign. Take the next right, at the stop sign, to head north on Route 14A. At the next stop sign, where Route 14A turns right, continue straight on County Road 5. Turn left onto Route 245 at the flashing light, and watch left.

6.
Address: 1821 Route 245, Stanley, Town of Seneca
Style: Greek Revival

The front, east and rear sides were made with small, red, lake-washed cobbles, but the west side utilized field cobbles. One of the west windows is fake with shutters covering a rough stone wall. The front and side porches and the garage were added in the 20th century. Today it sports a dilapidated front porch.

Continue west on Route 245, and take the next left onto Little Church Road. Take the third right onto Gorham Hill Road at the stop sign, and watch right in 1.5 miles.

7. Morabito House
Address: 2464 Gorham Road, Stanley, Town of Seneca
Original Owner: Luigi Morabito
Style: Greek Revival

The Doric portico with 4 scalloped columns across the front is unusual in that it spans the long side of the house. Shutters on the west side conceal a fake window. Notice the banded masonry — flat fieldstones where the slant reverses every 4 rows.

Continue west on Gorham Hill Road and continue straight at the stop sign onto Route 245 in Gorham. Take a left onto West Swamp Road, and watch right in 0.5 mile.

8. Mapes House
Address: 4892 West Swamp Road, Town of Gorham
Original Owner: Henry Mapes
Year Built: 1845
Period: Late

Style: Greek Revival

This late period, 2-story home was built with field cobbles in neat rows, 4 courses per quoin on the front. The wide frieze has belly windows. Again, there's a fake window covered by closed shutters on the west wall; added for symmetry. This home retains its original Victorian multi-colored slate shingle roof.

The second owner of this home was the Robson sisters, who then gave it to their handyman.

Mapes House, 4892 West Swamp Road, Stanley,

Continue south on West Swamp Road and take the first right onto Walters Road. Take the next right onto Bassage Road at the yield sign and watch right at the stop sign at the corner of Route 245.

9. George-Stell House
Address: 3315 Route 245, Town of Gorham
Original Owner: George brothers
Year Built: 1845
Style: Greek Revival

This 2-story home was built by or for two brothers named George, then was owned by the Stell family. It sat vacant through the 1960s. It was built using uniform dark red, lake-washed cobbles on the front and mixed field cobbles on the back. Limestone with tooled borders and hammered panels were used for the quoins and lintels. The wide friezes contain grills. There's a limestone water table over a cut-stone foundation.

Turn left onto Route 245, and pass Yautzy/Crowe Road, then watch left.

10. Clark-Rex House
Address: 3631 Route 245 (Rushville-Gorham Road),
Town of Gorham
Original Owner: Alanson and Mary Clark

Mason: Same mason as the Whitman-Fox-Snider House, #11 on this tour.
Year Built: 1845
Style: Greek Revival

Alanson and Mary Clark had this 2-story home built with its slate shingle roof, set at an angle to the road. The original door was on the west side. The three Italianate porches were later additions. The walls are a mixture of field and lake-washed cobbles. The gray limestone quoins have hammered panels and tooled edges. The smokehouse in the rear still has its original wood shingle roof.

Mr. and Mrs. William Rex owned this home for over 50 years in the mid-1900s.

Continue west on Route 245 into Rushville. Turn left at the stop sign to stay on Route 245. In the village, take a right onto Railroad Avenue. It will turn into Townline Road. Watch right at the crest of a hill.

11. Whitman-Fox-Snider House
Address: 4450 Townline Road, Rushville, Town of Gorham
Original Owner: Henry Whitman
Mason: Same mason as the Clark-Rex House, #10 on this tour.
Year Built: 1849
Period: Late
Style: Greek Revival

Beza and Alice Whitman arrived from Massachusetts via oxcart about 1800 and built a log cabin at the corner of Main and Railroad Streets in Rushville. One of their 5 children, Marcus was a medical missionary who led the first wagon train to Oregon. Another child, Henry, began building this cobblestone home in 1847. Henry had worked in sawmills to earn money for the land, and then turned to farming. He brought the cobbles back from Sodus Point after 2-day trips to get wheat to Lake Ontario for shipment to Montreal. His brother Augustus helped with construction, along with an unnamed mason who may have also worked on the Clark-Rex House (#10 on this tour).

This 2-story home with a wing, had an early central heating brick furnace and was built using the same floor plan as house, #8 on this tour (4892 West Swamp Road). The foundation is cut stone capped by a high water table. The quoins, lintels and water table are all cut gray limestone.

Continue west on Townline Road, then take the next left onto Lindsley/Arnold Road. Turn right onto Gray Road at the stop sign, then turn right onto Route 245 south at the stop sign. Take the next right onto Pierce Hill Road and right again at the stop sign onto Route 364 north. In 1.6 miles, watch right at the corner of Town Line Road.

12. Bates House

Address: 5521 Route 364, Gorham, Town of Middlesex
Year Built: ~1836
Style: Greek Revival, although the narrow, plain cornice reflects the older Federal style

This small, 1-story fieldstone house was built as a tenant house and is very plain. Except, if you look closely you'll see 2 rows of herringbone pattern above the windows on the right side (front) only. There is no tooling on the sills, lintels or quoins, and the doorway is narrow and plain. The interior is intact.

Continue north on Route 364. Pass Town Line Road, then turn left onto Twitchell Road, then a quick right onto Jones Road. At the end, turn right on East Lake Road (County Road 11), and watch left.

13.

Address: 4880 County Road 11 (East Lake Road), Rushville, Town of Gorham
Year Built: ~1830 (sometimes listed as early 1840s)

Set along the shore of Canandaigua Lake, this small, 1.5-story home was built with squarish fieldstones. Notice the cut stone lintels set on edge and the rough quoins. The basement is as high as a modern 11-course cinder block basement and contains a large Dutch oven fireplace. The picture window on the south side, wooden addition to the rear, and porch on the front are 20th century additions.

Continue north on East Lake Road, then turn left onto Route 364 north at the stop sign. After Deep Run Park, take a right onto Kipp Road. It will turn into Powell Road. At the end, turn

Cobblestone smokehouse at Isenhour Farmhouse, 3301 Algerine Street, Stanley

left onto Route 247 north, then right onto Route 5 & 20 east. Take the sixth left onto Algerine Street, and watch right.

14. Isenhour Farmhouse
Address: 3301 Algerine Street, Stanley, Town of Seneca
Original Owner: Jacob and Mary Isenhour
Year Built: 1842
Style: Greek Revival

Here's a cute 1.5-story home built using large field cobbles of various colors. It has a nonsymmetrical facade. The doorway was recently rebuilt to include sidelights and a transom as per the original design.
Peer behind the house to see a cobblestone smokehouse that was moved to this location as a pile of loose stones. Originally built in 1841 at Lake-to-Lake Road in the Town of Seneca, it was rescued from the bulldozer and reconstructed (complete with its datestone) behind Isenhour Farmhouse by Ross Marshall in 2001.

Continue north on Algerine Street (passing an original trolley stop building on the left) to the end. Turn left on County Road 4, then right on Malone Road. At the end, turn right onto Route 488. Pass Shekell Road, and look right.

15. Warner House (now Landmark Farms)
Address: 2607 Route 488, Clifton Springs, Town of Hopewell
Original Owner: Oliver Warner
Year Built: 1840
Style: Federal

This stately 2-story farmhouse has a wrap-around porch. The front entrance has freestanding columns between the door and sidelights. Notice the arch over the door and the stone fanlight in the gable. The house was obviously built in stages, with the Federal style front and west wing being built first. Notice the metal 4-point star tie bars on the front and sides. The limestone water table becomes brick at the rear — a common practice of using coarser materials on the sides and/or back of a cobblestone building. Hitching posts remain in the front lawn.

Continue east on Route 488. Turn right onto County Road 20, then take an immediate left onto County Road 23. Watch right, for the first house after the flashing light at Melvin Hill Road.

16. Ottley House
Address: 1523 County Road 23, Phelps
Original Owner: First son of William Ottley
Mason: Lorenzo Judd of Geneva
Year Built: 1848
Period: Late

William Ottley had this home built for his eldest son, perhaps as a wedding gift. It's a plain box, 1.5-story building with a simple porch. The red sandstone cobbles were carefully selected for size and laid 5 courses per quoin.

Continue a little further east on County Road 23, again watching right.

17. Ottley House
Address: 1379 County Road 23, Phelps
Original Owner: Second son of William Ottley
Mason: Lorenzo Judd of Geneva
Year Built: 1854
Period: Late

This T-shaped, 2-story home with a 1-story wing was built with a mixture of glacial and water-washed cobbles, some laid on a slant to the left. It sports a wide frieze with grills, a wide water table, and windows in the basement. The front door is inset with sidelights, a transom, and 2 columns. Small columns also support the porch. The quoins have tooled borders and hammered center panels. The foundation is carefully cut limestone blocks. The east wall has a fake, louvered window added for symmetry.

Contrast this home with the previous one. The same mason built both, but 6 years apart. William Ottley hired Lorenzo Judd to build this house for his second son.

Continue east on County Road 23, and go straight as it turns into McIvor Road. Turn right on Johnson Road, and watch right in 1.7 miles.

2916 Johnson Road, Geneva

18.
Address: 2916 Johnson Road, Geneva

Built of round, multi-color field cobbles, this house is adorned with random rows of herringbone pattern on the front. The top courses below the frieze are oval cobbles laid horizontally. It's a design also used on house #18 (921 Maryland Street, Phelps) on Tour 15.

Continue south on Johnson Road to the stop sign at the end. Turn right on County Road 4. Pass Prospect Hill Road, then turn left onto Sutton Road. At Route 5 & 20 turn left, and watch left.

19. Barron-Gracey House

Address: 1160 Route 5 & 20 (Canandaigua-Geneva Road), Geneva, Town of Seneca
Original Owner: Thomas Barron
Mason: Workmen who built this home may also have worked on the Rippey-Banfield House (#3 on this tour)
Year Built: 1848-1850 ("T. Barron 1848" is etched in the lintel over the main door.)
Period: Late
Style: Greek Revival

The Barron family arrived from England in the late 1790s, followed the Genesee Turnpike, built a log cabin and prospered at farming. Thomas Barron carted red sandstone cobbles 30 miles from Sodus on Lake Ontario in returning wheat wagons for 3 years to build his house. Construction took 2 years and cost $2,100. The Barron family owned this home until the 1920s. Mr. and Mrs. Lawrence W. Gracey purchased it in 1938.

The home has a 2-story central building with a portico, two 1.5-story wings and a slate roof. Four huge columns adorn the middle section with 3 columns on each wing. The door on the west wing is a fake, constructed to balance with the door on the east wing. Greek Revival was common architecture in 1848 for wealthier homes. There's a 3-inch beveled door on the front flanked by original stenciled sidelights. The brick steps and porch floor were added in the 20th century to replace the wooden originals.

Continue east on Route 5 & 20 to the starting point and Geneva.

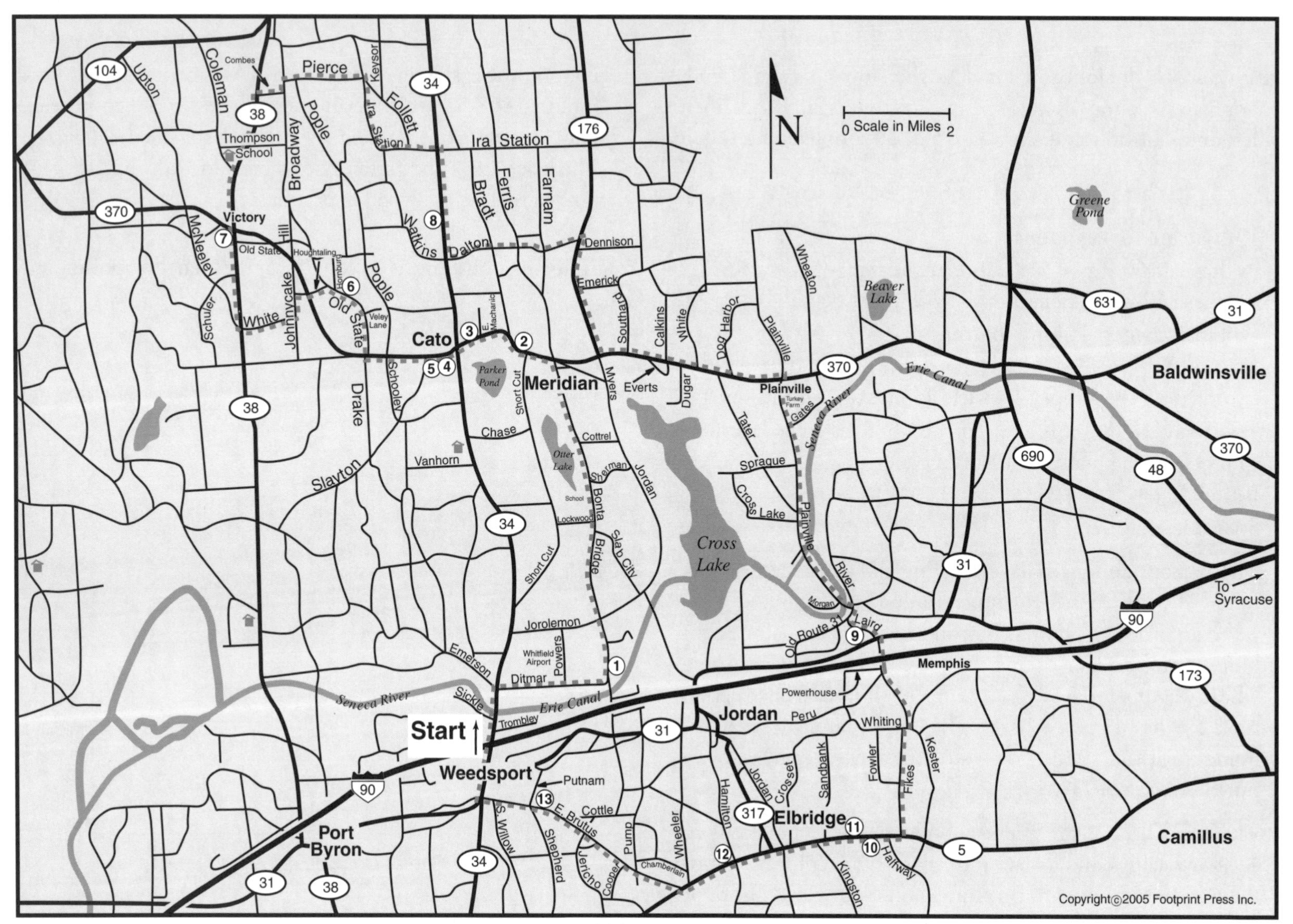

Cobblestone Tour 17

Cobblestone Tour 17

Weedsport, Cato and Elbridge in Cayuga and Onondaga Counties
Total Miles: 53
Approximate Time: 2.5 hours

On this tour you'll visit two cemeteries (in addition to many houses), each with a different cobblestone structure. One is a tall obelisk tombstone, the other is a burial vault.

Begin in Weedsport (I-90, exit 40) and head north on Route 34. Cross over the Erie Canal and take a right onto Ditmar Road. At the end, turn left (north) on Bonta Bridge Road (no sign) and watch right.

1.
Address: 9650 Bonta Bridge Road, Cato

This 1.5-story home was built with large field cobbles set on edge with V mortar joints. The lintels and quoins are limestone.

Continue north on Bonta Bridge Road. North of Lockwood Road, watch to the left to see a brick schoolhouse built in 1870.

Kimball Tombstone, Route 370, Meridian

At the end of Bonta Bridge Road, turn left onto Route 370 west in Meridian. In 0.3 mile look right, uphill in the cemetery or pull right into the cemetery to park and walk.

2. Kimball Tombstone
Address: Route 370, Meridian

Part way up the hill in the middle of this cemetery stands a 15-foot-tall tapered, conical cobblestone obelisk. It's a burial marker for the Kimball clan, including:

Robert G. Kimball, died 1889, age 89
Margaret Kimball, died 1876, age 78
Their 6 children: Harriet A. (1 year), Cornelia (8 years, 1840), Elizabeth (5 days), Henry Eugene (3 years, 1855), Robert W. (3 years, 1842), E. Mortimeur (4 months, 1831).
John Kimball, died 1860, age 26
Charles M. Kimball, died 1889, age 59.

This shows how tough life on the frontier must have been, especially for young children. The obelisk was built with small, multi-colored, lake-washed cobbles. It sits on a square stone and concrete base. At the top is a stone finial.

Continue west on Route 370. Enter Cato and watch right shortly after East Mechanic Street.

3.
Address: 2587 East Main Street, Cato
Year Built: ~1853 (Not listed in 1850 census but is listed in 1854 census.)

This 2-story home, with yellow trim, was built with field cobbles. The wings are more recent additions. It has a wide frieze on the side. Larger fieldstones were used on the back. (You can view the back from the St. Patrick's Church parking lot on E. Mechanic Street.)

Continue west on Route 370, cross Route 34, and watch left after Community Bank.

4. Savery House
Address: 2512 West Main Street, Cato
Original Owner: John Savery
Style: Federal

This 2-story home sports metal lions on each side of the limestone lintel above the front door and sidelights framing the door.

This home's original owner was a dentist and became a major in the Civil War. It's currently an apartment house.

Continue west on Route 370, watching left.

5.
Address: 2466 West Main Street, Cato

This 1.5 story home was built with multi-colored field cobbles and rough limestone lintels and quoins. There's a frieze across the front and two doors, one on the front and one on the side. The single gable peak faces Route 370.

Continue west on Route 370. Pass Pople Road, then turn right onto Old State Road. Pass Veley Lane, then watch right.

11676 Old State Road, Victory

6.
Address: 11676 Old State Road, Victory
Mason: Probably the same mason as the previous house, #5, 2466 West Main Street.

This 2-story farmhouse has a cut limestone water table and foundation, as well as limestone quoins and lintels. A few cobblestone courses on the front are set in a herringbone pattern. The front door is inset and framed by sidelights and a transom. The wing has an inset porch with four square columns. Notice the oval window in the gable end.

Continue northwest on Old State Road, and take the first left onto Houghtaling Road (no sign). Cross Route 370, and at the end, turn left onto Johnnycake Hill Road. Take the next right onto White Road, then right again onto Route 38 (north). Pass Schuler Road, then Old State Road, and watch left in Victory, at the corner of Route 370.

7. Select School
Address: 12027 Route 38, Victory
Original Owner: J. D. Woodford
Mason: Probably the same mason as houses # 5, 2466 West Main Street and #6, 11676 Old State Road on this tour.
Year Built: 1836

This cobblestone building was used as a select school with a ballroom on the second floor. A datestone in the peak reads

"J. D. Woodford 1836." The wooden addition on the rear was once a creamery, manufacturing butter.

Notice the herringbone pattern on some rows on the front and less commonly, on the sides.

Continue north on Route 38. Pass Coleman Road and Thompson School Road, then turn right onto Combes Road. At the end turn left onto Broadway Road, then take a quick right onto Pierce Road. At the end, turn right onto Ira Station Road ,and bear right at the Y to follow Ira Station Road. Turn right onto Route 34 south, and watch right after the silo on the left.

8. Havens House

Address: 12085 Route 34, Cato

This house passed ownership from its original owner, the elder Mr. Havens, to his son Glen Havens. It's a small, square, 1.5-story farmhouse with slit windows in a wide frieze on the front and sides. The sides are beginning to bow and crack.

Continue south on Route 38, and take the next left onto Dalton Road. Follow Dalton until it ends at Route 176, then turn right onto Route 176 south. Turn left onto Route 370 east. Take the fifth right onto Plainville Road. Cross two bridges over the Seneca River/Erie Canal. At the end, turn right onto Old Route 31 then a quick left onto Laird Road, and watch right.

9.

Address: 6629 Laird Road, Cato

Here's a simple, two-story box house with few embellishments. The original field cobblestones were set at an angle, but mortar has been applied to be flush with the stones. The lintels are limestone set on edge.

Continue south on Laird Road to the end. Turn left onto Route 31, then take a quick right onto another segment of Laird Road. Cross the NYS Thruway (I-90). At the end, turn right onto Whiting Hall Road, and take a quick left onto Fikes Road (no sign). At Route 5, turn right (west), and watch to the left for Old Elbridge Rural Cemetery. At the far end of the cemetery, turn left into the grass track, and park just off Route 5. Look ahead, left to see the cobblestone vault or get out of your vehicle and walk 120 feet, slightly downhill to view it.

10. Cobblestone Vault

Address: Elbridge Rural Cemetery, Route 5, Elbridge

Year Built: 1879

Built with field cobblestones, the horizontal mortar joints of this building are eroding over time. A limestone arch over the metal door has a limestone block engraved "1879." This vault was built to house those awaiting burial after the spring thaw. It was built while John Munro was president of the cemetery. It may have been his influence (see house #12 on this tour) that resulted in the use of cobblestones. The metal door is open, so you can peek inside.

Continue west on Route 5, and pull right into the parking lot for Squire Farms Garden Center after the large "Squire Farms" green and white sign.

Brown Barn, 1133 Route 5, Elbridge

11. Brown Barn (now Squire Farms Garden Center)
Address: 1133 Route 5, Elbridge
Original Owner: Squire M. Brown
Year Built: 1850

Squire M. Brown built this barn using large field cobbles, set 3 courses per quoin with V mortar joints.

Return to Route 5, heading right (west) through Elbridge. Just after the traffic light for Hamilton Road, pull into the right shoulder, and stop at the gap in the arborvitae hedgerow.

12. Munro House
Address: Route 5, Elbridge (at corner of Hamilton Road)
Original Owner: John Munro
Year Built: 1850-51
Style: Scholarly Gothic

This beautiful home is set back, behind a row of arborvitae hedges, making it difficult to see. The Munro family settled here in 1799. John, one of 4 Munro sons, prospered and built this home in 1850-51. It was designed by English architect Thomas Atkinson, and built with gingerbread common to the gothic style. The very small, greenish-gray cobbles came from Lake Ontario near Oswego. The slate roof and diamond-paned sashes in the windows are all original.

Continue west on Route 5. Pass Wheeler Road, then turn right onto East Brutus Street at the caution light. Follow this toward Weedsport. After a cemetery on the left, watch right.

13. Putnam House

Address: 2977 East Brutus Street, Weedsport, Town of Brutus

Year Built: Pre-1834 (The deed dates back to 1834.)

Lewis Putnam moved to Brutus in 1804 and built grist and saw mills. Most likely a Putnam descendant (with a similar name) built this house. The 1830 census records a Lewis Putnam, Jr. and the 1840 census lists an L. Putnam, but neither describe a dwelling type. It isn't until the 1855 census that a Lewis Putnam is listed as living in a "stone" house.

In the late 1980s, owner Kenneth Weller spent 5 hours hammering a hole for a doorway through an 18-inch-thick wall.

The 2-story farmhouse, with a 1-story cobblestone wing, is much easier to see than the previous house. It has a brick 2-story addition. The cobbles were set 4 courses per quoin. It sports limestone lintels, quoins and a water table, and is set on a cut limestone foundation. A triangular fan decorates the gable end of the 2-story portion, and a round decoration is in the gable end of the 1-story portion.

Continue west on East Brutus Street, and turn right onto Route 34 north to return to the NYS Thruway.

Definitions

Ashlar mortar - Traditional ashlar jointing and bedding mortars were made with lime and crushed chalk, usually with a small amount of crushed stone or sand added for bulk. This was mixed on a marble slab with just enough linseed oil to grease the tools, it was made up into a consistency similar to stiff glazing putty, wrapped in oiled cloths and stored until required.

Balustrade - A row of repeating balusters or small posts that support the upper rail of a railing. Staircases and porches often have balustrades.

Bay - One unit of a building that consists of a series of similar units, commonly defined by the number of window and door openings per floor or by the space between columns or piers.

Bead -A projecting half circle of mortar about 1 inch wide, formed with a specialized metal form, to embellish the joints.

Beaded joints - The mortar between cobbles that is formed with a special tool that leaves a half-rounded ridge to emulate wood moldings.

Bee - A gathering of people to perform a common function, such as collect and sort stones

Belly window - This is folk terminology for frieze windows, the rectangular windows, 1/3 to ½ the height of a normal window, placed under the eves, often in Greek Revival houses. Some were placed at belly height. To look out others, you had to lay on your belly.

Chiseled lintels and quoins - A decorative tooled finish on the quoin created by repeated chisel strikes to the stone surface. The dimpled central panel of these quoins was often created with a tool called a brush hammer— the stone mason's equivalent to the meat tenderizer.

Cobblestone - A small stone that can be held in one hand.

Coffin door - A door in the parlor, generally on the side of the house for easy access to remove a coffin. Home funerals were commonly held in the deceased person's residence before the establishment of funeral homes. Also called death doors and funeral doors.

Cord - 128 cubic feet of stone in the wall (4 x 4 x 8 feet).

Cornice - The projecting ornamental molding along the top of a building or wall.

Course - Each horizontal layer of a stone wall is called a course.

Cut stone - Stone used as a building support, that was either chiseled or sawn into blocks. Limestone was commonly used because of its abundance in this area.

Datestone - A stone plaque or building block indicating the year the structure was built. Most are located on the front of the building or over the front door.

Death door - See coffin door.

Doric column - The primary type of classical Greek column comprised of a rectangular slab (called the capital) above a circular column. Made famous by the Greek Parthenon, Doric columns stand plain and smooth.

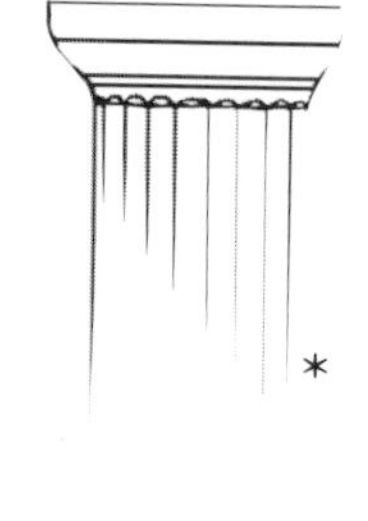

Egyptian Revival - An architectural style that references the visual motifs and imagery of Ancient Egypt. It is comparable to Greek Revival.

Eves - The projecting overhang at the lower edge of a roof.

Fanlight - A semicircular or fan-shaped window set over a door or window.

Federal - An architectural style popular from the 1780s-1830s characterized by simple rectangular boxes, unadorned, symmetrical facades and shallow, low-pitched roofs. It's sometimes referred to as Post-colonial style.

Finial - A vertical termination; a cast, carved, or turned ornament capping another form.

Flute/fluted - Wavy around the edges.

Foundation - The part of a building that meets the ground, where all loads are transferred to the ground.

Frieze - In house construction, a horizontal member connecting the top of the siding with the soffit of the cornice.

Frieze window - Rectangular windows, 1/3 to ½ the height of a normal window, placed under the eves, often in Greek Revival houses. Sometimes called a belly window.

Gable - The triangular wall segment at the end of a double-pitch or gable roof.

Gothic - A general term for a style of architecture and ornament characterized by pointed arches, ribbed vaulting, and flying buttresses.

Gothic Revival - An architectural style popular from the 1830s to the 1880s, characterized by steeply pitched gables, often containing an arched window, and elaborate porches and moldings.

Greek Revival - An architectural style popular from the 1820s to the 1850s, characterized by wide friezes, heavy cornices, columns supporting porches, doors surrounded with sidelights and rectangular transom windows, and either gable or hipped roofs.

Grill - A framework of metal or wood bars used as a partition or a grate.

Herringbone - Brick or stone laid in alternate diagonal courses.

Hip Roof - A roof where all four sides slope upward.

* Diagrams used with permission of The Landmark Society of Western New York.

Ionic column - A column of classical Greek architecture characterized by an elegantly molded base, tall, slender fluted shafts, and prominent spiral, scroll-shaped ornaments on the capitals (the top part).

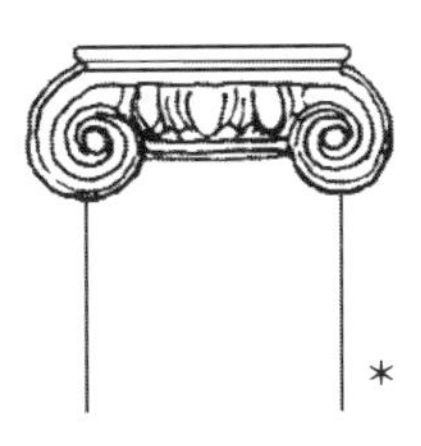

Italianate - An architectural style popular from the 1840s to the 1880s, characterized by shallow roof angles, deep eves, decorative brackets supporting the eves, and paired windows with rounded arches.

Joint - Mortar divisions between the stones on a stone wall. There can be horizontal and vertical joints. Joints are often described as being in V or pyramid shapes.

Keystone - The stone at the top or middle of an arch or vault, which, being wider at the top than at the bottom, enters like a wedge and binds the work; sometimes they project and are ornamented.

Lime mortar - A mortar made from lime, sand and water. Wide variations occurred in proportions of ingredients, quality of ingredients, method of obtaining and mixing them and storage methods. Lime mortar is soft and flexible. It sets in a few hours but takes months to years to harden. The slow hardening allowed cobblestone buildings to settle without cracking.

Limekiln - A furnace, sometimes built into a hill, where native limestone was burned to create quicklime.

Lintel - A horizontal architectural member spanning the top of a door or window, usually carrying the load. Cobblestone building lintels are most often cut stone (limestone or sandstone) but can also be brick, wood or fieldstone.

Mansard Roof - A roof with two slopes or pitches on each of the four sides. The lower portion has a steeper slope than the upper portion.

Mortar - A mixture, as of lime or cement, sand, and water, which hardens in the air and is used for binding together bricks or stones.

Mortar joint - The space between stone or brick where mortar is placed.

Mudded/mudding - The process of placing mortar on a brick or stone.

Obelisk - An upright, 4-sided, usually monolithic pillar that gradually tapers as it rises and usually terminates in a pyramid.

Occulus - A round window.

Pilaster - A shallow post attached to a wall, often decorated to resemble a column.

Perch - 16 ½ cubic feet of rubble stone.

Pointing - The process of filling joints with mortar.

Portico - A major porch, usually with a roof supported by columns.

Portland cement - A mortar used since the 1880s that is a patented formula for an exceptionally strong and unyielding, waterproof cement.

Quicklime - Burned or decarbonated limestone ($CaCO_3$ + heat = CaO + CO_2 gas), sold by the bushel. It was used as fertilizer, for tanning, as a whitewash, for plaster, and in building mortar.

Quoins - Offset corner blocks, often made of quarried limestone, including Lockport dolostone and Onondaga limestone used in cobblestone building to add structural integrity to corners. The word derives from the French word for "corner."

Rubble - Rough, irregular stone fragments used in construction of a wall or wall surface.

Shaft - The middle portion of a column. The shaft sits on a base and has a capital on the top.

Sidelight - A window beside a door forming part of the door unit.

Sill - A main horizontal member forming the bottom of the frame of a window or door.

Six-over-six window - (6/6) - A window containing 6 panes of glass in the upper sash and 6 in the lower sash.

Slaked - A process of adding water to quicklime to create hydrated lime.

Sorting board - A plank with a few holes of various sizes, through which cobblestones were sorted.

Stone boat - A flat sled drawn by horses or oxen on which to collect stones from the fields.

Tie bar - Steel cable or rod running the entire length or width of a building terminating on the outside wall. Each end is threaded and a large bolt or decorative end piece is attached. Used to add strength to the structure.

Transom - A small, often hinged window or multi-paned window opening above a door or another window.

Triangular joint - The mortar between cobbles that is formed with a special tool that leaves a three-sided pointed ridge.

V joint - The mortar between cobbles that is formed with a special tool that leaves a pointed ridge.

Water table - A line of sill-like cut stone that protrudes 2 to 3 inches from the face of the wall and separates the foundation wall below and the cobblestone wall above. Water tables can be found on the front wall only, on 3 walls or on all 4 walls of a cobblestone house. They prevent water from soaking up from the ground by capillary action.

Cobblestone Museums

Tour #	House #	Name	Page #
2	2	Babcock House Museum	26-24
2	4	Hartland Historical Society District 10 Schoolhouse	27
3	3-7	Cobblestone Society Museum	34-37
6	8	Alexander Town Museum in Alexander Classical School	73-74
7	1	Livingston County Historical Museum in Geneseo District #5 Schoolhouse	76
8	18	Chili Schoolhouse Museum, District #4 Schoolhouse	88
9	6	Tinker Homestead and Farm Museum, Tinker House	94-95
12	10	Wallington District #8 Schoolhouse	126-127

Cobblestone Bed & Breakfasts

Tour #	House #	Name	Page #
11	11	Captain Throop	118
12	6	Maxwell Creek Inn B&B	125-126
15	20	Peppermint Cottage and Jackson Schoolhouse B&B	159

Cobblestone Restaurants

Tour #	House #	Name	Page #
1	4	Wilson House Inn	20-21
16	1	The Cobblestone Restaurant	162-163

Cobblestone Antique Shops and Galleries

Tour #	House #	Name	Page #
9	12	Golden Lynx Art Gallery	99
9	17	Cobblestone Antiques	101
13	12	Cobble Ridge Antiques	137

For Cobblestone Building Owners

The State of New York offers a special "fast track" system for getting cobblestone buildings listed as officially designated landmarks in the National Register of Historic Places. Established in 1966, the National Register is the federal government's official landmark program. It is administered in New York State by the New York State Office of Parks, Recreation and Historic Preservation. Owners of cobblestone buildings who would like assistance in getting their buildings officially designated as landmarks in the National Register should contact:

NYS Office of Parks, Recreation and Historic Preservation
Historic Preservation Field Services Bureau
Peebles Island
PO Box 189
Waterford, NY 12188
(518) 237-8643

Word Index

A

B

C

H

L

M

N

O

S

Bibliography

A series of annual tour guides, The Cobblestone Society

Architecture Worth Saving in Pittsford, Elegant Village, 1969, Historic Pittsford, Inc.

Brockport Post articles, circa 1979 by William Aeberli

Cayuga's Cobblestones, Ward O'Hara, 1991

Church Tales of the Niagara Frontier, Austin M. Fox, 1994, Western New York Wares

Cobblestone Architecture, Carl F. Schmidt, 1944

Cobblestone Architecture: Bounty of the Field & Shore, 1979

Cobblestone Buildings of orleans County, N.Y., A Local History, Delia Robinson, 1996

Cobblestone: Glacier's Gifts, 1994 video, Ann Esch, Jean Hayes, Dan Reardon, and Ann Esch's 4th grade class

Cobblestone Landmarks of NY State, 1978, Olaf William Shelgren Jr., Cary Lattin and Robert W. Frash, Syracuse University Press, 1978

Cobblestone Masonry, by Carl F. Schmidt, 1961 house tour booklet

Cobblestone Masonry, 1966, Carl Schmidt

Cobblestone Masonry in the Town of Hamlin, unpublished manuscript by Mary E. Smith

Cobblestone Structures of Wayne County by Verlyn Edward Klahn, 1955

Cobblestone Tours of Rainbow Country, Niagara County Economic Development & Planning Department

Cobblestones of Orleans County, compiled by Robert Roudabush, 1977

Details of Cobblestone Masonry Construction in North America, Robert Frasch and Delia Robinson, 1993

Flint Architecture of East Anglica, by Stephen Hart, 2000

Geology and the Development of Upstate New York's Distinctive Cobblestone Architecture, from the NYS Geological Association Field Trip Guide, approx. 2000. D. Brooks McKinney

Historic Homes In & Around Arcadia, by Cecilia Jackson, 1982

Historic Sites in Orleans County, New York, by Irene M. Gibson, 1979

Hoffman Essay - Cobblestone of Marion Section, Verlyn E. Klahn

Mendon's Cobblestone Landmarks, Diane C. Ham, 1997

Newspaper Articles (Cobblestone Architecture file at Rundel Library):
- *A Cobblestone & Tickertape Farm*, Times Union, May 7, 1968
- *A Tour of Geneva's Cobblestones*, Democrat & Chronicle, May 23, 1965
- *Area Cobblestone Houses are Magazine Rock Stars,* Democrat & Chronicle, July 20, 2001
- *Buildings of Glacial Cobblestones*, Times Union, June 6, 1970
- *Round Cobblestone on Mile Square Road*, Democrat & Chronicle
- *The Old Cobblestone House on the Hill*, Greece Post, December 24, 1970
- *Those Cobblestone Houses*, Times Union, June 9, 1967

Niagara USA - Cobblestone Landmark Guide, Niagara County Planning & industrial Development Department

Ontario County Cobblestones, Barbara Swartout, 1981, Ontario County Historical Society and Geneva Historical Society

Our Cobblestone Heritage, published by The Cobblestone Society, 1970

Palmyra - A Bicentennial Celebration 1789-1989, edited by Betty Troskosky, Heart of the Lakes Publishing, 1989

Robert Roudabush compiled data on cobblestone buildings.

The Architectural Heritage of Genesee County, New York, project coordinator Catharine Ross, Landmark Society of Genesee County, 1988

The Cobblestone Houses of Orleans County, map, The Cobblestone Society

The Octagon Fad, Carl F. Schmidt, 1958

Village of Webster Historic Sites Survey, 1992

Wayne County Cobblestone Architecture: Bounty of the Field & Shore

About the Authors

Rich and Sue Freeman decided to make their living from what they love—being outdoors. In 1996 they left corporate jobs to spend six months hiking 2,200 miles on the Appalachian Trail from Georgia to Maine. That adventure deepened their love of the outdoors and inspired them to share this love by introducing others to the joys of hiking.

Since most people don't have the option (let alone the desire) to undertake a six-month trek, they decided to focus on short hikes, near home. The result was the first edition of *Take A Hike! Family Walks in the Rochester Area*. They went on to explore hiking, backpacking, bicycling, skiing, and snowshoeing trails, waterfalls, and waterways for paddling throughout central and western New York State.

Along the way, they kept discovering unique and beautiful places in this region. Driving to the trails and waterways often took them down back country roads were they saw unusual "potato" houses (to quote an architectural student visiting the area from New York City). Of course, these weren't potato houses at all. They were cobblestone houses. They not only inspired the architectural student, but they inspired the Freemans to find out more and share their find with others. *Cobblestone Quest* is the result of that curiosity. This is the Freemans' 14th guidebook.

Rich and Sue have a passion for adventure and an inquisitiveness that continues. They have hiked the 500-mile-long Bruce Trail in Ontario, Canada, hiked on the Florida Trail, hiked across northern Spain on the Camino de Santiago Trail and hiked a 500-mile section of the International Appalachian Trail in Quebec, Canada. They have trekked to the top of Mt. Kilimanjaro, the highest mountain in Africa. Recently (in addition to exploring New York's cobblestone buildings), they hiked the tropical forests and volcanic peaks of wild Hawaii and hiked across England.

On bicycles they have crossed New York State on the Erie Canalway Trail and pedaled the C&O Canal Trail from Washington D.C. to Cumberland, Maryland.

Since beginning their new career writing and publishing guidebooks, the Freemans' have pared down their living expenses and are enjoying a simpler lifestyle. They now have control of their own destiny and the freedom to head out for a refreshing respite or to follow a new interest when the urge strikes. Still, their life is infinitely more cluttered than when they carried all their worldly needs on their backs for six months on the Appalachian Trail.

Other Books Available from Footprint Press, Inc.

Paddling:

Take A Paddle - Western New York Quiet Water for Canoes & Kayaks
ISBN# 1-930480-23-7 U.S. $18.95
20 ponds and lakes plus over 250 miles of flat-water creeks and rivers in western New York for fun on the water.

Take A Paddle - Finger Lakes New York Quiet Water for Canoes & Kayaks
ISBN# 1-930480-24-5 U.S. $18.95
35 ponds and lakes plus over 370 miles of flat-water creeks and rivers throughout the Finger Lakes region and central New York for fun on the water.

Cross-country Skiing and Snowshoeing:

Snow Trails – Cross-country Ski and Snowshoe in Central and Western New York
ISBN# 0-9656974-52 U.S. $16.95
80 mapped locations for winter fun on skis or snowshoes.

Hiking:

Peak Experiences – Hiking the Highest Summits in NY, County by County
ISBN# 0-9656974-01 U.S. $16.95
A guide to the highest point in each county of New York State.

New York State County Summit Club Patch
ISBN# None U.S. $2.00
A colorful embroidered patch to commemorate your *Peak Experiences.*

Take A Hike! Family Walks in the Rochester Area
ISBN# 0-9656974-79 U.S. $16.95
60 day hikes within a 15-mile radius of Rochester, New York.

Take A Hike! Family Walks in the Finger Lakes & Genesee Valley Region
ISBN# 0-9656974-95 U.S. $16.95
51 day hike trails throughout central and western New York.

Bruce Trail – An Adventure Along the Niagara Escarpment
ISBN# 0-9656974-36 U.S. $16.95
Learn the secrets of long-distance backpackers on a five-week hike in Ontario, Canada, as they explore the abandoned Welland Canal routes, caves, ancient cedar forests, and white cobblestone beaches along Georgian Bay.

Backpacking Trails of Central & Western New York State
ISBN# none U.S. $2.00
A 10-page booklet describing the backpackable trails of central and western New York State with contact information to obtain maps and trail guides.

Bicycling:

Take Your Bike! Family Rides in the Rochester Area
ISBN# 1-930480-02-4 U.S. $18.95
Converted railroad beds, paved bike paths and woods trails combine to create the 42 safe bicycle adventures within an easy drive of Rochester, New York.

Take Your Bike! Family Rides in the Finger Lakes & Genesee Valley Region
ISBN# 0-9656974-44 U.S. $16.95
Converted railroad beds, woods trails, and little-used country roads combine to create the 40 safe bicycle adventures through central and western New York State.

Bird Watching:

Birding in Central & Western New York – Best Trails & Water Routes for Finding Birds

ISBN# 1-930480-00-8 U.S. $16.95

70 of the best places to spot birds on foot, from a car, or from a canoe.

Waterfall Fun:

200 Waterfalls in Central and Western New York – A Finders' Guide

ISBN# 1-930480-00-8 U.S. $18.95

Explore the many diverse waterfalls that dot the creeks and gorges of central and western New York State.

Self-help:

Alter – A Simple Path to Emotional Wellness

ISBN# 0-9656974-87 U.S. $16.95

A self-help manual that assists in recognizing and changing emotional blocks and limiting belief systems, using easy-to-learn techniques of biofeedback to retrieve subliminal information and achieve personal transformation.

For sample maps and chapters, explore:

www.footprintpress.com

Yes, I'd Like to Order Footprint Press, Inc. Guidebooks:

#	Title	Price
____	*Cobblestone Quest*	$19.95
____	*Take A Paddle - Western NY*	$18.95
____	*Take A Paddle - Finger Lakes NY*	$18.95
____	*200 Waterfalls in Central & Western NY*	$18.95
____	*Peak Experiences—Hiking the Highest Summits of NY*	$16.95
____	*NYS County Summit Club Patch*	$ 2.00
____	*Snow Trails—Cross-country Ski & Snowshoe*	$16.95
____	*Birding in Central & Western NY*	$16.95
____	*Take A Hike! Family Walks in the Rochester Area*	$16.95
____	*Take A Hike! Family Walks in the Finger Lakes*	$16.95
____	*Take Your Bike! Family Rides in the Rochester Area*	$18.95
____	*Take Your Bike! Family Rides in the Finger Lakes*	$16.95
____	*Bruce Trail—Adventure Along the Niagara Escarpment*	$16.95
____	*Backpacking Trails of Central & Western NYS*	$ 2.00
____	*Alter—A Simple Path to Emotional Wellness*	$16.95

Sub-total $________

Florida and Canadian residents add 7% tax

$________

Shipping is FREE (when pre-paid by check)

Total enclosed: $________

Your Name: ________________________________

Address: ________________________________

City: ________________ State (Province): __________

Zip (Postal Code): ____________ Country: __________

Make check payable and mail to:

Footprint Press, Inc.
303 Pine Glen Court, Englewood, FL 34223

Or, order through www.footprintpress.com

Footprint Press books are available at special discounts when purchased in bulk for sales promotions, premiums, or fund raising. Call (941) 474-8316.